MY NOVA SCOTIA
HOME

Nova Scotia's best writers riff on the place they call home

Copyright 2019 Vernon Oickle

All rights reserved. No part of this book covered by the copyrights hereon may be reproduced or used in any form or by any means — graphic, electronic, or mechanical — without the prior written permission of the publisher. Any request for photocopying, recording, taping, or information storage and retrieval systems of any part of this book shall be directed in writing to the Canadian Reprography Collective, 379 Adelaide Street West, Suite M1, Toronto, Ontario, M5V 1S5.

MacIntyre Purcell Publishing Inc.
194 Hospital Rd.
Lunenburg, Nova Scotia
B0J 2C0
(902) 640-3350

www.macintyrepurcell.com
info@macintyrepurcell.com

Printed and bound in Canada by Friesens

Design and layout: Alex Hickey
Cover design: Denis Cunningham

ISBN: 978-1-77276-111-5

Library and Archives Canada Cataloguing in Publication

Title: My Nova Scotia home : Nova Scotia's best writers riff on the place they call home / Vernon Oickle, editor.
Names: Oickle, Vernon L., editor.
Identifiers: Canadiana 20190054832 | ISBN 9781772761115 (softcover)
Subjects: LCSH: Nova Scotia—Anecdotes. | LCSH: Nova Scotia—Social life and customs—Anecdotes.
Classification: LCC FC2318 .M96 2019 | DDC 971.6—dc23

MacIntyre Purcell Publishing Inc. would like to acknowledge the financial support of the Government of Canada and the Nova Scotia Department of Tourism, Culture and Heritage.

CONTENTS

FROM THE EDITOR / Vernon Oickle 5
i have now seen / George Elliott Clarke 7
HOMEOIR (HOME MEMOIR) / Sheldon Currie 11
NOVA SCOTIA — MY HOME / Theresa Meuse 15
THIS IS HOME / Jonathan Torrens 17
IT IS NOT ABOUT THE GEESE / Elaine McCluskey 23
WHEN NURSES WORE WHITE / Carol Bruneau 31
YOU GET A LINE ... / Jan L. Coates 41
AN ISLAND JUST IN TIME / Silver Donald Cameron 47
HOME / Chris Benjamin 53
A WHITE-WASHED HISTORY / Dr. Daniel N. Paul 61
THE SUPERLATIVE ANNAPOLIS VALLEY / Allan Lynch 77
THE SAFE ZONE / Tareq Hadhad 87
WELL GROUNDED / Clara Dugas 97
**MAKING NOVA SCOTIA HOME: A MATTER OF CHOICE
  AND RESISTANCE** / John J. Guiney Yallop, Phd 107
CFA VS. HBC VS. BRH / Vernon Oickle 115
SETTLING IN / Glenna Jenkins 119
RETURNING TO MY NOVA SCOTIA HOME / Dr. Peter J. Ricketts .. 127
MY BEAUTIFUL NOVA SCOTIA HOME / Neville Mackay 139
HOME IS WHERE THE HEART IS / Starr Cunningham 149
THE BOOK / Robert Hirtle 153
THE KEEPERS OF THE LIGHT / Janice Landry 161
LETTER TO CANADA / Lesley Choyce 173
A HOMECOMING / Ian Colford 179
THE COME-FROM-AWAY SPEAKS ABOUT FAMILY LIFE /
  Phil Milner 193
SAVING HOME / Janet Barkhouse 203
PLACES IN EIGHT ACTS / Alice Burdick 211
MY HOME IN NOVA SCOTIA / Monica Graham 217

FROM THE EDITOR

Vernon Oickle

Somebody much smarter than me once said that life is essentially a search for home. Whether you've "come from away" or you have had only a fling with this "Wharf of the Atlantic" as historian J. Murray Beck described Nova Scotia.

Writers are inspired by people, places, events and things they encounter in their lives. I asked these writers, both seasoned and accomplished, and some who are aspiring to success, to tell us their stories; to share their thoughts; to enlighten us.

I urged these contributors to tell us what is the nature of their relationship with Nova Scotia. How has it changed over the years? Has its embrace loosened or tightened with the passage of time? What drives them absolutely stark raving mad about Nova Scotia, and what experiences have the sweetness of fresh honey? What inspires them and what turns them off?

We wanted it all, the bad with the good; the mud with the blossoms; the guts with the glory; the disenfranchised with the grounded.

In this collection, the writers were given an opportunity to riff and to capture and captivate. In many respects it is a map of their lives. The door was wide open for each of them to take whatever approach they desired, but in My Nova Scotia Home, we wanted stories that convey the "Nova Scotia" experience from their perspective — we got all of that and more.

What you are about to discover between these two covers is a collection of work by many of the best writers, poets and researchers to ever come out of this province. So then, on behalf of all my friends who are assembled on the proceeding pages, allow me to say, welcome to "my Nova Scotia home."

i have now seen....

George Elliott Clarke

i have now seen—
nestled twixt warped ties of rusted train tracks,
snow, aged dingy, grey and black,
frosting loose, brown dirt and jumbled gravel,
while a stream hisses neath thin, dull ice,
and i look out over fields flecked with patches
of *grisaille* grass —
the tint of putty —
and wind, subdued, gasps
intimations of winter's seasonal assassinations....
under ledges of runaway clouds,
my love-hunting eyes view
stark outhouses the dirty snow frames
under a dustbowl sun.
the pothole-pocked, dirt road sprawls toward
the pine-serrated horizon,
where rough-edged hills,
lined with chicken-wire fences, sagging barns,
and derelict farms,
unfurl also.
i see rag-tag scarecrows murdered
by knifing winds, bleeding straw
in the snow-snuffed fields,
among broken wagon wheels,

the last monuments
to red-dust cowboys
who once twanged moon-June-silver-spoon tunes
to hay-ride madonnas
on rickety house steps
bordered by violently ruddy roses
and dead conches holding the ocean's roar.
this is the "now and then,"
"the future and the past" :
the hollow corpse of a '57 Chevy
lays half-interred in a rambling drift,
half-smothered by the ivory quicksand.
suddenly, the shrieking banshee horn
of a rushing, steel juggernaut, boxcar hauler,
resounds and detonates across these hilly plains,
where fir trees, evergreen, point directly
to stars, visible or not,
that pinpoint where Aquarius strides
with his medicine water of galaxies gleaming,
pouring silver against indigo velvet.....
An ancestral African rocks his wooden rocker
in a clapboard cabin,
heated by an iron-black wood stove,
that percolates scents of cornbread and rabbit stew—
a still-life or Home-Sweet-Home vignette,
presenting a weeping, folk guitar
and white smoke lifting from a gnarled, mahogany pipe.
add a disordered woodpile, a dead orange tractor,
and evacuated dreams.
i have this old man's Zulu spear
(actually a Micmac cane),
and i perforate snowbanks
with the crooked, wooden point.

from now on, if i must cry,
let the tears signal Joy.

— *George Elliott Clarke*
[Three Mile Plains (Nova Scotia) 19 février mcmlxxvii]

The fourth Poet Laureate of Toronto (2012-15) and seventh Parliamentary Poet Laureate (2016-17), George Elliott Clarke is a revered artist in song, drama, fiction, screenplay, essays, and poetry. Now teaching African-Canadian literature at the University of Toronto, Clarke has taught at Duke, McGill, the University of British Columbia, and Harvard. He holds eight honorary doctorates, plus appointments to the Order of Nova Scotia and the Order of Canada.

His recognitions include the Pierre Elliott Trudeau Fellows Prize, the Governor-General's Award for Poetry, the National Magazine Gold Award for Poetry, the Premiul Poesis (Romania), the Dartmouth Book Award for Fiction, the Eric Hoffer Book Award for Poetry (US), and the Dr. Martin Luther King Jr. Achievement Award. Clarke's work is the subject of Africadian Atlantic: Essays on George Elliott Clarke (2012), *edited by Joseph Pivato.*

HOMEOIR
(HOME MEMOIR)

Sheldon Currie

WHEN I WAS A TEENAGER, dancing was the fun activity in industrial Cape Breton, for adults and teenagers alike. Dances were weekly performances by the two top bandleaders, trumpet player Emilio Pace and Gib Whitney on sax. The bands offered dances at the Strand gym in New Waterford, The Venetian Gardens in Sydney, and at St. Anne's Parish high-school gym in Glace Bay.

Emilio Pace's singer Kay Peters' repertoire included the song, *Vagabond Shoes: vagabond shoes you've gone astray, vagabond shoes why do you roam, take me home again, home again, home again vagabond shoes.*

I had never been more than 25 miles from home, and the song made me yearn for the experience of leaving. As soon as I graduated from high school and went to the prom in that same St. Anne's gym, I left my home and my hometown.

High school behind me, I was 17, and after a few short-term, part-time jobs, I got on a train, travelled to Halifax and joined the Royal Canadian Air Force; got on another train and travelled to London, Ontario. An Air Force corporal transported me to the air base and I settled into my home away from home and began basic training and officer cadet training.

I came back and forth several times for varying lengths of time, to home and away again; I was, when away from home, never homesick, and I often wondered, why?

Thomas Wolfe's famous novel makes a challenging statement: "You Can't Go Home Again." OK.

But why not?

There are plenty of clichés about home. One of the most common: HOME IS WHERE THE HEART IS hangs on walls of kitchens, pinned on kitchen bulletin boards, attached with magnets or scotch tape to fridge doors. But there are more trenchant statements about home. The American poet Robert Frost observed: "Home is the place, where if you show up at the door, they have to take you in."

The Canadian Oxford Dictionary displays more than two and a half pages of words that begin with home. *Roget's Pocket Thesaurus, A Treasury of Synonyms and Antonyms*, under the heading HABITATION, offers a multitude of possibilities if you are looking for an alternative word to replace home. Google offers a choice of 66 or more songs about home.

The home, in your hometown, if you are not there, is a place where you used to live. Many people have multiple places where they used to live. Even when I was home, I often lived with my grandparents, who lived in another area of my hometown. But, I've lived in several places where I lived in my home. So, home is an ambiguous word, signifying a variety of sites. Teachers and students have homerooms. Baseball players have a home base, where they love to leave, and love to run to, but they never stay for more than a few seconds.

William Faulkner, famous American novelist and Nobel Prize winner, wrote: "The past is not dead. It's not even past."

What does he mean?

Jean-Paul Sartre, the French existential philosopher, wrote a full-page essay in *Le Monde*, the French "progressive" newspaper, about Faulkner's novels, especially *Absalom, Absalom* and *The Sound and the Fury*. Sartre wrote: "Reading Faulkner is like driving down the highway in a convertible while looking in the rear-view mirror." That means, I take it, that the present is nothing but an invisible gateway from the past into the unknown.

For human beings, our home, and our many homes, are our past. Our present home is a gateway to the future, the unknown. We only know where we have been years ago and a split second ago.

Thomas Wolfe's novel, *You Can't Go Home Again*, is often interpreted as: because when you get there, it is no longer there, or it's not the same. But what it probably means is: you can't go home again because wherever you go, home is like an indelible tattoo on your brain, in your mind, wherever you take it, or wherever it takes you.

Your home always goes with you, an invisible backpack in the subconscious of your brain. Yes, when you go back home for a visit, everything is different, but everything is the same.

When my home was Tuscaloosa, Alabama for two years while I took courses toward a Ph.D, I also taught two first-year English Literature courses for engineering students who were training for the US space program in Huntsville, Ala. When I gave the students the task of writing an essay on any topic of their choice, well over half of them chose to write on a topic related to the War

Between the States, The Civil War. Where these students lived, their home, the war, long past in years, but ever present in the minds of the citizens of the southern US states. The past is not dead, it is not even the past.

When I go to visit the home of my mother and father, the home of my birth, my parents are both gone, my sisters and one of my brothers are gone, living in other parts of the country. The two houses we lived in are both radically changed, the roads are changed, the stores, the churches, the vehicles are changed, or gone, but in my nostalgic mind the changes are superficial, the changes change nothing in my perception.

I will often take a walk up a now-paved road, to a dirt road leading to another dirt road through the woods until it meets up with what we called back main street, a tributary of the main street where the Catholic Church still sits but is not so busy, and the United Church, the credit union and co-op grocery store, plus the schools are now empty spaces once filled with well-kept buildings.

In my mind, they are all where they used to be; they are absent spaces haunted by ghosts. My hometown.

The road to my hometown's main street is through a wooded area, the trees and bushes on either side hide fallen-in holes in the ground, holes that were once bootleg coalmines with shaft and tunnel, where my cousin Basil and I provided unpaid labour to the miners. We weren't allowed into the tunnels, although we would sometimes sneak down when left alone, but we worked on the platform on the surface and winched the buckets the miners below filled with coal, up the shaft, and dumped them beside the mine to be loaded onto sleigh or dump cart to be pulled by horse to the customers. These businesses would be particularly active during strikes and layoffs.

Once we loaded the coal on the dump-cart or the sleigh and hitched the horses between the shafts, we rode on the load of coal and helped dump or shovel it in the yards of schools, churches and company houses or homes of coal mining families.

During the prolonged strike of 1947 that stretched well into a nasty winter, the striking miners from Reserve Mines blocked the highway to Glace Bay and Sydney to prevent delivery of coal to commercial businesses, so the owners would urge the government to force the coal company to settle the strike.

For school children there were two upsides to the strike. Because money was scarce for families, charity organizations offered at least one meal a day in the schools. And bands of musicians and dancers toured the coal town to entertain the population with free concerts.

But otherwise it was, especially for the parents of large families and the children, an unforgettable, miserable winter, and in the end the owners or their representatives in Montreal made all the decisions, the miners and their families were no better off, and life went on as before.

Unforgettable indeed: Home is where the head is.

Sheldon Currie was born in Reserve Mines, Cape Breton, and often draws from the mining experience in his writing. His novel, The Glace Bay Miners' Museum, *was adapted for film under the title* Margaret's Museum, *which won international accolades, and was also the basis of a CBC radio play by Wendy Lill. A recent stage adaptation of his novel,* The Company Store, *concluded runs in theatres across Canada just last year. His play* Lauchie, Liza and Rory *toured across Canada and in five venues at the New Zealand festival.*

After a short spell in the RCAF and several jobs, Sheldon attended the Xavier Junior College and St. Francis Xavier University. He did post-graduate work at the University of New Brunswick and the University of Alabama. He taught high school and English Literature for two years at St. Thomas University and 35 years at St. Francis Xavier University. Sheldon is now retired from teaching and writes full time.

NOVA SCOTIA — MY HOME

Theresa Meuse

GROWING UP IN A MI'KMAQ First Nation Community in the Annapolis Valley prevented me from knowing life was different depending on where you lived. As a child I was unaware of the grownup things that influenced a person's life — visiting places, people, and sites.

My time was spent playing with friends in the vast, beautiful forest; visiting the ocean beach to dig clams, preparing for clam boils with family and friends and travelling on the old wood roads to locate the best fishing holes. We may have been considered poor by today's standards, but we enjoyed being part of what Mother Earth had to offer. Growing up enabled exploration of this beautiful, picturesque province.

Today, it may be known as Nova Scotia, but for our culture, Nova Scotia makes up part of the land we know as Mi'kma'ki — land of the Mi'kmaq. I soon came to learn that this part of Mi'kma'ki has so much to offer, from Yarmouth to Cape Breton.

Along the Bay of Fundy, you can play in the ocean waves, dig for clams, find seashells, collect beach glass or even do a little surfing — there is something for everyone. A few of my favourite spots are the beaches of Digby and Annapolis County when the tide has gone down, Peggy's Cove along the South Shore, Lawrencetown Beach along the Eastern Shore and Cape Breton along the shores of the Bras d'Or Lakes. Although picturesque, one must never forget that the oceans are powerful.

We are fortunate to have protected forested lands that provide wonderful trails for walking or canoe trips. Kejimikujik National Park, also known as Keji, has a great history that starts with the Mi'kmaq. It is home to a traditional

Mi'kmaw burial site and petroglyph area, two protected areas that can be visited with the assistance of a Mi'kmaw guide. Keji Park also provides for all sorts of camping, social celebrations, swimming at the lakes, short and long hiking trails, a scenic environment where you can see protected wildlife like the deer and turtle.

Visiting the Cabot Trail in Cape Breton leaves everyone in awe. Travelling up and down the mountains and stopping along the way to view the sites makes this trip most enjoyable. You can even visit a few Mi'kmaw communities along the way and purchase many beautiful handcrafts like the traditional ash baskets or porcupine jewellery.

Throughout the province there are provincial walking trails available to walkers, runners, and bicyclers. And yes, dogs are always welcomed too, as long as they remain on a leash. Each trail is unique in its sceneries and views, and my favourite are those that allow me to walk along the lake, like in Lower Sackville.

A person can't forget the many wonderful eateries throughout Nova Scotia. In the city of Halifax, some of my favourites spots are: The Wooden Monkey located in both Halifax and Dartmouth, Agricola Street, Chives, The Auction House and many others located in downtown Halifax. Nova Scotia is known for its seafood and I always enjoy a good feed of haddie tips or seafood chowder made at most restaurants. If you get to partake at feast time during the annual powwow, you might even get to sample traditional Mi'kmaw bannock called Lu'sknikn; Luskie (loo ski) for short.

Besides shopping at malls, visiting rural tourist shops, walking the city waterfronts in Halifax or Sydney, one should always take in the many festivals that happen throughout the summer months. Music, culture, crafts, and buskers are always entertaining. As are the Mi'kmaw powwows, which can be enjoyed by everyone. Starting in June and ending in September, the Powwow Trail offers the opportunity to take part in Mi'kmaw culture. From Yarmouth to Cape Breton, a Powwow can always be found.

Although I still prefer the peacefulness of what the forest and lakes have to offer, visiting other areas is always a nice change of pace.

Theresa Meuse grew up in the Bear River First Nation Mi'kmaq Community. She attended Dalhousie University as a mature student and after graduating worked for two Mi'kmaw organizations in various programs. She went on to become a cultural educator and advisor for several years. She continues to share her culture by working as an Aboriginal student support worker in the Halifax area. She has written articles for several publications and is the author of The Sharing Circle, L'nu'k *and* The Gathering. *Theresa is married, has three grown children and four grandchildren.*

THIS IS HOME

Jonathan Torrens

HOME. HOW CAN SUCH A simple word be such a complicated concept?

I was born in Charlottetown and when someone asks where I'm *from* that will always be the answer. As far as I'm concerned, PEI was the perfect place to grow up. You could somehow feel the comfort, security, and protection that an island offers. In fairness though, seeing as I haven't lived there since the early 80s I can hardly call it home.

In classic Maritimes fashion, my earliest memories of Nova Scotia are from the water. Not from the deck of a fishing boat as you might expect. Rather from the upper deck of the PEI ferry where Nova Scotia magically appeared out of the mist a little over an hour after leaving the dock in Wood Islands. For a relatively short journey, it felt worlds away.

Nova Scotia even smelled different the second you drove off the boat. It might have been the Scott Paper factory in Pictou County that we passed on the way to visit relatives.

My mother Susan grew up in New Glasgow where her father ran Ormond's Drugs. Her two brothers stayed there to raise families so when we'd visit I played with cousins in Merigomish and on Fraser's Mountain. We went to Melmerby Beach and I'd join them at church camp every summer. My grandmother lived on Marsh Street in New Glasgow and we'd wander downtown to poke around Zellers.

Nova Scotians sounded different too. Their "OATS" and "ABOATS" stood in sharp contrast to the "ROIGHTS" and "TANOIGHTS" of PEI. It seemed so exotic.

It was also intriguing to me that Nova Scotia wasn't landlocked. You could drive for as long and far as you wanted. This was very different from PEI before the fixed link was built. Often in storms the airport and ferries would shut down and you couldn't leave even if you wanted to.

We moved to Halifax when I was 12 to be nearer to my ailing grandmother and it might as well have been New York. We lived in a two-storey four-bedroom apartment with a wooden spiral staircase at 1544 Summer Street right across from the Public Gardens. If only I'd had the appreciation for architecture that I do now it would've blown my mind. All I knew then is that it wasn't where my friends lived and you couldn't play street hockey on Spring Garden road.

Over time though, Halifax started to feel like home. I took the Metro Transit bus almost two hours each way every day to Fairview Junior High, the only school to offer French Immersion at the time. You get to know a place pretty well on public transit. Not only the geography but the people too. Halifax is a peninsula and is pretty easy for a curious youngster to cover on foot. We'd roam from the pit in the North End to Point Pleasant Park at the tip of the South End. Take the ferry to Dartmouth on a nice summer day. It was walkable but big enough to keep me interested.

Halifax shaped me and I enjoyed my first sweet tastes of freedom there. In fact, I had a lot of firsts there. First job (McDonald's on Quinpool!), first car (Jeep Cherokee!), first kiss (not telling!) and first apartment of my own. The universities gave the city a vibrant worldly feel but as the cliché goes I moved away in my early 20s in search of work, adventure, and myself.

I'd been working on *Street Cents* for several years and was ready for a change of scenery.

As an extremely inquisitive kid, my mother always said she would answer any question I had with the exception of "what if" questions.

> *"What if we get there and it's closed?"*
> *"What if we get in a car accident on the way there?"*
> *"What if I slip and fall and break my collarbone?"*

Her feeling was there were enough difficult questions in life that there was no room for hypotheticals. Answering my own "what if" questions has driven many of the decisions I've made in life.

> *"What if I went to Toronto to work? What would* happen*?"*

So I did. But before I left I bought a house in the Annapolis Valley with the first money I ever made in television. An old apple farm 20 minutes outside of Windsor.

The house was more than 100 years old. It had a stone and dirt foundation and stood proudly atop a small hill framed by towering twin sugar maples. When I bought the house it was the perfect blend of 1870s and 1970s. Shag carpet served only to protect the wide pine plank floors underneath. Cardboard drop-down ceilings masked the huge hand-hewn beams hidden underneath.

I took great pride in accomplishing small projects there and found it satisfying to address the cosmetic issues, transforming it into my little fortress of solitude.

It was on a pretty good-sized acreage through which a narrow river wound its way. There were plenty of deer, pheasants, and even the odd bear to keep me company. I walked the land every day and found peace in the silence. It was like social quicksand that place. The longer I was there, the harder it became to leave.

But leave I did. Often and for extended periods. Surprisingly, there was little television work in rural Nova Scotia in those days.

And can you call a house a home if you're there for only a few weeks a year? It provided me enormous comfort to know it was there, waiting for me. I knew it was the place I could retreat to if the world became too much or the work became too scarce.

Although I stayed in Toronto for several years, I never really lived there. Always furnished sublets, never a proper home. Always left for Nova Scotia the moment my work there was done.

It seemed like for most of my 20s I was to and fro, living in one place but working in another and that suited me fine. In fairness, I didn't ever really give Toronto a fair shot. My head was there but my heart wasn't. Every weekend I'd drive my truck out of the city to find space. Quiet. Peace.

When I turned 30 I'd been working at CBC for 15 years. Once again anxious for a change of scenery I headed west to Los Angeles to answer another what if question.

"What would happen if I went to LA?"

Most of my preconceived notions about Los Angeles were born out of the 45-second montage in *Pretty Woman* where Richard Gere is trying to drive a standard around Beverly Hills. I thought every dog had a diamond collar and every guy in a suit was a sleazy agent.

It turns out LA is a big city of small towns and your experience there depends on which small town you live in. I chose Venice because a friend of a friend lived there and I hoped the beach and ocean might make it feel like home.

The clichés definitely are there but what I didn't expect was to find so many people like me. Ambitious, curious, creative. In some ways, it felt like I'd found my home. It took awhile to weed through the fakes and the flakes but I made friends for life there. There was a Main Street and coffee shops where people knew your name. The climate was hard to argue with. The work came eventually.

Most holidays I'd travel back to the little farm in Nova Scotia and while I loved being there, my feelings of guilt around it being empty most of the year started to weigh on me. I sold the place and committed to making Los Angeles my home. Could I do it? Live and work in the same place for the first time in my life?

Shortly thereafter, the bloom came off the rose for LA too. You start to do the math on how much of your life you're spending in traffic. "Only took me two hours to get to Burbank. Not bad!"

The work prospects were steady but ultimately unsatisfying.

The incidents involving shootings not too far away from where I lived started to get more frequent. There were police helicopters overhead most nights as I tried to sleep. I was escorted from my parking place to my apartment door by a cop with his weapon drawn on a few separate occasions because there was someone on the loose in the neighbourhood and they were just taking precautions. Real city stuff. Real different from what I was used to.

The other thing about living in California was finding a work/life balance. Living by the beach helped but you're in a hold pattern, waiting for the phone to ring if some director happened to mention you to some producer after talking to a casting person who liked your audition. You're so reliant on so many people to make it happen for you.

Between being unable to control all those variables and the complicated administrative stuff, filing taxes in two countries, keeping cars and homes in both countries started to get hard on the head.

LA was not unlike Toronto in that my head was there but my heart was still in Nova Scotia.

I'll never forget the moment Nova Scotia truly became my home.

On my long drive back from a forgettable audition I was stuck in traffic on the 405 freeway, talking to my mother on the phone back in Halifax. She had a dentist appointment the next day and wasn't looking forward to going alone.

I knew it was time to move back. Suddenly the things I used to find suffocating and limiting about Halifax felt comforting and familiar again. Did I want to be the guy who got hired to host a show he didn't care about or did I want to be the guy who took his mom to the dentist?

It was settled. I was moving back.

Damn clichés for being true. It took going away to appreciate what we have here. Once that desire clicked in, there was no stopping me.

Every traffic jam. Every day wasted waiting for a phone call. Every July 4th reminded me of what I was missing. Canada Day. Freedom. Control of my own life.

Nova Scotia doesn't come after your heart the way some places do. Nova Scotia lets you figure it out for yourself.

The artisans of Bear River. Whale watching on Brier Island. An uninterrupted walk on Martinique beach. A harbour cruise in Halifax followed by drinks on Argyle Street. A drive around the Cabot Trail in the Fall. A lobster roll in Lunenburg.

Suddenly I couldn't wait to get back. *Home.*

So I moved back and bought a house on Church Street that needed lots of work. With the help of my friend Mike, who is a photographer, I threw myself into the renovations while reacquainting myself with the city I grew up in but hadn't lived in for 20 years.

There was only one problem. I'd invested so much time and energy into carving out a niche for myself professionally in California that I didn't know what I'd do for a living. Should I go back to school? Become a realtor? This was a new twist on my predicament. I was living somewhere but not working.

As the place was finished and I moved in, I started to formulate a plan for work. In Canada, I could create my own opportunities in television without relying on so many others. The first thing I needed was new headshots. Mike suggested we take pictures in the space we'd renovated to mark the end of the project. He suggested his friend Carole could come help.

Long story longer, Carole is the love of my life and we've been married for 10 years this year. We have two daughters, nine and seven, and we live just outside Truro within a mile of Carole's folks.

Funny how if you start tracing back all the seemingly inconsequential decisions you make in life, how they all conspire to deliver you to exactly where you're supposed to be at that very moment. If I hadn't always had a burning desire to answer "what if" questions, if my mother hadn't had a dentist appointment, if I had become a realtor.

Carole and I built the log home of our dreams in a farmer's field outside of Truro. The wind whistles pretty hard off the Bay of Fundy but we have space, we have privacy, and we have each other.

As I write this on a cold Saturday morning in the country, with a rare empty house and a full teapot and a few lazy snowflakes landing on the deck outside my window, there is little doubt in my mind that I am home.

Carole is my home. Our daughters are my home. And as a result, our house is my home.

Every scratch on the floor. Every giggle. Every tiny flawed potato we grow in the garden. Every sunrise, sunset and snowstorm.

I am home.

Jonathan Torrens has worked in Canadian TV for 30 years as a performer, writer, director and producer. A winner of multiple Gemini Awards and Canadian Screen Awards, Jonathan started as one of the hosts of Street Cents, *CBC's International Emmy Award-winning consumer affairs show for teenagers. From there he hosted his own critically acclaimed talk show* Jonovision *for five years.*

Most audiences know him as J-Roc, the rapper character from Trailer Park Boys. *Other credits include* Air Farce, 22 Minutes, The Joe Schmo Show *and* Letterkenny Problems.

These days Jonathan is one half of the popular podcast duo Taggart & Torrens *with Jeremy Taggart (former drummer of Our Lady Peace). TnT has more than four million downloads and their book* Canadianity *(published by HarperCollins) is a bestseller. Winner of the 2018 Canadian Comedy Award for Best Audio Program, TnT is releasing a record on the Dine Alone label in 2019.*

IT IS NOT ABOUT THE GEESE

Elaine McCluskey

IF YOU THINK IT IS strange that 70 well-meaning people in Tilley hats and yellow ponchos staged a slightly surreal memorial service in Dartmouth, Nova Scotia, for two domesticated geese, and someone played "Blackbird" on a guitar and someone wrote a haiku poem, you are only half right.

The geese, you see, were not normal geese.

They were snippy and white and imperious, and they did what they pleased.

For years, they and roughly seven others had presided over Sullivan's Pond, which has a small island and a totem pole from British Columbia. They routinely waddled across a busy street named Prince Albert Road in a marked crosswalk. And cars routinely stopped, and people took their photos as though they were The Beatles on the cover of *Abbey Road*, and everyone in my hometown missed them when they left the pond for the winter, and everyone was happy when they came back.

They weren't normal geese.

On another street by the pond lives an extremely badass orange cat. And he's not normal either. OK? He walks through traffic five or six times a day like he is Moses parting the Red Sea. Wades out onto wet rocks. Enters houses. When people open the doors of their parked cars, he audaciously jumps inside and settles himself on their rear window like he is one of those "winky cats" people used to buy, the ones with illuminated eyes that blinked on turns.

Part of the collective psyche, Pekoe is celebrated enough to be on a mural. So ingrained that his owner went online and thanked the community for its kindness to her irrepressible cat.

And I pray to God that some unlucky driver never accidentally hits him, like that driver hit the now-departed geese, because people would probably lose their minds again. And the wise guys would ridicule them. And try to turn their public sadness into a Christopher Guest mockumentary full of oddballs from *Best in Show* and *Waiting for Guffman*.

And that's too bad. Because some of the best parts of Nova Scotia are strange. And sometimes that's where the joy lives, in between the sweetness and the naïveté that take the sting out of life.

Sullivan's Pond: where an unnamed driver ran down three geese in the summer of 2017, killing two and injuring one. Hashtag DartmouthGeese. Let me explain.

The pond is a favourite backdrop for wedding and graduation photos. It has an open-air concert pavilion. A while back, at the urging of a group of mothers, a small park was added in memory of children gone too soon. It has benches and flowers, and as its focal point, a silver-coloured dragonfly sculpture that appears to soar above the water. It is, for many, a place of reflection and love.

Sullivan's Pond was dug, according to historians, in the 1830s for a practical purpose — to complete a waterway of lakes to connect Halifax Harbour with the Bay of Fundy. Above the pond is Lake Banook, one of 25 in The City of Lakes, known for the purposes of this piece as Dartmouth, not Halifax, Darkside, Darkness, or other dopey names.

People swim in Lake Banook, from beaches or the seawall. They skate.

Long before the British settlement of Halifax in 1749, the principal lakes (Banook, Micmac and Charles) had been used for thousands of years by the seminomadic Mi'kmaq as part of a trans-provincial canoe route from Chebucto (Halifax) to Cobequid (head of the Bay of Fundy). (*Canadian Encyclopedia*)

Lake Banook is near a Superstore and a Robin's, but it transcends its mundane setting. It is one of those places in Nova Scotia with singular power, accrued through history and use and accidental beauty. When you are on the lake, you could be navigating a Mi'kmaw birch-bark canoe through streams past beavers and bald eagles. You could be in Lane 4 at the Olympic Games.

Lake Banook is grand enough to have hosted the world canoe/kayak championships and the junior worlds. People walk around it all year. They bike. And paddlers run around, flighty pre-teens still strapped to yellow lifebelts, and buff tanned people in red Canada singlets.

I don't have the numbers for you, but Dartmouth has, I swear, more sprint canoe/kayak paddlers than any town or city in Canada. Olympians. Canada Games medallists. Pan Am champs. In summer, you will see dozens of kayaks and canoes at a time, tippy carbon fibre slivers of speed that are made in Poland and Portugal and come in custom colours. Zebra stripes. Polka dots. Shark heads.

Lake Banook is that place where you can imagine being on podium in Slovenia or the Czech Republic with "Oh Canada" playing and tears streaming down your mother's cheeks. Next to someone named Yurii or Marko. It is — as much as the hockey rink where Sidney Crosby grew up — a place of dreams.

Lake Banook also has rowers, dragon boats, and stand-up paddleboards. Like all places magical, there are myths and conflicting stories; there is lore and there are lies. If you were to look up Lake Banook on Wikipedia some time ago, you would have found this astounding fact:

> *Lake Banook has also become known internationally for a naturally occurring phenomenon, which allows its water temperature to remain at relatively warm temperatures year-round. This is due to the large amount of sediment dumped into the lake during construction for the 1989 Junior World Championships. The high amount of phosphorus in the lake has led the water to remain at such a high temperature. Records dating back to 1989 indicate that the water temperature of Lake Banook has never fallen below 8.3 degrees, which was an all-time low in January, 1997. This makes Lake Banook a very desirable destination for paddlers, for the simple fact that they may train year-round without the requirement of a safety belt. (Wikipedia, deleted)*

That, of course, is entirely untrue, and was written by paddlers balking at orders to wear safety belts during "cold-water" conditions in the spring. And yes, it was a joke, but it lasted for years, and maybe, like many jokes, it was wishful thinking.

I love Lake Banook, but we are on a break right now.

I am seeing other places, and it's all on me, *that* time, *that* place in my life.

On Canada Day, my husband and I drove two and a half hours to the South Shore town of Lockeport, which has a mile-long sandy beach. A beach you might find in a glossy travel brochure, the kind of beach that clears your mind and smells like freedom. A geodesic dome of calm. When you are on that ion-charged beach, the waves are writing pages of your novel for you, the sand is massaging years from your bones.

Nova Scotians have long understood the power of the ocean, but neuroscientists at a conference in California tried to break it down. There is, they suggested, a "similarity in chemical composition of the brain, body water, and seawater." There is a sense of safety instilled by a flat horizon that allows humans to spot incoming threats.

According to a story in the *Santa Cruz Sentinel*, the experts believe that the ocean's *whoosh* is calming because of its regular pattern. Noxious noise is random. The ocean heightens your awareness of your emotions by creating a mild meditative state. The salt-air ions and the colour blue play party tricks with your mind.

In Lockeport, years ago, you could see schooners returning from the Grand Banks heavy with cod. Back in the days when small town Nova Scotia hummed with factories and mills, when people made their living from farms or the sea, before men marched off to war and troop ships filled Halifax Harbour, before it all became so different.

The day we were there, we drove past the beach to the centre of town. We saw young couples holding hands; we saw a man in an 81 shirt. We walked by a house that had a Boston Bruins shrine in a window and, proving that there *may, just may*, be love out there for the anti-Sid, Brad Marchand, we saw a woman wearing a knee brace with a Bruins logo.

There was a cake. Speeches. And then Lockeport — a rugged town of 530 people, a town you wouldn't want to pick a fight with — held a children's parade. And some children drove motorized miniature cars decorated to the nines. And flag-festooned bicycles. Some were pulled in wagons. Others walked in costume, and one girl wore a red felt cape with white fake-fur trim and she seemed as sweet and guileless as the heroine in one of my favourite movies, *Little Miss Sunshine*. And it was strangely lovely.

An American writer, John Koenig, coined the word *sonder* to mean the psychological state of discovering that everyone has a life as exciting and as complex as yours. That's what I'm discovering about Nova Scotia towns. They are as exciting and as complex as mine.

One day, we went to the Acadian shore, stopping on the way at a McDonald's in Barrington Passage, where we overheard the staff casually note: "There's a shark down at the causeway and it's eating seals." In Lower Woods Harbour, we saw fishing boats with inspired names like *Stairway to Heaven*, *Grampy's Boys*, and *Big Bucks*, the last name a play on words with a deer motif.

We drove through Yarmouth to the municipality of Clare, which consists of a chain of Acadian communities along St. Mary's Bay, places like Meteghan, Saulnieville, and Comeauville. Places with giant skies, brilliant sunsets, and *rapure* pie.

The early Acadians were expelled in the 1750s, but they returned, bringing with them a culture celebrated with flags, food, and a French-language university. Next to Université Sainte-Anne in Church Point (Pointe-de-l'Église) is a structure reputed to be the largest wooden church in the Americas. *Paroisse Ste Marie, Fondée en 1799. Musée Religieux*, which is open to the public. A towering comeback to history.

According to its website, the "church is based on the French Breton style and it is the only church in the world with this style of architecture, which is built out of wood."

> *A historical place of worship, the church, with its steeple rising 56.4 m (185 feet) above the ground, is the largest wooden church in North America. Built over*

> a period of two years, from 1903 to 1905, by 1500 volunteers under the supervision of a master carpenter who could neither read nor write, it features large columns which are actually complete 20 m (70ft) tall tree trunks. The tall steeple is anchored down using 40 tons of rocks and contains 3 large bells with a combined weight of almost 2 tons.'" (http://www.museeeglisesaintemariemuseum.ca/en/)

And, then, if you drive a short distance further, in a landscape of humble wooden houses and fishing boats, of boatyards and car dealerships, you will see another magnificent church, this one made of granite.

> Église Saint-Bernard
> Construction 1910-1942
> Première Messe 1942

Spectacularly dwarfing everything around it. A gothic testament to will.

The granite was brought in by rail car and then transported by ox cart to the site, and the rocks were put in place, patiently and expertly, over 32 years as money was raised. Three sets of red double doors welcome you. When we went inside, the church was empty of people, and the silence reverberated like one long prayer and light shone through high windows halfway to heaven, and we felt in awe.

I was born in Nova Scotia, but I don't have the centuries of history the Acadians have; my genetic memory is rooted in red Island clay and a death ship from Ireland and a small cemetery in Iona, PEI, filled with names like Murphy and McCluskey. But this I know — in a land of long winters and hard beginnings, of unplowed roads and treacherous online trolls, it is easy to retreat to a warm safe room and stay there; it is easy to be lonely. According to Statistics Canada, more Canadians than ever — 28.2 per cent — now live alone, and according to media reports, many describe themselves as lonely.

In a *Globe and Mail* story, experts linked loneliness with depression, anxiety, and a suppressed immune system and cardiovascular function. The story quoted *Happy City: Transforming Our Lives Through Urban Design*, by Charles Montgomery: "Social isolation just may be the greatest environmental hazard of city living — worse than noise, pollution, or even crowding." Montgomery then told the paper: "The way we've built cities — suburbs with no central meeting place, prioritizing the car and the condo tower, passing restrictive zoning bylaws — has made the problem worse." Technology, some argue, is contributing to our loneliness.

All of that loneliness makes some people sad and it makes, I believe, some people angry, an anger all too often manifested in nastiness. In Halifax, a man — not a goose — was struck in a crosswalk, a shockingly common occurrence that has defied explanation. (Around 200 people are hit in Halifax each year, over half in crosswalks.)

The struck man was charged with a summary offence ticket under the Motor Vehicle Act and given a hefty fine, which should have been the end of it. But the online horde was not sated; they rose in a chorus of vengeance.

"If he dies, I hope his family gets billed for the damage to the car!!"

"What no law against being a dumb ass?" wrote one.

"Dumb ass deserves a ticket and more," wrote another. "This is what laws are for."

And they didn't care about the sanctity of our laws. They didn't care about the safety of our streets. They were simply people so angry and so disappointed with their own lives that they wanted — more than they wanted happiness or an all-inclusive trip to Jamaica — to see misery heaped upon others.

They were the people who would show up for a British navy flogging during the Napoleonic wars, the "chattering mob" chillingly depicted by Thomas Raddall in *Hangman's Beach*.

And people did the same thing when the Sullivan's Pond geese were killed; they went online and called for the head of the driver, and they whipped themselves into a frenzy of opprobrium and reprisal. And then others lashed out at the poncho-wearing gatherers and called them names.

And Nova Scotians, after all we've been through, are better than that. We just *are*.

In Dartmouth, there is a tiny Italian man named Carmine, who drives his bicycle around Lake Banook like clockwork. Some days, he wears a white sleeveless undershirt and white gloves. Knee socks. He is, people who know him say, well over 80 years of age and he used to run a fish-and-chip shop from the storefront where he still lives. You will see him at the Superstore, getting groceries with his bike.

And he is awesome, and everyone knows him, and it's a good day when you see Carmine, fearlessly, and some might say perilously, driving through a frenzied rotary like he is Lance freaking Armstrong.

People and things can bond us in an unspoken way — a common object, a common person — someone we respect for their perseverance, their audacity, their willingness to just be who they are. An invariable that is there when other things aren't — jobs, relationships, or grown children like mine who have fled the nest, children who not that long ago were racing kayaks on Lake Banook and in a strange country for Canada while I stood on the side of a course, my heart pounding, their inevitable departure leaving me so bereft that I now drive across Nova Scotia seeking new and wondrous sights to inspire me. To move me. And they do.

Elaine McCluskey is the author of three short-story collections and two novels. She has had stories featured in journals such as Geist, subTerrain, The Antigonish Review, The Dalhousie Review, Fiddlehead, Room, *and* Riddle Fence. *She placed second in the Fish international contest in Ireland. She was a Journey Prize finalist. She lives in Dartmouth; the McCluskeys are originally from PEI, where they landed in 1847 from Ireland. Elaine is working on her sixth book of fiction.*

WHEN NURSES WORE WHITE

Carol Bruneau

MY MOTHER HAS BEEN GONE longer than she was with me in this world. She died 36 years ago, three years younger than I am now. Reaching my auspicious birthday, I couldn't help feeling a sort of relief, but it was instantly swallowed by the regret that my mother didn't live longer, a lot longer.

My regret is mingled with the sad fact that life robs some — many, actually — of the chance to live it to its fullest, or long enough to glimpse in the present some sense of completeness. "In the fullness of time" — isn't that how we imagine the as-yet-unlived parts of our lives unfolding and their meaning, if we're lucky, playing out?

It's taken more than half of my life to be able to write this about my mother — no reflection on her but on me and the power of reticence, a strongbox containing emotion. This isn't to say that memories of her haven't leaked into my writing. They have, but in dribs and drabs and in the comfort of made-up stories about other mothers and daughters, friends, sisters, and aunts. But all of these are in a liminal way linked to her, I realize just now, linked by threads that are invisible but tough as dental floss and good old garden twine.

Reader of my earliest three-word sentences, my mother was the one to plant the seed: "Maybe you'll be a writer?" Maybe it's a little strange that it was her absence that prodded me into writing fiction? Or maybe this isn't strange at all, her absence a daredevil coaxing me to write what I want, spared the worry of offending her. Writers write for all sorts of reasons but, last time I checked, doing it to please our moms isn't generally one of them. My mother never saw any of my stories or my name in print, but this is minor compared to the fact that she never saw my sons; the youngest is older than the age at which I lost her. Yet she remains with me, her absence a presence. One that's been with me all along, it's a distant but radiant force in the wings of my writing: an indelible muse, my softer, smarter alter-ego, an ideal listener, the kindest possible reader.

To write nakedly of my mother is to write nakedly of me. It's like stripping off for a tandem polar bear dip, the two of us plunging into the North Atlantic on some never-ending New Year's Day. There's ice, lots of ice, and our skins' winter paleness — which is no accident since both figure in a memory from before I could talk: Mom and I watching an ice-breaker cut its way up the Northwest Arm. Bundled against a bitter wind, she was carrying me, we were joined at the hip. It's no accident either, that other memories of her are veiled in white, as she died in the dead of a soulless January.

Because of the illness she suffered, her life ended some time before she died. But who's to say what a single ending means?

My mother was a nurse and though I've been without her longer than I was lucky enough to have her, some of my best memories of her — also some of my saddest — place her in hospitals. For most of her relatively short life, she loved hospitals — although after she died, her sisters' stories about Mom's early queasiness at the very smell of a hospital surprised and sustained me. These still do, in a funny way, despite her having passed away in one.

They say home is where the heart is. My mom used to say a person was in the best of hands in hospital, that there was no safer, kinder place to be than among those who cared for the sick. Maybe it was self-reflective: meeting her profession's demands was a point of pride.

My earliest recollections are tied to her preparing for work: waiting in the back of her blue Volkswagen while she picked up her caps from the Chinese laundry — a freshly starched stack like steamrolled wings. Before work, she took pains straight-pinning her RN's black velvet ribbons to their stiff white cotton — a marvel, to me, that such things could be shaped into caps, even more of a marvel that with a few bobby pins she could keep one on her head. Next came dabbing whitener on her oxfords, the stuff in a tube like a bingo dauber, then putting on white stockings held up with garters. An understatement to say the invention of pantyhose delighted her.

Just as vividly, I recall her Saturdays on the job. It's bizarre to think of now, but back then, in the late fifties, if my dad was also working and my aunt couldn't babysit, Mom brought me along. One of her best friends ran the EEG department, conducting electro-encephalographs in the little pavilion at the top of the Victoria General. It sat on the roof like a toque and, second only to Citadel Hill, was the city's highest vantage point, its wall of windows facing out to sea. But at age four I had no interest in scenery, not when there were people to watch — human specimens suffering brain injuries and what were probably debilitating cases of mental and neurological disorders. To me they were like large, mostly silent dolls or mannequins; I remember few of them speaking, most showing little response as my mother shaved their heads, marked their scalps with red grease pencil, then helped to affix electrodes. The women looked like brides of Frankenstein or Phyllis Diller, their poor heads sprouting wires. I can still almost hear my mother and her friend's easy, cheerful chitchat intended, probably, to put the patients at ease.

I would sit quietly in a corner and scribble on any fudged sheets of graph paper the EEG machine spat out. I still remember the high-pitched, irregular *scritching* sounds of its wiry fingers tracing brainwaves, their evidence recorded in jagged red lines. Another marvel of my mother's professional bearing was how easily she ignored me — and how very unprofessional of her to have her child there at work, in her comfort zone. How would that be viewed today? Yet she and her friend comported themselves with an undivided attention and an unflappable calm that seem impossible now: theirs was a steadiness that could've withstood nuclear attack, I think, looking back. But I was much too young to think then of my mother being extraordinary; she was just my mom and this work was what mothers did.

Valedictorian of her nursing class, Mom trained at the Children's Hospital and kept up her friendships there. On days off she volunteered at the IWK's gloomy predecessor housed in a grim red brick building beside the even grimmer Civic Hospital, both long gone. While she socialized, I watched cartoons on TV in the street-facing playroom, such as it was — a dingy room with children in johnny shirts and in wheelchairs colouring and doing, sort of, things that most little kids do. Being among them I never felt odd or out of place or fortunate in the ways you might imagine. I was far too young to think, however childishly, that having a nurse for a mom might confer a special status. I was too healthy and naïve to realize that the simple pleasures of being well weren't to be taken for granted. Mostly I liked being among other *Huckleberry Hound* fans and resented being dragged away from *Yogi Bear* when it was time to leave.

My mother was at her best in these settings. She was happiest working — not in the home, as we say, but in her profession surrounded by her comrades. She was a terrible cook, though she could bake circles around anyone. She loved to sing, and she was full of stories. Her best ones were, of course, from the hospital, and though she edited them (slightly) while within earshot of me, I savoured their dark, unseemly edges of sickness and the dangers lurking in each corridor and doorway, dangers that people like my mom worked to fend off. At age four I was all curiosity, a tiny voyeur, and on those Saturdays, before she could rush me past the open wards I'd steal good long looks at people in bed, family members murmuring around them. It must have been their solicitude, decency or exhaustion that kept anyone from asking, "What's that kid doing here?" Visiting hours generally precluded children.

My mom would tug me away, give me a gentle scolding. But nobody else said a word. To me these people were the intruders. The hospital was her purview and I was her guest; in my preschooler's mind, it was our house, our rules. Kids, like cats and dogs, can be territorial, and to me my mother's confidence marked the hospital as hers. Not only her territory, but a realm where sad, bad things could happen only to strangers.

"What do you wanna be when you grow up?" someone else's mother once asked. My mom and I were sitting together at my Grade One closing concert. Like a cat reacting to the sound of a can opener I trilled, "A nurse!" — the brightest, boldest answer in my worldview, and offered to please.

I can still feel my warm bubble of pride and the icy chill when my mother punctured it, her response a cynical laugh and an offhand comment that nursing was too much hard, unrecognized work. "Don't ever be a nurse," she instructed straight away, neglecting to suggest an alternative, like being a doctor. It was the early 60s and no one in her blue-collar, working-class family would ever have entertained such an uppity notion. Doctors were gods, or at the very least a higher form of human being: *Doctor Kildare* and *Ben Casey* would eventually replace the cartoon animals in my TV-land.

What I remember most about that day is feeling betrayed, as if the cheerful example of my mother's attention to hygiene, well-made beds and routine — the rigours of the hospital that she imprinted on our household — was suspect, worse, untrue.

It wasn't long after this that she said, "Maybe you'll be a writer," having few if any clues about the rigours of writing, and contradicting her later advice that every woman, no matter what, must be able to earn her own living. It was a no-nonsense dictum that paralleled Virginia Woolf's about women writers having rooms of their own, though I'm pretty sure my mother never read Woolf. It doesn't matter. My mother was very smart and valued discipline — the best way most of us know for fending off, or trying to fend off, life's dark clouds and chaotic shadows.

Yet there's something mesmerizing about darkness, the kind that comes of knowing life is fragile. I often wonder if, as a very young woman, a teenager, she was drawn to it the way I am as a writer: because darkness adds value to colour. The second-youngest in a family of nine children, she witnessed her share of it growing up in a Cape Breton coal-mining town. God only knows what prompted her to go into nursing. Her sisters — four in total, only one still living — remembered taking her along to visit someone in the town's tiny hospital, which back in the 1940s occupied a former mine manager's home. Mom barely got past the door before fainting; so much for bringing some cheer. You could've knocked my aunts over with a feather, apparently, when she announced she was going to nursing school.

But Mom had this calm about her — a sort of resignation — as well as a Cape Bretoner's sense of humour, bred by an un-blinkered awareness of hardships. When her father lost his leg to diabetes, it was her job to wait ashore with his crutches while he swam the length of the beach. She had a fatalistic streak that located itself in people's suffering, yet she nursed zero tolerance for self-pity and any kind of hypochondria, especially if used as a ploy. As long as you were still breathing, you could go to school. I suspect that it tired her, upholding this standard among the healthy, and that she found it easier dealing with the sick.

In the way a novelist turns to conflict for shaping plot, something in my mother gravitated toward the ill. She had experience aplenty — not just at others' bedsides but at her own, dealing with her body's failings, and from a young age. She was one smart cookie, my beloved mom. But all the smarts in the world can't protect you from bad luck. Never a person of much faith, she succumbed — she believed she did — to the predictions of a palm-reader who once amused "the girls" by telling fortunes under the hospital stairs. Mom's indicated that she wouldn't graduate with her class — in fact, her graduation was sidelined when she contracted tuberculosis and spent two years in the Kentville San, as it was known, and recuperating in Cape Breton. That she went back to school and graduated at all was feat enough, and then she topped her class.

As a little kid, I accompanied her year after year to her annual chest x-rays. She'd strip down to her slip before disappearing into the cubicle, then, afterwards, get back into her dress — I recall a tailored shirt dress with a full skirt — and her high-heeled pumps. I remember her jaunty mood at hearing that the slides were clean for another year: her relief and, perhaps, a measured disbelief, for she never quite escaped a nagging pessimism.

It always seemed she was dodging something — the eight balls of disease, accidents and the other assorted tragedies that she and my aunts discussed whenever they gathered at my grandmother's. Instead of sitting in the kitchen with my uncles and my dad, they would occupy the "dining room," so-named because it contained a small table at which no one, to my recollection, ever ate. A tiny spotless room, it had a coal fireplace, lace curtains fluttering at two narrow windows that faced my grandmother's garden, and, because it was next to the bathroom, a pervasive smell of toothpaste.

It was here that stories of the sick, dying and dead were shared, as well as stories about other live comings and goings, mostly goings, because this was Cape Breton in King Coal's last throes.

It was in this room, I think, that my mother's natural tendency to await some large, non-velvet hammer or wrecking ball from heaven sprouted from a seed and grew roots. I think of her now in that room as a twenty-something lying on a daybed pushed against the papered wall, her muscles weakened by the torpor of bed rest. How that very weakness must've lit a firecracker of resolve to get herself back on her feet, get away and make her own life.

Later, she would say that if she hadn't left Cape Breton she never would've gotten sick. That might well have been true about the TB, which she no doubt caught from a patient in an era when the disease was rampant and nurses-in-training learned all their skills from hands-on duty — duty that included peeling potatoes. No romantic views here of Florence Nightingale with her oil lamp beaming light from patient to patient, so it's no wonder Mom warned me off following in her footsteps.

None of this touches on the fact that I would've made a terrible nurse. It's funny, sobering, to note that before Nightingale's day nurses were dragooned from society's most desperate orders, women with no other options and cast as reprobates whose selfless work only gained respect once it was elevated by Nightingale's famous virtue. By the time my mom became an RN, nurses were like secular nuns, professional saints whose pristine white uniforms signalled a higher power second to — a distant second to — that of doctors.

My mother loved the ideal Cape Breton — St. Ann's lookoff was her idea of Earth's most heavenly view — and I believe she loved the ideals of her profession even more. When I was nine and my sister just turned two, anxious to have an income of her own and a purpose besides homemaking, she joined the nursery staff at the old Grace Maternity. Caring for the newborns, she was in seventh heaven, and her favourite 3-11 shifts were with the premmies, as she called them — not preemies, as they're called today. Hands down, she loved the premmies best, some no bigger than a pound of butter, hooked up to tubes in their incubators. She'd call home each night before her shift's end to check with Dad on how we were. When I was old enough to stay up and answer the phone I'd struggle to hear her voice above the crying — the ferocious *ahh-waahhh, ahh-waaaah* of all those tiny babies. A teenager, I asked how she could stand it, all the noise, all the crying. She could've been on a beach or looking down over St. Ann's gut, her voice that amused and charged, no doubt with adrenalin, as she said with conviction, "I love it."

She did, too. She loved the babies and the "girls" she worked with. She liked many of the mothers, too, except those who considered the hospital an all-in resort, nurses at their beck and call. The ones who demanded to have their beds "wound up" while watching TV and smoking — this back in the days when smoking was allowed everywhere — those whom she considered to be perfectly capable of looking after themselves and struck her as lazy. My mother hated smoking and she hated laziness, in any form, real or imagined — maybe because the place she came from was nicknamed Lazytown?

She believed in keeping busy. She loved the busyness of mending bees and coffee klatches undertaken as part of the charity work she did with other like-minded women, on evenings she hosted. When she wasn't at the hospital she was volunteering for organizations like the Ottawa-based Unitarian Service Committee, collecting clothing, arranging its shipment to the needy in far-flung places like Korea. One rainy fall day, I remember her driving its founder, Dr. Lotta Hitschmanova, around town to interviews on one of the noted humanitarian's visits to Halifax. If you're of a certain age and disposition, you might remember Dr. Hitschmanova's military garb and heavy Eastern European accent from ads on TV. I remember my mother's awe barely contained by her calm efficiency as they chatted and I listened from the Volkswagen's backseat.

Back in the *Huckleberry Hound* days, Mom had me in tow when she sorted donations in a temporary depot, an abandoned army barrack wangled for the Committee's purpose. I remember the clothes' musty smell and the chill of the empty rooms still charged with the vibe of past activity — the palpable absence of soldiers who had bunked there, is how I'd describe it now. Its woodwork echoed the fullness of lost bravery, an absence my preschooler's imagination tried to fill with the faces and voices of invisible people. A small, active child, I should've been bored and fidgety, but I wasn't. I was fully absorbed, my imaginings as mesmerizing to me as the curiosities I glimpsed in the hospital.

In a more ordinary, warm-blooded way, I was content just to be Mom's sidekick — but unbeknownst to her and to me, this might've been the start of a double perspective, weighing the world that exists with the parallel universe in my imagination, full of living dimensions. Out of nothing I tried to conjure the presence of the absent, those who, at one time, had filled the place with their eating, breathing, sleeping, and yes, using the toilet — men who, I realize now, had squeezed ordinary activities around work that must have been dangerous, even heroic. Some physical traces of their fuzzy, restless spirits were what I longed to see, because restlessness wasn't strange or threatening to me: it was a feeling that my mother — for all her calm — exuded.

She gave off the lingering sense that she had a lengthy list of tasks to accomplish, and ever-dwindling hours and chances in which to do so. This fed an occasional silence that was hard for a child to fathom, the silence behind headaches that kept her in bed on Sundays, leaving our dad to take over — a silence that permeated the house and made us tiptoe around, as if on eggshells.

There was a darkness there, all right. Some call it the black dog, and by turns it plagues most if not all of us. In retrospect — all things considered, weighed by experience and knowing that most people do the best they can with what they're given — my mother had a good life. A quiet, ordinary, decent life. But maybe it was too quiet, too ordinary, because always simmering beneath her smile was a dissatisfaction — an urge to want what lay just beyond the horizon somewhere, perhaps not so far from sight but inaccessible.

And doesn't this describe the writing life and writing itself, trying to nail real things down with mere words? To host, then find good homes for our ideas? It's taken entering life's final third for me to realize and accept that this is okay: we try and fall short and often fail, yet accepting with grace the limits of our ordinariness is what living's all about.

My mother did not go gently into her dark night, however — certainly not so quietly as we seem to be called to do. It's because she wasn't ready — old enough — to.

She was diagnosed — or misdiagnosed because, of a slew of doctors, few could or would put a name to her grab-bag of symptoms as anything worse than

Parkinson's disease — when I was 17. My sister was only 10. It started as a weakness in one arm, then a tremor dismissed by one doctor as symptomatic of "the change of life." Was it ever. It soon progressed to the rest of her limbs, turning her walk into a shuffle and destroying her body's sense of balance. Accompanying her to her endless appointments, I watched in frustration as the neurologist she'd placed her final hopes in asked her to walk for him. What a sad, humiliating exercise, this woman who had cared for the most fragile, delicate human beings imaginable summoning everything she had to walk a straight line without looking as if she were three sheets to the wind — my mother who reviled alcohol and, in my entire memory of her, never touched anything stronger than tea.

I remember how this doctor swiftly and, to us, cavalierly confirmed the worst — or what Mom thought at the time was the worst, Parkinson's, but ended up being a lot worse: a baffling systemic degeneration that combined Parkinson's symptoms with the more extreme ones of Lou Gehrig's disease.

My heart still sinks, somehow, all these years later, at the naming of such death sentences after their victims. "And what are you famous for?" I imagine the small talk on the other, inaccessible side of the veil that separates them from us, the living.

I remember my mother's panic attacks as she lay in bed for nearly a decade before the suffering ceased — I remember her rage, her furious, frustrated tears, and most of all, her speechlessness, how the disease stole her ability to talk. I remember her choked attempts at vocalizations. I remember when she stopped trying. I have not forgotten the anguish when my dad would phone to say she thought she was expiring — and we would gather around her bed, the bed my parents still shared, as she silently raged against the machine, whatever the machine is or was. The mechanisms, the channels, the gears and cogs that put us in our places, that chain and confine us to or shake us forever from our comfort zones, whether we approve of them or not.

I remember before any of the worst of it, when she could still walk, talk, feed, and bathe herself and even cook and do dishes — Mom sitting in her wingback chair in her yellow sweater, rust-coloured skirt, pantyhose, and the battered Hushpuppies she wore around the house, and the bitter despair in her voice: "I'm just waiting to die."

And so she was. That's how she handled it. Waiting. Waiting all through the ministrations of nurses in and out of hospital, those my father hired to care for her when he was working. Waiting for the next pill — how my throat still tightens at the trade names Sinemet and Levodopa — for someone to pop down her throat. Waiting while the rest of us — my dad, my aunt, my sister and I — tried to decipher what on Earth she meant as she spelled out each word letter by letter on the alphabet Mom's eldest sister printed on a piece of pantyhose cardboard. It was anger that kept my mother moving her index finger, pure rage that fuelled her determination to be heard — I do not know if at this point it had anything to do with love of life. My mother's *joie de vivre* had been in working; and her life —

any traces of joy in it — ended when the illness forced her to quit her job, around the same time she gave up driving.

The very last time she drove was giving me a lift to school, one autumn day after an early snowfall. I remember thanking her and getting out and stepping into the snow, and how not a single thing about any of it felt extraordinary.

She recanted her old, naïve words about being in the best of hands in a hospital, eventually refusing to darken the doors of one, but before that, sitting through a Thanksgiving dinner with a broken hip after falling, and only relenting, slowly, when the ambulance arrived.

This was the beginning of the long, slow ending. Once bedridden, she never stood or walked or did much of anything on her own again.

I see those news clips on TV now of music therapy for Parkinson's patients, how music resets the damaged wiring in their brains, setting them free enough to dance.

I daydream about what it would have been like, dragging, pulling my mother up from her bed, holding her in my youthful arms and putting on her favourite records — the Inkspots, Mantovani, Patty Page, Vera Lynn — not to mention singing with her all the songs she used to sing when she was healthy and I was small —*Spanish Eyes, Rock of Gibraltar, Moon River* — the list is long and though I can still imagine her voice, most of their tunes and lyrics now escape me. I imagine her putting on her coral lipstick, beige high heels, and an apron over her nice shirtdress, throwing potatoes in a pot and boiling them to mush while twirling like Julie Andrews in *The Sound of Music*, the steam giving her cheeks a rosy flush.

I close my eyes to picture her dancing. And when I do, her face appears, looms, warm and smiling in whatever lobe of the brain and whatever chemically-driven impulses — sparks leaping from synapse to synapse — memories and the imagination reside in. There, in a certain sense, they do not die.

The very end of her life is too harsh, too painful to recount — no less because it was inevitable. The hardest part has been her physical absence, especially as I've navigated my own experiences of motherhood without the benefit of her motherly wisdom. I know she would have loved my boys, and I suspect, speaking optimistically, that if she had made it into the final third of life she'd have found contentment.

But who knows? We're given what we're given, our bodies and ourselves and our short allotments of days: call them destinies. As surely as my mother became a nurse, the world should be thankful I didn't follow in her footsteps — ones I never could have filled. But we pick our spots and we pick up threads and suture our wounds with them. Writers write. Nurses will always be. When the last of my sons was born at the Grace — the old Grace, just before it closed for good and was razed — some of my mother's old friends were there in the nursery to receive him. So she was present, somewhere, somehow, in some free-floating version of whiteness — her absence a presence, a muse, a consolation spun of air, as real as fiction can be. In the strangest way, somehow, she was right there, at home.

Carol Bruneau is the author of eight books, the most recent of which are the story collection A Bird on Every Tree, *published in 2017 by Nimbus/ Vagrant Press, and the novel* A Circle on the Surface, *published in 2018 by Vagrant. Bruneau's stories, articles and reviews have appeared in newspapers and journals nationwide, and two of her novels have been published internationally. She lives in Halifax with her husband and their critters, a small black dog and a large tabby cat.*

YOU GET A LINE ...

Jan L. Coates

I'M IN LOW GEAR, BUT I'm still sucking wind by the time I get to the top of Rabbit Hill. The yard at Grampy's old place is full of faded plastic toys and dog crap. Wonder if the new renters like the tree house me and Grampy built back when I was six.

And the brook. Best trout brook in all of Cumberland County right here in my backyard, he always said. He grew up in that big, old house, then he and Gram lived there for the whole 52 years they were married. Mom always says it's a good thing Gram went first since seeing Grampy now would've broken her heart in two.

Lakeview Villa looks about like the run-down elementary school I went to for Grades Four and Five before they bulldozed it. Built in the 60s by somebody with zero imagination. You'd think somebody might at least think to cut the grass every now and then. And water the planters. Dead flowers outside a nursing home? Pretty sure in a book or a story, my English teacher would call that symbolism.

I lock my bike to a post beside the main doors and look down to where I know the lake is. You can see a corner of it, barely, shining in between all the pine trees, way off in the distance. Some view. First time I've been here by myself. Mom's working double-time since they laid off the other woman at Suds 'n Duds. Moron that owns the laundromat's an idiot, but we can use the money.

Did Mom try to guilt me into coming? Hell, yeah.

Did I moan and groan? Heck, yeah. But here I am, and feeling kind of weird about it. It creeps me out thinking I might walk in someday and Grampy will be there dead, and nobody even noticed 'til I showed up.

The heavy glass door slams shut behind me. The smell of sick slams into me at the same time. Like a fist to the nose. Hospital with a hint of cafeteria, toilet and bleach. And piss. Don't forget the piss. I nod to the lady in the little office, but she's busy talking on the phone. They've always got these random baskets of fake flowers hanging around in the lobby. Like funeral flowers or the ones people put on headstones. Flowers are supposed to cheer people up, but these ones are straight-up as depressing as the rest of this place.

All the wards have tree names: Maple, Birch, Oak, Pine. Grampy's on the Willow Ward, a name he'd like since he planted lots of weeping willows all along the brook when he was young. It's the dementia ward. Which he wouldn't like at all. He used to visit his best buddy here, before Elmer finally died of Alzheimer's. He had it even worse than Grampy.

I check the faces, some staring, some sleeping, in the circle of wheelchairs and walkers around the desk and nod at the nurse. Clarissa, her nametag says. Lucky for me, she's one of the all-business ones. Not like some of them that start yakking about everything under the sun the minute you show up. Like they've been waiting all day to pounce on somebody "normal." Clarissa just nods toward his wing. "He'll be so happy to see you. Hasn't had much appetite lately; keeps asking for pan-fried brook trout. Just sits and stares out the window most of the day. I think he's homesick."

I take my time walking down the hall. I like looking at the pictures they put up outside each door. The faces in them are always changing. Not too many people get out of here alive. Grampy's only been in the Villa for eight months, and he's already on his third roommate. It's hard to keep track. Grampy used to call this place Last View Villa, back when he still had a sense of humour.

I stop outside his door and check the name of his latest roommate. Oh, yeah—Johnny Mercer. But not the Johnny Mercer that wrote that old song, *Moon River*, according to Mom. This dude's picture looks like some prison mug shot. They should put up old black-and-white pictures, too, of what the people used to look like when they were young. Before and after shots. There's a note taped under Johnny's picture: *Please check Mr. Mercer's garbage before emptying to make sure there's nothing important in it.*

He's what the nurses call a wanderer, and he's always bringing other people's stuff back to the room. Candy, books, jewellery, stuffed animals. We even found Grampy's glasses on top of his head one time.

Even though it's 3 p.m., Grampy's in bed, still wearing his pyjamas. One of the nurses told Mom he gets a little contrary some days and won't get dressed. His eyes are closed, and he's got his big hands folded across his chest, which, lucky for me, is still moving up and down. He needs his nails cut. And cleaned. I tiptoe across the tile floor, sit down in the only chair, start breathing along with him. Deep breath in; deep breath out. Mr. Mercer must be out wandering.

The sun's shining right in on Grampy's face. He looks rough, like he hasn't shaved for a few days. He gets contrary about that sometimes, too. The nurses say they understand it's a hard thing for a man, having to let somebody else do what he's been doing for himself for 60-plus years. I figure it's gotta be even harder having somebody change your diaper when you've been using the toilet on your own for 80-odd years.

I look around the room. It's a decent colour, pale blue with dark blue trim. His bulletin board's full of pictures of us that Mom put up, to help Grampy remember us. So that didn't happen. He's always asking us who the people are, staring down at him from the wall. There's a couple of big ones of Charlie. Grampy loves our old yellow Lab, but the smells in this place drive Charlie freakin' crazy, and he's even wilder than usual when we bring him in, nosing in everywhere like he's at an all-you-can-sniff buffet. There's a little TV on the dresser and a couple of books beside the bed. But they're just for looks. Grampy hasn't read a book in years. He used to be the best at reading me bedtime stories. He could do all the voices in the Pooh books. His squeaky Piglet voice was just like on TV. Sometimes we read to him, but he mostly falls asleep now, a couple of pages in.

"Benny?"

"Hey, Grampy. No, it's me, Eli." Benny was his big brother who died in the war at the age of 19. Juno Beach, France, 1944. When Gram was alive she always said I was the spitting image of Benny.

He tries to push himself up so he's sitting, but he keeps sliding back down in the skinny bed. I can hear the plastic rustling underneath the sheet. "Don't know what I'm doin', snoozin' the whole day away." His eyes start watering when he squints up at the sun. "What time of day is it?"

I check my watch. "3:30."

"Good lord!" He feels around on the bedside table. "You're lookin' good today, Benny. Too good. Let me get my specs so I can see what you really look like."

I get up and look inside the little drawer. "Don't see them."

He feels around on top of his head. His sproingy grey hair is all mashed down on one side, like a used-up piece of steel wool. "Must have left them downstairs." Except the Villa's only got one floor. "Or did you hide 'em on me again, you rascal?"

"Hang on, Grampy." I pull Mr. Mercer's garbage can out from under his bedside table. "Found 'em!"

He frowns. "Why in tarnation would I put my glasses in there?"

I shrug and whisper, "I think your roommate's got sticky fingers."

He looks up at me without blinking. Did he get the joke? I polish the glasses on my T-shirt, then help him put them on.

He squints up at me. "Now I see — you're just as ugly as ever." He tries to punch my arm, only he misses, just about hits himself in the shoulder. "What's the date again?"

"April 23rd," I say. My 18th birthday, but I don't say that. It would get too confusing.

"What? You mean to tell me we already missed the first three weeks of fishing season! Them trout are waiting for us, boy. Give me a hand getting up, will you, Benny?"

I would if I could, but these days we always get a nurse to help get him into his wheelchair. Sometimes two nurses. It's some insurance rule. The home doesn't want to get sued if he wipes out. "In a minute, Grampy. What'd you have for lunch today?"

That's what Mom always asks, probably since it's the only thing that changes every day. No wonder people in nursing homes lose track of time. It's like the days are on forever repeat.

"Same thing as you, Benny Boy," he says, closing his eyes and patting his flat stomach that used to be a beer gut. "Mmmm… Roast pork with all the fixings and Ma's apple dumplings. Don't you remember?"

I laugh. "Oh, yeah. We got to have seconds on the dumplings."

"Just fetch my jacket out of the closet, will ya? And why do you keep calling me Grampy? What happened to Ralphy?"

I open the closet door. Three pairs of neatly-folded blue cotton pyjamas are stacked on the low shelf. On hangers above, there are three pairs of pants, a flannel housecoat and three plaid shirts. I pick the quilted red plaid one we got him for Christmas and help him get his stick arms into the sleeves. My arms are twice the size of his. I finished growing up and started filling out about the same time he started shrinking. He fumbles around with the shirt buttons for a minute, then I do them up. There's no way I'm gonna wrestle him into a pair of pants. At least he smells fresher than he sometimes does. Pretty sure he'd rather be dead than stuck here sitting in a diaper full of shit. When he was more with it, he'd ask for help. Not so much anymore.

"Now, where's my rubber boots?"

I make like I'm looking for them under the bed. People who can't walk don't need boots. I reach under and pull out his slippers. When I stand back up, he's got his scrawny chicken legs dangling over the side of the bed. His ankles are as big around as my wrists.

"Hang on now, Grampy," I say. "Let's get your boots on." I lean over and slide his bony white feet into the green plaid slippers. They're slipping off him, like somebody bought him the wrong size. Maybe feet shrink, too. Seems he's about half the size he was two years ago.

He sticks out his arms. "Just give me a lift, Benny."

I look toward the hallway, think about calling for the nurse.

But he's smiling so big when I look back at him that instead, I line up the wheelchair with where I hope to hell his butt lands. I make sure the brakes are on, the footpads up, then grab hold of his hands. They're icy cold.

"Cold hands, warm heart," he says, grinning up at me.

I give him a tug, get him up on his feet, then put my arms around his waist, try to turn him so he'll drop down into the wheelchair. Like we're slow dancing. His whole body's vibrating, like Charlie in a thunderstorm. When he finally drops, he's puffing and sweating like crazy, holding onto the chair arms tight. But smiling. "Well, what're you waiting for? Grab the gear and let's hightail it out of here. The fish are bitin', boy!"

I release the brakes, wheel him out into the hall, smile at Clarissa at the nurses' station and stop in front of the locked door to the lobby. On nice days, we're allowed to take him outside for a bit of fresh air. What did Mom say the code was? I try W.I.L.L.O.W. and the door buzzes and swings open. The lady in the lobby office is still on the phone and doesn't look up.

"Yee hah!" He throws his arms up in the air, roller-coaster style, as I push him through the outside door. It slams shut behind us, trapping the sick smell inside. I suck in a bunch of fresh air, hold my face up so the wind will blow the stink off me. Two fat robins are hopping around on the grass, big juicy worms dangling from their beaks.

"Should take those fellas with us to dig us up some bait. What a beauty of a day! It's great to be alive, isn't it Benny?"

I take a deep breath and smile. "Sure is," I say, pushing him along the sidewalk toward the little park at one end of the Villa.

"Where you goin'?" He looks up at me, then points toward the road. "You lost? Home's up that-a-way."

I haven't been down to the brook since we rented his place out while we're waiting for it to sell. Wonder if the fishing gear's still in the barn. And if the renters have been keeping the brook path mowed.

I look down at his hopeful face smiling up at me, his pale blue eyes twinkling, then spin the chair around. "Don't know what I was thinking, Ralphy."

"How's that fishin' song go again?" he asks. "That one Dad used to sing?"

I glance over my shoulder back at the main doors, then start running.

"You get a line, I'll get a pole, Honey," I sing.

He holds on tight to the arms and joins in on the second line. "You get a line, I'll get a pole, Babe."

"All together now," I sing. "You get a line, I'll get a pole. We'll go fishin' in the crawdad hole. Honey, Baby mine."

Then we laugh like fools, all the way home.

Jan Coates lives and writes in Wolfville. She started writing for young readers because of her own love of words and stories, and a passion for helping kids become lifelong readers and writers. Besides writing and reading, Jan plays badminton, bikes, travels, and shops for all things second-hand.

Her first picture book, Rainbows in the Dark, *was published by Second Story Press in 2005. She has also written 16 ESL illustrated chapter books for Caramel Tree, a Korean-based English Language publisher, and two non-fiction workbooks for Quebec ESL students. Her debut novel,* A Hare in the Elephant's Trunk *(Red Deer Press, 2010), was a finalist for the Governor General's Literary Award (Children's Text) in 2011, as well as an Ann Connor Brimer Award finalist.*

She has also written four middle-grade novels: Say What You Mean *(Nevermore Press, 2019);* Talking to the Moon *(Red Deer Press, 2018);* The Power of Harmony *(Red Deer, 2013), also a Brimer finalist, and* Rocket Man, *a YALSA Quick Pick for Reluctant Readers (Red Deer Press, 2014). Jan's other picture books include:* Dancing With Daisy *(Running the Goat Press, 2019);* Sky Pig *(Pajama Press, 2016),* The King of Keji *(Nimbus, 2015), and* A Halifax Time-Travelling Tune *(Nimbus, 2018).*

AN ISLAND JUST IN TIME

Silver Donald Cameron

THE NIGHT SKY IS DARK, and the land is darker. The sea is darkest of all, its charcoal surface relieved only by the restless white curl of the breakers. The water is hissing up the sand, then seething with the sound of pebbles clicking and rolling in the backwash.

It is a cool June night in Isle Madame, Nova Scotia, a fly-speck on the map just off the southeastern corner of Cape Breton Island, and the air is sharp with the iodine smell of rockweed strewn across the beachface, wrenched from the bottom by a recent storm.

At the edge of the waves stand 10 or 12 silhouettes, hushed figures with dip-nets and buckets. Eastward, to the left, flashes of light pierce the darkness from the lighthouse on Green Island. Unseen beyond the flashes, the open Atlantic stretches away to Ireland. Closer to us, just across the bay in Petit de Grat, the house windows glow yellow. But there is no light here on Rocky Bay Beach. Light would scare away the fish. So would loud voices.

The fish, when they come — if they come — will be capelin, small silvery fish rather like smelts. Capelin live their lives in deep water, the prey of cod and haddock. In June they move inshore to breed in swarms on the beaches, chiefly in Newfoundland, where they pack into schools dense enough to slow a powerboat. They live in sex-segregated herds, and the two sexes meet only on the beach. Two males capture a female between them on a falling tide, and hustle her up through the breakers to the sand. She releases ova while the males cloud the water with milt. Then most of them die.

People net the capelin on the shore by the hundreds and thousands. They fry them and smoke them and "corn" them, lightly salting them and drying them in the sun. The capelin constitute an enormous annual gift from the sea.

"Come down for a feed, have you?" murmurs a young man next to me.

"No, just to look."

"Seen this before?"

"Never."

"Me neither. Lived all me life on Isle Madame, and I never seen the capelin come ashore."

If the capelin came ashore in Rocky Bay that night, I didn't see them; I went home before they arrived. But the image of the silent watchers on the beach will linger. This is the magic of Isle Madame: its fecundity, its endless subtlety, the things it offers up to those who live with it and love it, who patiently watch and listen. I have been here more than 25 years, and my island is still unfolding.

Thirty-five square miles. Forty-three hundred people. But the island's allure is endless: infinite riches in a little room. A land tender with spring green, blazing with autumn crimson, stark black against the white of winter. Branches glittering in sheathings of ice. Low spruce-draped hills, none more than 150 feet high. A shoreline sprinkled with villages: Arichat, West Arichat, D'Escousse, Petit de Grat, Janvrin's Harbour, Little Anse.

Little islands ring the shores, an archipelago with haunting names conferred by the Acadians who have lived here for 300 years: Île á Couteau, Île Verte, Île Quetique, Île Cascarette. Names which sound like a kiss in French, but a burp in English: Île á Patate, Gros Nez: Potato Island and Big Nose. P'tato Island 'n' Groany, say the Irish families who came to Rocky Bay when the potatoes failed in Ireland.

Rockbound coves and stillwater inlets, wetlands and beaches. Solid rock bluffs trembling under the attack of breakers which took shape in a tropical gale. Tree-fringed jewel lakes where eels and moon jellies are born. Magic.

This landscape is radiant with history. An 18th-century French colonial orchard left us with apple trees blooming and fruiting in the forests, in the fields, along the roadsides. The magnificent wooden cathedral church in Arichat was built in 1838. The tall solemn building across the street was the palace of the Bishop of Arichat before one of my clansmen, Bishop John Cameron — may the fleas of a thousand dogs infest his armpits — moved the seat of the diocese 60 miles to the Scottish town of Antigonish, along with the college that became St. Francis Xavier University. That was 135 years ago. But we still have the only cathedral and the only episcopal palace in Cape Breton ...

After 25 years, I learned only this year where the girls on horseback splash through the saltwater creeks to reach the Goulet Beach. This year, for the first time, I bought begonias from the big flower-choked greenhouses, which Andre Samson built in the woodland behind his house.

This year I asked Clarence David once again to take me out to visit his mackerel trap — the only such trap on the island. He was willing, but it didn't happen. So maybe the mackerel trap will be part of next year's learning.

Other years, other learnings. The year of the lobster, sailing out in the darkness with Tommy Kehoe and Freddie Samson and hauling traps all morning. The year of the credit union, when our own tiny people's bank, founded in 1937, was in danger of extinction and a group of villagers brought it back to life. The year of the schooner, when I bought a little ship in Lunenburg and fumbled my way along the coast to bring it home to D'Escousse. I met the Skipper, Leonard Pertus, who had been the master of the village's last trading schooner. At 83, he took out my little vessel and deftly sailed her through the reefs and islands, rejoicing to have a schooner under his command again, although to him she was really just a toy.

The year of the crisis, just four years ago, when there were no more fish in the sea. Isle Madame was a fishing community for 300 years; when the fishery collapsed, a third of the island's jobs disappeared. The governments and media don't seem to know what it means to belong to a community; they thought that people in places like Isle Madame should just give up and move away. In a pig's ear! snorted the islanders. (In French they used a much more pungent Acadian expression.) We were here before Canada was invented, and we aren't going anywhere.

Instead, we organized and we made new jobs for ourselves in aquaculture, tourism, communications. We brought some of our university graduates home from the cities and put them to work. We organized community investment funds and small manufacturing plants. Now we're exporting what we've learned about community economic development.

We? I don't "belong to" Isle Madame, as islanders say, or to D'Escousse. It's not a rejection, it's simply a fact. A person "belongs to" the place that shaped him. Not me: I came here when I was 34. I drove along the shore on a wind-tossed autumn day, looking at the pastel shingled houses, the blue water, the green islands. A lovely place, I thought, and I was looking for a place to live. A month later I owned a house here, in a field that ran down to the water. I will never belong to D'Escousse as a native-born islander does. But I will never belong anywhere else.

The year of the wars, 1993, when I learned about the dozens of island elders who had fought in Normandy, Hong Kong, Sicily, Iceland. I did a TV show to honour them. They were only teenagers, but they fought in trenches, sailed in destroyers, flew fighter-bombers, drove tanks, blew up bridges. They starved in prison camps, cut bullets out of their flesh, and had comrades die in their arms.

This is not an insular island. Isle Madame people sail supertankers to the Persian Gulf, crew the Lake boats in the St. Lawrence Seaway, "work construction" in Calgary and Vancouver, serve as peacemakers in Bosnia and teach in distant universities. They come home for the winter, or for weddings and funerals, or for vacations. Eventually they come home to retire. In war and peace, the island's people fan out across the globe.

The year of the first boat shop, 1976, when I decided the schooner would not serve for long cruises and resolved to build a boat myself. I knew nothing about boatbuilding and little about carpentry. But a century ago, Isle Madame men built brigantines, topsail schooners, full-rigged ships, and sailed them to Venice and Valparaiso. They were smart and strong and courageous, and I revere their memory. But they cannot all have been smarter than me. If they could build a big ship, I could build a small one.

I met a girl who loved to sail. Lulu was 30, but still a wee slip of a thing, full of gaiety and ardour. She was divorced, with a toddler. She had lived in Europe for eight years, but she had grown up in a house I can see from my window. We married and finished building the red-sailed cutter together and we sailed it into ports in four provinces. Her little boy, Mark, became my adopted son.

The year of the house, 1983. The roomy, run-down dwelling on the harbour had been built in 1890 by a doctor, sold to a teacher, and then acquired by Captain Frederick Poirier, whose family kept it for four generations until Lulu and I bought it. We took a year to dismantle it and put it back together again, working with our carpenters and plumbers and dry-wallers to make it ready for its second century.

Then came the year of the deep tolling bell of mortality, after nearly 17 laughing years together. A lump in Lulu's breast. Doctors, hospitals, operations, medications. And my body failing, too. I turned grey and gaunt, listless and trembling. Maybe you both have cancer, said the doctors. We were too sick even to care for ourselves.

Isle Madame enfolded us. Friends did our work, cleaned our house, shovelled our driveway. Neighbours fed us, brought us flowers and music, prayed for us. At a clinic in Germany we got a six-foot fax of Christmas greetings from home, signed by everyone who had been in church that night.

My illness proved treatable. But Lulu's slowly killed her. After 21 brave months — with her unquenchable laughter still rising above her pain — she died in our house, held by six people who loved her.

Now our neighbours wrapped Mark and me in their care, like shipwrecked sailors in rescuers' blankets. They crowded the church, stayed with us, wept with us, helped with the endless tasks and duties, which attend the end of a life. "Lulu's team" — the people who had eased Lulu through her dying — came together again to build a garden in her memory. Her friends planted flowers in it. We held another service and buried her ashes among the blossoms.

And then, gently, this island taught me about healing. Let go, people said. Move on. Yes, we loved her, and we will never forget her. But we are together in this place for only a little while. Be strong. Make yourself whole again. Life is still sweet, and love is still possible.

Isle Madame has taught me about time and mortality and the brilliant interlude between birth and death. I have been here now for more than a quarter of a century, a watchful navigator in the flowing stream of time. People mature and flourish and fade. The Skipper and his generation are gone. Those who were middle-aged when I came are moving into the serenity of age. The active ones who run our affairs were teenagers when I first moved here. Their own children are becoming young lawyers and school bus drivers, woodworkers and programmers.

I did not expect to spend a lifetime here. But I have, and I am, and this island never ceases to give me joy. One glorious spring day I stood by outside the gas station with Claude Poirier, who with his brother Russell has spent a lifetime operating it. I drew a deep breath and looked around me at the hills and the sea, the trees and fields and houses.

"What a day, Claude!" I said happily.

"Yeah." Claude lifted his head and drank in the scene for a moment. He smiled. "We need another lifetime in this place," he said.

Silver Donald Cameron, CM, ONS, DCL, Dlitt, PhD, is currently the host and executive producer of the ambitious environmental web site, TheGreenInterview.com, *and the writer and narrator of its recently released feature documentary,* Green Rights: The Human Right to a Healthy World. *A professional writer since 1971, Dr. Cameron has written numerous plays, films, magazine articles, radio and TV scripts. His classic 1998 book on shorelines,* The Living Beach *(1998), was re-issued in 2014, and his 18th book,* Warrior Lawyers: From Manila to Manhattan, Attorneys for the Earth, *— a companion volume to the* Green Rights *documentary — appeared in September, 2016. His next book,* Midnight Slider, *about the killing of a poacher in Isle Madame, will be published by Penguin in 2020, and he was recently appointed the inaugural Farley Mowat Chair of Environmental Studies at Cape Breton University.*

HOME

Chris Benjamin

HE STRIDES ACROSS THE HIPPIE diner toward her, hand extended, mispronouncing her name slightly. He pronounces it 'Buyer Ma.'

"Are you Dan?"

"I figured it was you, going by the name."

She smiles. She is practically Canadian now.

"Ready to see the place?"

"Yes, sir."

"Out back." Dan walks down the aisle. He steps on a dropped soother as he passes a young mother breastfeeding her infant. He doesn't break stride, doesn't seem to notice the pacifier under his sneaker.

Bayarmaa follows Dan through a grey metallic side door and up a flight of wooden stairs with jagged lettering all over it — some of it carved and some inked. She recognizes a variation on the famous Robert Frost line about the road less travelled, next to a swastika.

They come to a hallway with three doors. Dan sticks the key in the middle door and opens it. There is a small room, or a large closet, with a desk and a single futon on the floor, off-white with yellower stains. It has a large vertical window with no curtain or blinds. She looks out the window.

"It's a great view," Dan says.

It isn't bad. She can see the bridge but not the water under it. And it's quiet, sturdy enough to keep out the noises from the street and restaurant. "Where's the bathroom? And kitchen? And laundry?"

"Basement. All in the basement."

She follows him back down the stairs, this time noticing how steep they are, how loose the thin wooden railing is. Outside there is a concrete set of steps going down to a door, which Dan opens. "This is Del's apartment. He's a cool dude — a drummer. He's really made it his own."

Bayarmaa's eyes are slow to adjust to the darkness. "Can you turn a light on?"

Dan laughs. "I did. Del likes it dark though."

A lamp covered by a black shade is lit in the middle of the apartment. The objects in the apartment are divided in groups according to what room you'd expect to find them in — an open toilet and bathtub in one area, a stove, beer fridge and sink full of dishes in another area, futon, coffee table and lamp in the middle, with drum pieces lying around. But there are no walls separating these things.

Bayarmaa wonders how she is supposed to use the bathroom when Del is home. Is he supposed to leave his apartment every time she has to relieve herself?

"Well," Dan says, "it ain't much but what can you expect for the price?"

She expects more. "And the laundry?"

"Laundromat's three blocks north."

Once she's on the street again she sees things she should have noticed on the way in, obvious things like the couple sitting on the sidewalk next to a shopping cart full of bulging garbage bags, the two of them yelling slurred words back and forth. And the men in front of the shelter smoking something foul.

She walks away from the harbour, back up toward the Common, where her second cousins live. She had hoped to never see them again. She doesn't like the way they stay up late drinking vodka on the couch, which is where she sleeps when she can. Bayarmaa has to stay there another night.

She spends three more nights on her cousins' couch before she finds an apartment she can barely afford. It's nothing special and it is stressful paying more that she budgeted for, but it has what she needs and at least she doesn't have to walk through anyone else's space to go pee. She imagines standing in the cold, pounding on Del the drummer's door with a full bladder.

The mold at the new place is disconcerting and it's cold living in the basement. The woman who owns the house, an artist with several cats and a bewildered fish, is kind and lets her use the washer and dryer.

Across the road is a compound of apartment buildings. They remind her of her old Soviet building, back when she worked for the Bank of Mongolia in Ulaanbaatar. Much bigger city than Halifax. And colder. Her building was a monolithic grate of vertical concrete, punctured by pockets of glass, built over permafrost. An imperialist postcard.

From her window she could see the suburbs, which were comprised nearly entirely of sprawling little white yurts. The sight of them took her back to her early childhood following Mother around to help milk the livestock and leading little sisters about gathering dried dung for fuel. When she left, her parents made it clear she was not to come home without a driver, personal assistant and the cash to pay back the loans they'd taken for her schooling.

One thing she likes about the new place is watching the liveliness of the compound across the street, which has a large rectangular common area in the middle where children run around throwing snowballs at each other, wrestling or kicking a half-inflated soccer ball across the ice. Sometimes some of the parents join in the games. The families are mostly Black. It's nice to see people watching each other's kids. That happened sometimes when she was a child, but only rarely, when the adults weren't busy herding or milking or butchering the animals.

Mongolian government men promised her the world through education and now here she is. She did well in junior management at the Bank of Mongolia, researching and monitoring policies to maintain a stable currency, but everyone told her if she wanted to make any real money she had to be in North America.

The currency she worked to stabilize wasn't worth much in the wider world. She has to start over here, work her way back up to the middle. She submitted hundreds of resumes as soon as she arrived and was granted not a single interview, not even for the jobs she thought herself overqualified. To get the kind of job she did back home she has to pass her exam, the one proving that her graduate degree and work experience are as good as the ones you get in Canada. She's paid half her savings for tuition fees and books — binders full of photocopied sheets. It's a self-directed course that lasts eight months. In the meantime, she needs to work to pay her bills. Which is how she ends up handing out flyers.

She has to catch the morning's first bus, transfer twice, pick up her flyers and take two more buses to get to the wealthy neighbourhood where she delivers them. The homes here are of sizes that stretch the very definition of the word "house," they are nearly as large as some of the apartment buildings across from her, only they look more like the White House. They even have the white pillars, some of them, and fences surrounding acres of flat land. A lot of their otherwise unmarred doors are stuck with little signs saying, "No Flyers Please."

Bayarmaa has learned to keep her head down, as if she doesn't see or can't read those signs. The only people who acknowledge her existence are those chiding her for failing to heed the rule of signage.

"Can you read English?" a woman says to her.

Bayarmaa doesn't register the voice at first, lost as she is in her own thoughts, unaware that the people in these homes are capable of seeing her. But the woman repeats herself as Bayarmaa turns away, and her voice is sharp, inquisitorial but somehow not quite invasive. It is late morning and Bayarmaa is nearly finished her route.

She turns back to face the woman, who stands in the doorway sipping a cup of coffee. Bayarmaa tells her that she wrote her master's thesis in English.

"The flyer girl has a graduate degree?"

Bayarmaa nods.

The woman clicks her tongue against the roof of her mouth. "What a waste."

"It's temporary."

Bayarmaa hates explaining herself to this Canadian woman. Aren't they supposed to be equals, even if one lives in a mansion and the other in a moldy basement apartment? There is nothing and yet everything to explain.

The woman sips her coffee and looks over Bayarmaa's head to the horizon. "Would you like a better job?" she asks.

Bayarmaa looks over her shoulder, trying to figure out what the woman is looking at. What kind of person offers a stranger a job? Only the kind of person who wants something in return, some pound of flesh.

"I need childcare," the woman says, raising her voice and speaking slowly, annunciating for Bayarmaa. "I've been waiting on the government's foreign domestic workers program forever. Frankly, I'm desperate."

Bayarmaa shakes her head. She doesn't mind children, in reasonable doses, from a safe distance, but she has avoided having them for good reason. "Are you asking me to watch your children?"

"My child," the woman says. "Olive. She's three and she's got so much creative energy." The woman espouses opinions against daycares, calling them "childcare factories," and apologizes for being "forward."

"I know it's sudden," she says. She wants Bayarmaa to come in and meet the girl. "You'll love her. She's very intelligent." She says Bayarmaa will a need police check and references. That will be no problem; the first thing Bayarmaa did in Canada was get her paperwork done: MSI, SIN, and getting the resume done at the employment centre. The workers there are always willing to serve as references.

Bayarmaa hears the child's voice yelling from inside. Making some repetitive, wailing sound like she urgently needs something. Bayarmaa tilts her head slightly and asks what the job pays, preparing herself to negotiate for far more because the woman is desperate, and rich. But the woman offers Bayarmaa the impossible: free room and board. No mold. She's signed a lease with the artist who owns her basement apartment. She'll have to skip out.

"Build me this," Olive tells Bayarmaa. She points at a diagram of a Lego spaceship.

Bayarmaa smiles and says she will as soon as she finishes her breakfast. The household is vegetarian and the lack of meat makes it harder to get up in the morning. Toast is a poor motivator. She quickly spoons the wet, candied cereal into her mouth as Olive runs circles around the kitchen table making spaceship noises: engines firing up, lasers shooting.

Bayarmaa finds the Lego in Olive's toy closet. The girl's bedroom is the size of two yurts. Bayarmaa enjoys building the spaceship, like a 3-D puzzle involving hunting out the right pieces — size and shape — and layering them together. It takes some time.

Olive watches intently for short spurts in between showing Bayarmaa her somersaults, then how high she can jump, then how she can do a backward somersault if she pushes off the wall.

"Look Olive, I've done it," Bayarmaa says.

"Are you proud?" Olive asks.

Bayarmaa nods, surprised to find she does in fact feel she has accomplished something.

"Watch this!" Olive says, grabbing a toy metal fire truck and swinging it down on the spaceship until the pieces lie scattered across the hardwood. "Are you sad, Bye-maa?"

Bayarmaa shakes her head. Sorrow, no, but she would like to grab the fire truck and avenge the fallen Lego spaceship.

"Build it again!" Olive squeals, dropping the fire truck and tearing across the room and into the hallway.

Chloe, Olive's mother, was right; Olive is energetic. Bayarmaa takes her to parks, the library, train stations, the Discovery Centre, McDonald's, anywhere to let her blow off steam while Chloe does her volunteer work. Chloe's husband owns a consulting firm and spends most of his time in Ukraine helping the government recycle.

Bayarmaa is running out of ideas. She brings Olive to the compound across from her old basement apartment. The grandmothers are out with their morning teas in thermoses chatting and watching the children, who are having a snowball fight before school.

"Fine morning," the eldest grandmother says.

"Say hello, Olive." Olive clutches Bayarmaa's leg.

"Morning, Olive," another grandmother says.

"Want to play?" a boy about Olive's size says.

Olive shakes her head.

The boy grabs a mitten full of snow from the ground and throws it at her. It is hardly a snowball, more a loose clump that disintegrates as he throws it.

Olive wails. "I want Mommy." Over and over.

Bayarmaa scoops up the child, apologizes to the boy and grandmothers and walks to the bus stop.

The grandmothers nod and the boy waves.

Chloe is horrified when Olive tells her what happened. "What were you thinking taking her there?"

"What's wrong with it?"

"Nothing, Bayarmaa. Nothing's wrong with it."

Olive sniffles and buries her face in Bayarmaa's leg, hiding from her mother.

Bayarmaa should let it go but she knows Chloe's scorn is unfair. Bayarmaa has done nothing wrong and pushes the issue, asking politely as polite can be what exactly she did wrong.

Chloe says they will discuss it later and begins her usual complaints about the "Ladies Who Lunch," the wealthy wives of faraway husbands. She has just now returned from a meeting with them to plan a fundraiser for homeless youth. "What controversy erupts when lonely old ladies plan a fireman auction!"

Bayarmaa forces herself to smile. "I can only imagine."

"Oh, I wish you could join me. You've got that Zen quality."

Bayarmaa nods and picks up Olive, carries her to bed. She is shaking. Two months she has been in this meatless home entertaining a toddler. Bayarmaa tries to keep her head down but Chloe wants conversation, companionship, whatever she doesn't get from Olive, her husband or the Ladies Who Lunch. Bayarmaa does not feel gratitude for this form of inclusion. She feels only fatigue and despair. She needs to study her textbooks, her photocopied sheets in binders.

When Olive finally sleeps Bayarmaa tries to study, but the text blurs. Every night it's the same. Sometimes Chloe shakes her awake from her snoring and invites her to come have a drink and girl talk. "It's too early for bed," she says. Bayarmaa can't say no. Chloe relays the headlines of the day, shaking her head and speaking as if she is a magnanimous force of goodness. "I try to do my part. So many lost souls."

"We can only each do our part," Bayarmaa says, but the irony is lost on Chloe.

She passes the familiar graffiti; the swastika is still there but the paraphrased Robert Frost lines have been spray painted over. She tries not to think about the lurch she left Chloe in. She didn't say goodbye, simply left them a note and took off one morning before anyone else was awake. She couldn't risk being talked into staying.

Her parents' debts; she had no choice. She has to study. Maybe Chloe will bond with Olive while she waits for another live-in. Bayarmaa knocks on the grey metallic side door and waits, squinting against the morning sun.

Dan answers wearing jogging pants and a hockey jersey. "Can I help you?" he says.

"You showed me an apartment a couple months ago."

"That one's gone. Another one's available. You want it?"

The new unit is next to the one she's seen before. It looks the same and she takes it anyway. She'll have to buy a bucket to pee in at night. She'll work it out somehow. The priority has to be studying, and she starts in on the binders as soon as she's got the futon covered with bedsheets. She's on page two when the crying starts. The light wail of an infant. And two other voices murmuring, a man and a woman. Some parents at the park use leashes on their children, she recalls.

The crying worsens by page three. Inconsolable wails. Like Olive's, but less conscious, less intent. Pained, hungry, lonesome convulsed screaming. Bayarmaa can no longer hear the adult voices. She leaves her room and knocks on the neighbour's door. The crying stops for an instant and re-starts. She knocks again, waits. She will offer help, just this once. Parenting is a life sentence. She will offer a few minutes of respite, that's all. Only there is no answer. More crying. Then a hoarse male whisper. She can't make out the words.

Bayarmaa knocks again and calls to them. "Hello? Need any help?" She tries the door but it is locked.

Screaming, crying, wailing, choking on sorrow. Until it finally stops.

Bayarmaa puts her hand on the door. Feeling for what, she does not know. She presses her ear to it and hears nothing.

"OK in there?" She calls it softly, not daring to yell in case she wakes it again. Still receiving no answer, she returns to her room, desperate to study, unable to concentrate.

In a few days the police come for the father of the baby. They question every resident about what was going on with the parents, demand to know why no one intervened on behalf of the baby. Surely the police notice the conditions of the building but they say nothing to Dan about that. Bayarmaa tells the police she has often heard the baby wailing and wondered if the parents were home with it, but their door was always locked. It is hard not to mention that if she cannot pass her exam she will have to return to her parents a failure. But she manages to keep everything to herself.

Chris Benjamin is a writer and editor living in Halifax. He has written three award-winning books: Drive-by Saviours, *a novel;* Eco-Innovators: Sustainability in Atlantic Canada; *and* Indian School Road: Legacies of the Shubenacadie Residential School. *He has had short stories published in literary journals, newspapers and anthologies across Canada. He is also managing editor with* Atlantic Books Today *magazine. Chris has had the privilege of working abroad as a journalist and researcher in Asia, Europe and Africa, and he has visited every Canadian province. But he has always called Halifax home (even that time when he lived in Toronto).*

A WHITE-WASHED HISTORY

Dr. Daniel N. Paul

NOVA SOCTIA'S BEAUTIFUL SCENERY IS in need of an inclusive society.

My love of the section of Mi'kma'ki, now known as Nova Scotia, and dislike for the racism that has burdened our People since the British invaders assumed control of our land in 1713, have been with me for my lifetime. I have written at length on that history in my book, *We Were Not the Savages*. Here, I offer a brief summary of the ways First Nations history has been whitewashed, that is, covered over with colonial propaganda that demonizes First Nations Peoples in an attempt to subdue and destroy them. I have come to believe that re-education of both First Nations and non-First Nations people is the only way forward, to correct this historical wrong.

I'll start with the land itself. Nova Scotia has 55,284 square kilometres (21,300 sq. mi) of land and besides Cape Breton, has another 3,800 coastal islands. Only, approximately, 29,000 acres are Indian Reserve land, which consist mainly of bogs, swamps, mountains and clay pits.

The Province has a coastline that is 7,400 kms long. It ranges from lovely beaches to rock faced cliffs. In my younger years, I've walked hundreds of miles along the coast and have wonderful memories of its magnificent beauty. Also, my wife Patricia and I have visited, by automobile, every nook and cranny of the province, savouring the wonderful scenery from such places as Cape Blomidon and the Cabot Trail.

I've also seen some terrible destruction of Mother Nature's pristine forests, i.e. clear cutting and the befouling of pristine waterways. The worst water befouling in Nova Scotia was the use of Boat Harbour, near Pictou Landing, as an industrial waste lagoon. It went from a beautiful Harbour in the early 1960s to a stinking mess by 1966.

I was deeply involved in the Boat Harbour fiasco from 1981 to 1991. In fact, I put my family's security on the line while I was still employed by the Department of Indian Affairs and Northern Development as District Superintendent of Lands, Revenues and Trusts, up to 1985 by doing so, from then to 1991, as executive director of the Confederacy of Mainland Mi'kmaq I did it openly. I've only been reimbursed for my expenses associated with the suit.

I was the mover and shaker in shaping and moving the lawsuit. Without my expertise in Indian law and the Indian Act, and regulations made thereunder, it's quite likely that it would still be gathering dust. Before I got involved in 1981, the Chief of the Pictou Landing First Nation, Raymond Francis, had for 15 years tried every means he could to get action to make the provincial government take responsibility for industrial waste effluent flowing into Boat Harbour, i.e., Union of Nova Scotia Indians legal expertise and Indian Affairs funded lawyers, and got nowhere until he came to see me. Within a few short years, under my guidance, we had the thing headed for settlement.

I'm still suitably pissed off at the Federal Crown for permitting Boat Harbour to exist. The following are some observations.

We, as Registered Indians have, what is called Usufructuary Rights to Indian Reserve lands. We cannot hold title to it as the title is vested in the Federal Crown, authorized by Section 91.24 of the BNA, part of the Canadian Constitution, or alienate any of it without the approval of the Crown, etc., and the Crown cannot alienate any of it without our informed consent. This saddles the Federal Crown with fiduciary responsibility for the proper management and use of Indian Reserve lands. The neglect by the Crown of its legal responsibilities to the Pictou Landing Band members is why we won our lawsuit against Canada. It did not manage the Band's Usufructuary interest in the land in the best interests of the Band Members. We can sue the Federal Crown for mismanagement, but we cannot sue a third party for damaging reserve lands that the title to which belongs to another party, in this case the Federal Crown.

Provincial assurances. In the 1960s, the province assured the band members that they would be able to use the harbour for recreation, swimming, fish farming, and that its use for an industrial waste lagoon would not have any adverse affect on the harbour, or their health. Indian Affairs was well aware that such was an out and out lie, and did nothing to stop it. In fact, both the Federal Department of Justice and the department's own engineers advised the department that to proceed with the project would not be in the best interests of the Band members or the Federal Crown itself, yet the Department gave full support in getting it done. This was one of the aces we had in our lawsuit that was eventually settled by the Crown out of court. The Band received 35 million dollars and some land.

But, the most positive fallout is that the cleanup of the harbour is mandated to begin in 2020.

I'll start the racism section of this story with the following quotes from the portion of *We Were Not the Savages* that was devoted to telling the tale of Boat Harbour. For surrendering its Usufructuary Rights in Boat Harbour in 1965 the Band received $60,000.

During this time the province, knowing the area around Boat Harbour would become unfit for human habitation, purchased or expropriated all non-Indian lands adjacent to the harbour. In many cases, the non-Indians were paid far in excess of $60,000 for their properties. Unbelievably, the province was doing this at the same time Band members were being assured that Boat Harbour would suffer no dramatic environmental changes. Asked about the welfare of the Mi'kmaq who were to be left living next to the polluted mess, an engineer involved in the project replied, "So, they're only Indians."

When Armand F. Wigglesworth was asked under oath at a discovery hearing held March 13, 1987, in Halifax if he knew the system wouldn't function properly, he replied, "As I say, my part was to get the easement rights across the lands and for the use (of Boat Harbour), not to tell them that." Believe it or not, he was inducted into the Order of Canada in 1994.

On November 23, 2007, as Chairman of the Mi'kmaq Education Advisory Council I submitted the following paper to a Teacher's Education Panel chaired by former Nova Scotia Lieutenant Governor of Nova Scotia Myra Freeman. It was meant to provide a format to start the process of ending the systemic racism that has impeded the progress of the Mi'kmaq People.

TEACHER'S REVIEW PANEL PRESENTATION

> *"Our nation was born in genocide when it embraced the doctrine that the original American, the Indian, was an inferior race."* — Martin Luther King Jr.

Martin Luther King made the statement in reference to his country, the USA; however, it can easily be applied to Canada.

I'll start this discourse by thanking the panel for providing the council with an opportunity to put forward a proposal for reforming Nova Scotia's teacher-training program to the extent that graduating students will leave a training school with a positive opinion of the Mi'kmaq Nation. To achieve this goal we will advocate that true Mi'kmaq history be a required course for teacher training students. As matters now stand, most teachers graduating from teacher-training institutions in this province know little, or nothing, about First Nations Peoples. And, unfortunately, much of what they do know can be categorized as "whitewashed history."

> *I want to get rid of the Indian problem. I do not think, as a matter of fact, that the country ought to continuously protect a class of people who are able to stand alone ... Our objective is to continue until there is not a single Indian in*

Canada that has not been absorbed into the body politic and there is no Indian question, and no Indian Department, that is the whole object of this Bill.
— Dr. Duncan Campbell Scott, 1920.

Scott made his mark in Canadian history as the head of the Department of Indian Affairs from 1913 to 1932, a department he had served since joining the federal civil service in 1879.

Even before Confederation, the Canadian government adopted a policy of assimilation (actually, it was the continuation of a policy that British colonial officials had pursued since 1713). The long-term goal was to bring the Native peoples from their "savage and unproductive state" and force (English-style) civilization upon them, thus making Canada a homogeneous society in the Anglo-Saxon and Christian tradition.

In 1920, under Scott's direction, it became mandatory for all Native children between the ages of seven and 15 to attend one of Canada's residential schools.

Before proceeding further, I want to diverge from the subject for a moment to state, related to the fact that systemic racism has often caused me to suffer the indignity of being discriminated against because of who I am, that this opportunity to propose positive proactive action to correct a historical wrong through education is something that I've been wanting to do for years. If our proposal is accepted, and followed through, it will eventually help realize a long-sought-after result; non-First Nation peoples accepting our People as equals from a different progressive culture.

Therefore, because I see it as essential for the success of the Mi'kmaq People's future endeavours and prosperity in Nova Scotia, I do hope that during our discourse we can persuade the panel to embrace what we will propose.

THE WHY AND HOW

In *The Arrogance of Ignorance; Hidden Away, Out of Sight and Out of Mind*, an article from October 15, 2006 Stephanie M. Schwartz wrote:

> *This is an article of facts about the lives of modern-day American Indians, a topic most mainstream American news organizations will not discuss. ... It is not a plea for charity. It is not a promotion for non-profit organizations. It is not aimed for pity. ... It is, however, an effort to dispel ignorance ... a massive, pervasive, societal ignorance filled with illusions and caricatures which, ultimately, serve only to corrupt the intelligence and decent intent of the average mainstream citizen. Only through knowledge and understanding can solutions be found ....*

I recently received an e-mail from an American Indian leader asking if I could offer an explanation about why racial discrimination in the United States against First Nation Peoples is yet so widespread and pervasive. The following is an edited version of my reply:

"It's the same on both sides of the border. Somehow, someway, pride in origins needs to be re-instilled in our People, and the non-First Nation population must be educated about the true histories of our Peoples. Then, somehow, someway, a desire to return to the self-sufficiency that was part and parcel of pre-European invasion First Nation existence must be reinstated into the expectations of our Peoples. Depending on another race of people's charity for survival is degrading and fosters feelings of inferiority and insecurity. The end result is that the idleness created for able-bodied People by living on handouts leads to drug, alcohol, family abuse, etc."

TWO MAJOR PROBLEMS
First: The white man's condescending paternalism. The following is essential for First Nations Peoples to restore self-esteem. We need to come to know, and promote the truth; our intellectual abilities are equal to those of any race of people on the face of Mother Earth! We have the intellectual capability to do things for ourselves; we don't need others to do things for us.

Because we've been treated as mental incompetents, incapable of managing our own affairs by another race of people for centuries, doesn't mean that we have to accept the fabrication as fact. We have much to be proud of. Our People survived the hell on Mother Earth that the European invasion begot them, and are still here. That alone is something to be immensely proud of.

Second: The lack of knowledge about the true histories of First Nations among ourselves, and the general population is almost universal, with very negative results for First Nations. This is a vacuum that Canadian provinces can easily correct by proactive reform, if the will can be found, of education systems, which will require mandatory teaching of real First Nations history in schools. Such won't be easy to accomplish. Elected officials will have to muster the fortitude to override the obstruction efforts of influential closet white supremacist individuals, who will fight diligently to preserve the status quo, which presently excludes real First Nations history from being included in the Province's school curriculums.

One of the most serious problems arising for our Peoples, out of our historical exclusion, is, as mentioned, most First Nations Peoples have very little knowledge about their histories. For instance, most Mi'kmaq haven't any knowledge whatsoever about the fact that their ancestors, trying to save their country from theft by invaders, fought the British bravely for more than 130 years. Regarding our culture, most people know only of dancing and artwork.

The before-mentioned lack of awareness can be attributed in a large part to the hunter writing the history. Read most history books written by white men about the invasion and colonizing of the eastern seaboard of North America by Europeans, and you will find nary a positive comment about the heroic efforts made by the area's original inhabitants to preserve their cultures and homelands. Most of them do not even acknowledge the existence of the great First Nations that once prospered in the area. When they do, it generally is in the most unflattering terms: barbarous people, savages, heathens, etc.

One notable exception was made by Joseph Howe (http://www.danielnpaul.com/JosephHowe'sReport-1843.html) in an anti-Confederation speech he delivered in Dartmouth, Nova Scotia, in 1867:

"The Indians who fought your forefathers were open enemies, and had good reason for what they did. They were fighting for their country, which they loved, as we have loved it in these latter years. It was a wilderness. There was perhaps not a square mile of cultivation, or a road or a bridge anywhere. But it was their home, and what God in His bounty had given them they defended like brave and true men. They fought the old pioneers of our civilization for a hundred and thirty years, and during all that time they were true to each other and to their country, wilderness though it was …."

EUROPEAN COLONIAL HISTORY

The European subjugation of the Indigenous Peoples of the Americas was a crime against humanity that knows no equal in human history. By the time the invaders had managed to appropriate all the lands in the Americas that our ancestors had owned and occupied for millennia, of the hundreds of diverse civilizations that had existed prior to Columbus, not one was left intact, and tens of millions were dead. During the process, Indigenous Peoples suffered every barbarity imaginable — mass murder, germ warfare, enslavement, rape, enforced starvation, relocation, etc. One of the favourite means used by the English to ethnically cleanse the land of its original inhabitants in North America were proclamations offering bounties for the scalps of First Nations men, women, and children. A barbarous means used by them in Nova Scotia, on three occasions against the Mi'kmaq. Stemming from it, some United States jurisdictions continued to use these ungodly proclamations until the 1860s to try to eliminate some First Nations populations.

The following contains examples of some of the abhorrent acts that were visited upon First Nations Peoples, related to the systemic racism that was created for them by demonizing colonial propaganda. One can be certain, if enlightened action is not taken to stop it, similar abhorrent acts will continue to occur for the foreseeable future.

WHY RACISM AND OTHER FORMS OF INTOLERANT ATTITUDES PERSIST

In his discourse, *Lessons at the Halfway Point*, Michael Levine accurately identifies why intolerance exists: "If you don't personally get to know people from other racial, religious or cultural groups, it's very easy to believe ugly things about them and make them frightening in your mind."

If Europeans had gotten to know, and had accepted Indigenous Americans and Africans as equals during colonial times, instead of adopting white supremacist racist beliefs that negatively, and erroneously, depicted both Peoples as wild inhuman savages for the better part of five centuries, these peoples of colour would not have suffered the indescribable hells they did across the Americas, and, in far too many cases, still do.

The following shows how the racism problem that First Nation Peoples suffer is pervasive and why a nation of civilized people must fight together to overcome it!

FIRST NATION INVISIBILITY

Buffy Saint-Marie, a member of the Cree Nation, acclaimed singer and human rights activist, stated during an October 1970, interview with the Los Angeles Times, that Indian children "are not taught to be proud they're Indian. Here the melting pot stands with arms open — if you're willing to get bleached first."

This statement made by Dalhousie University professor Susan Sherwin, about the underlying cause of racism, is the best description I've ever read. It puts into words why it is so hard to get society to recognize, and accept that the systemic racism that victimizes First Nations Peoples exists: ".... the greatest danger of oppression lies where bias is so pervasive as to be invisible ..."

REVISIONIST HISTORY

In the case of First Nations, we need factual First Nations History to replace the fairy-tale version that is still widely accepted and used by many Caucasian writers as fact. When my book, *We Were Not the Savages* — which outed the use of scalp proclamations by the British and other atrocities committed against Eastern North American First Nations Peoples by them — was first published, I was roundly condemned by many Anglo individuals, from across the spectrum of society, as a "revisionist."

SYSTEMIC RACISM

Systemic racism is an evil that demeans civilized societies. The systemic racism that burdens First Nations Peoples, as mentioned previously, stems from colonial propaganda that demonizes its targets. Although both claim to be compassionate countries, with justice for all as a core value, governments in Canada and the United States (with a few notable exceptions such as Maine and Montana) are not making any viable effort to replace colonial propaganda with the truth.

On April 4, 2007, Don Imus, a radio talk show host, made a sexist racist remark about members of a female sports team whose players were mostly of African American heritage, calling them "nappy headed hos." Rightfully, there was condemnation across the board and he was fired. During the two weeks prior to that event, I saw three shows on North American television where the following degrading terms, describing First Nation Peoples, were used: "Injuns," "Savage Redskins," "Indian givers," "Acting like a bunch of wild Indians."

Not a word of condemnation. Why not? The answer is simple — a subconscious belief among the majority that the statements are true.

During the colonization of the Americas by invading Europeans, tens of millions of First Nations People died at their hands from genocidal practices including starvation and the deliberate spreading of European diseases. The following is a prime example of how religiously the catastrophe is ignored by Canada and the United States.

VIRGINIA TECH MURDERS

In 2007, following the Virginia Tech murders, these were some of the headlines in the United States and Canada: "The worst shooting rampage in American history…" "Massacre and Mourning, 33 die in worst shooting in U.S. History," "Rampage called worst mass shooting in U.S. history." "What first appeared to be a single shooting death unfolded into the worst gun massacre in the nation's history."

In response, a First Nations person might want to know: What about the Massacre at Sand Creek in Colorado, where Methodist minister Col. Chivington and his soldiers massacred between 200 and 400 Cheyenne and Arapaho Indians, most of them women, children, and elderly men?

Chivington specifically ordered the killing of children. When asked why, he said, "Kill and scalp all. Big and little; nits make lice."

At Wounded Knee Creek in South Dakota, the US 7th Cavalry, on December 29, 1890, attacked, while they were engaged in a spiritual practice known as the "Ghost Dance," 350 unarmed Lakota Sioux. Approximately 90 warriors and 200 women and children were killed. Although the attack was officially reported by Field Commander General Nelson A. Miles as an "unjustifiable massacre," 23 soldiers were awarded the Medal of Honor for their participation in the slaughter. The unarmed Lakota men fought back with bare hands. The elderly men and women stood and sang their death songs while falling under the hail of bullets. Soldiers stripped the bodies of the dead Lakota, keeping their ceremonial religious clothing as souvenirs. In spite of this, modern US governments have been steadfast in refusing to revoke the medals.

Joan Redfern, a Lakota Sioux, remarks, "To say the Virginia shooting is the worst in all of US history is to pour salt on old wounds. It means erasing and forgetting all of our ancestors who were killed in the past."

A few examples of First Nations invisibility in Canada:

The following is a quote from a story published in the May 30, 2007 edition of the *Globe and Mail*. "Tim Horton's serves up some controversy" — No Drunken Indians Allowed. The sign was put up by a young employee at an Alberta outlet.

> *The incident provides a great example of how deeply ingrained in Canadian society systemic racist beliefs about First Nations Peoples are. When a young Caucasian teenager hangs a sign stating "No Drunken Indians Allowed," it shows that she has been taught by others that expressing such racist garbage about First Nations*

Peoples is not wrong. Her action exposes the reality that there is a long-festering sickness loose in Canadian society that needs to be dealt with effectively by federal and provincial governments. After all, it was their predecessors, and British colonial administrations, that instilled in the subconscious of this society, by using demonizing propaganda about First Nations Peoples, the systemic racism that plagues our Peoples today.

JUSTICE COMPARISON

In 1995, Paul Bernardo and Karla Homolka were accused and convicted of murdering, torturing, and raping two white girls, horrific crimes. After conviction, Bernardo was sentenced to life and designated a dangerous offender. He is kept in isolation and, in all likelihood, will never get out of prison. Karla, of course, swung a deal and is now out free.

At the same time in Saskatchewan, Paul Martin Crawford, a convicted murderer and rapist of a Cree woman in 1983, was tried and convicted for torturing, raping, and murdering three more Cree women. There is evidence that he may have killed and raped more, and he has a history of committing other violent acts. For these horrific acts, Crawford is serving three concurrent life sentences in open prison confinement, with no chance of parole for 20 years. He has not been declared a dangerous offender.

Crown prosecutor Terry Hinz stated during an interview: "There is no reason why the Paul Bernardo case should have received more publicity than the John Martin Crawford case."

These comments made by trial judge Wright during the conviction process answer best why the national media all but ignored this horrendous case: "What was it about these four victims that made Mr. Crawford feel that he could take their lives after sexually assaulting them, confining them, terrorizing them ...?

"And finally, what on earth can explain his actions in mutilating two of them? I refer to his conviction with respect to Ms. Serloin; she was left naked, the final indignity, on her back and exposed and mutilated by biting. Ms. Taysup's arm was cut off at the elbow, for what possible reason?

"It appears to me that Mr. Crawford was attracted to his victims for four reasons: one, they were young; second, they were women; third, they were Native; and fourth, they were prostitutes ... The accused treated them with contempt ... He seemed determined to destroy every vestige of their humanity. He left three of them naked and lying on the ground. There is a kind of ferocity in these actions that reminds me of a wild animal, a predator.

"The accused has shown no remorse, absolutely none, no regrets, there's been no effort to explain his actions and, in fact, we know from the tapes that he laughed about the killings."

Sensational horrific stuff, isn't it? Thus, there is no rational conclusion that can be drawn from the media's indifference, other than that these women were viewed by them as only "Indians" and, because they were, of no interest. An example of systemic racism at its worst.

The author of *Just Another Indian*, journalist Warren Goulding, offers his opinion of why Crawford's crime spree has largely been ignored by the media.

"Race, geography, incompetence, and economics all play a role. There are no easy answers to explain Canadians' indifference to this case then, or now, but as a society we must ask ourselves the questions."

I'd be remiss if I didn't mention the Junior Marshall case, in which a Nova Scotia Mi'kmaq boy was convicted of murder because he was a Mi'kmaq, which needs no elaboration here.

The following is a quote from the November 12 issue of the *Halifax Herald*:

> VANCOUVER — Frank Paul spent the last night of his life crawling on his hands and knees at the police station, from where he was dragged to a police wagon and then dumped, drunk and soaking wet, in a back alley where he died.
>
> But Paul's family heard a starkly different explanation from police when they were finally called about his death on the night of December 6, 1998.
>
> "They said he died in a hit-and-run and that he was found in a ditch," Paul's cousin, Peggy Clement, said from the New Brunswick community of Elsipogtog, formerly known as Big Cove."
>
> Paul's official cause of death was hypothermia.
>
> For Steven Kelleher, the lawyer representing the family, one big question about Paul's fate begs an answer: "Why?"
>
> "Why was there such a profound and unanimous indifference to this man's life and death? Lethal indifference."

The following is a quote from a column by Jonathan Kay, published by the *National Post*, October 23, 2007, which illustrates vividly that you can write and have published by a respected publishing entity in this country just about anything about First Nations Peoples, no matter how vile it is:

> ".... A proper native policy would be guided by the three principles listed above .... The most decrepit and remote reserves, ... would simply be torn down — their inhabitants installed at government expense in population centres of the residents' choice. The hundreds of millions of dollars that go into running these hell-holes would be used to teach job skills, detox the drunks, educate the children and otherwise integrate the families into mainstream Canadian life ....
>
> "Self-government would be possible, but only in the same limited way that any Canadian city or town is self-governing. The conceit that native reserves can be re-conceived as culturally distinct 'nations' would be given up in favour of a model that promotes integration ....
>
> Off the reservation: The reserve system is Canada's worst moral failing. Let's do the right thing and get rid of it."

I had published in the May 26, 2000 issue of the *Halifax Herald* a column entitled, *Where is society's outrage over proposed genocide?* The following is a quote from it:

> The headline "Book blames reserves for natives' plight" *appeared over a front-page story in the April 17 issue of this newspaper. The story revealed that in his soon-to-be-published book,* First Nations, Second Thoughts, *author Tom Flanagan (University of Calgary Professor) advocated the extinction by assimilation of Canada's First Nations Peoples as a means to solve the country's so-called "Indian Problem."*

Flanagan, who at the time was an influential Alliance Party policy advisor, was not expelled from the party for advocating in his book the extinction of our Peoples by assimilation. Nor did he suffer any penalty from society for asserting in it that First Nation Peoples, because their cultures were not identical to European models, were not civilized. In fact, he has been the recipient of many awards, i.e., the Donner Foundation awarded him its writing prize of $25,000. Alliance Party brass did not react in horror to his outrageous suggestions. Today, he is still used as a consultant by the federal government. In fact, he led the 2005 PC election campaign.

The before-mentioned examples are just a few of a multitude that could be cited to demonstrate that Canadians have a serious problem of systemically racist attitudes about First Nations Peoples to deal with. To see the relegation of the horrendous murders and abuse of our peoples to a footnote in the obscure corners of the news media, just because of their race, is unforgivable. This is even more so when the offending society promotes itself as a bastion of tolerance, justice and equality for all!

It should be noted that individuals such as Kay and Flanagan always blame First Nations Peoples for their sorry state, never the racism of their own ancestors that created the hardship that our Peoples still suffer today. I've yet to hear of an instance where one of them has called for an in-depth investigation into the historical performance of the Department of Indian Affairs.

Is it because it has been staffed over the years by white men who were hell-bent on solving the "Indian Problem" by engineering and promoting policies and programs to destroy First Nations by assimilation, not for their acceptance and prosperity? I can state, without hesitation, that such a report, if conducted with outing the unvarnished truth as its goal, would shock most Canadians profoundly.

I believe that the before-cited conduct by Caucasian society towards our Peoples explains why colonial Governor Edward Cornwallis, despite it having been amply proven that he indulged in what can be described as genocidal behaviour by trying to exterminate the Mi'kmaq, offering bounties for the scalps of men, women, and children, is still honoured by Nova Scotia and Canada. Can you imagine there being a statue of him in a public park, or having a junior high school, among many other things named after him, if he had tried to exterminate a white race? But, because he only tried to exterminate red people, it's okay to continue to honour him. By doing so society demeans itself and teaches its children to be racist.

EXAMPLES OF SYSTEMIC RACISM — NOVA SCOTIA STYLE
"Never attribute to malice what can be adequately explained by stupidity."

A great piece of wisdom! I don't know who coined it; therefore, proper accreditation cannot be given. However, when writing or talking about the intolerant views of people, I prefer to use ignorance as an excuse for the intolerance displayed. "Stupidity" only comes into play when people indicate by their continued prejudices that they are too stupid to learn how to recognize and cure their ignorance.

The following are examples of some of the negative incidents I've dealt with in recent times, caused by racist beliefs ingrained in society:

An elderly Scottish gentleman, after the first edition of my book, *We Were Not the Savages*, was published in 1993, told me in a shopping mall: "You creature you, how dare you be critical of those who have done so much for your people. My ancestors educated yours and made their lives complete!" He had not read the book, just some reviews. I suggested he read the book, gave him my card so that he could contact me afterwards, and haven't heard from him since.

The following is a quote from a speech that was delivered by a white male speaker at a business people's forum I attended in Dartmouth in the early 1990s: "Our ancestors came to the Americas five centuries ago, found, and started populating and developing two vast and vacant continents." He was most apologetic, and embarrassed, when I pointed out to him that when Columbus landed in the Americas in 1492, the estimated population of the two continents was around 95 million.

This nugget: "Since responsible government was established here by Europeans," was uttered in a speech made by a former speaker of the Nova Scotia legislature, Art Donahue, to a human rights conference at the Metro Centre, which I attended in the 1990s. He ignored, because of ignorance of history, the fact that the Mi'kmaq had developed and implemented responsible government in the area tens of centuries before the European invasion commenced.

The following is a racist insult, depicting us as irresponsible bloodthirsty hunters. It was made by an official of the Nova Scotia Wildlife Federation and published widely in newspapers, television, etc., after we had signed a hunting agreement with the province, without condemnation: "The Micmacs will coat the province, from Yarmouth to Sydney, with the blood of our wildlife." To counter this garbage, I spent, on behalf of the Confederacy of Mainland Mi'kmaq, approximately $25,000 on positive newspaper ads. Under the agreement we had an allocation of 2,000 deer for the first year; only 400 were harvested and, of course, wildlife still exist today in the province.

Three highway signs that I lobbied successfully to have changed:

This sign, *Annapolis Royal, established 1605, Canada's oldest settlement*, was placed at an exit from a newly constructed by-pass express highway to the village of Annapolis Royal. It did not recognize this fact: North America had First Nations settlements for millenniums before Europeans set up any.

After hearing about, and seeing it, I contacted the mayor of the Town of Annapolis Royal, the Warden of Annapolis County, and the Department of Transportation, and voiced my outrage. After they were reminded about the First Nations' existence, the mayor and warden were shocked that they had supported the wording of the sign. Within a few days the signs were removed and I was invited to a joint meeting of the councils so that they could formally apologize.

The sign now reads: *Annapolis Royal, established 1605, Stroll Through the Centuries*.

Signs on Highway 2, giving notice of Bedford exits, didn't acknowledge that the Mi'kmaq had been using the Bedford location as a stopping place for tens of centuries before Europeans did. The wording had been recommended by author Elsie Tolson to the Town of Bedford — *Bedford, a Stopping Place Since 1503*.

Because the Mi'kmaq had been stopping in the area for tens of centuries, I arranged a meeting with Elsie, and pointed out to her the erroneous message the sign portrayed. She was appalled by the fact that she had not taken into consideration the existence of our ancestors. With her cooperation, the sign now reads: *Bedford, a Traditional Stopping Place*.

This 1997 incident of highway naming borders on the unbelievable.

Background: In 1744, the Mi'kmaq and allies had laid siege on several occasions to the fort at Annapolis Royal. Mascarene, the fort's governor, appealed to the governor of Massachuetts Bay Colony, William Shirley, for military assistance. Shirley responded by declaring war on the Mi'kmaq, which included a bounty to be paid for the scalps of Mi'kmaq men, women, and children. To help enforce his declaration of war, he sent Captain John Gorham and his Rangers to Nova Scotia. They, by brutally killing many Mi'kmaq, soon established a reputation for barbarity that didn't take a backseat to the actions of other barbarians. His Rangers were also involved in enforcing Cornwallis's 1749 proclamation for Mi'kmaq scalps from men, women, and children. Because of their murderous reputations, even the British civilian and military populations of the Annapolis garrison did not welcome these barbarians with open arms. In fact — some say with good cause — many loyal British subjects were terrified of them.

In spite of having this knowledge, HRM municipal councillor Bob Harvey recommended to the Department of Highways that it name a connector highway, connecting Bedford and Sackville, *Captain John Gorham Boulevard*, which it did. The signs went up. I responded in January 1998 by writing a newspaper column detailing to some extent Gorham's barbarous history, which even prompted the *Halifax Herald* to write an opinion demanding that the sign be removed.

The Department of Highways could be excused to some extent because its employees were ignorant of our history, but Bob Harvey, a former school teacher, can not. He was well aware of Gorham's brutality. After I educated highway staff a bit, the sign came down, and the highway was renamed.

PROPOSAL

Please keep in mind that across the board acceptance of our People by all facets of Canadian society as equal players is essential for our future prosperity and wellbeing. This is so because, as demonstrated, systemic racism has marginalized and excluded us for centuries and it is the root of the discrimination we still suffer.

After considering various options that could be used to negate the systemic racism that colonial propaganda created to demean our People, some of them tried without success, I've concluded that there is no other way but through education that it can be effectively accomplished.

We now put on the table for consideration by government a proposal for creative, proactive reform of the Province's teacher-training education system, to be taught in teacher-training institutions, an accurate complementary picture of the Mi'kmaq Nation. In the future, if implemented, graduating students will know that our ancestors abided in a prosperous, socially caring, free, democratic, "YOU" society, prior to European invasion. Most important, course material must impart the fact that our ancestors fought the British to try to preserve their culture and country, not for the perverse pleasure of slaughtering innocent people.

With the goal of eliminating the systemic racism that colonial propaganda has created, to remove that impediment to a return to self-government by our Peoples, we propose that the Province's teacher-training institutions be required to adopt a mandatory course on the history of the Mi'kmaq Nation, with emphasis on post-European invasion events, and all the warts that go with it. This should be a course all students must pass to acquire a B.Ed.

I promote such a reform wholeheartedly, because I consider inclusion of true Mi'kmaq history in teacher-training curricula a vital element for successfully removing, in the foreseeable future, from the non-First Nations sub-conscience, the negative picture they hold of First Nations. It will have other positive benefits for the Province: among them, it will be used as a pioneering model of progressive racial education policy for the rest of the country. And a prosperous Mi'kmaq People will increase the prosperity of all Nova Scotians.

The structuring of a Mi'kmaq history course for teacher-training programs should not be hard. Such individuals as Don Julien, Professor John Reid, Professor Geoffrey Plank, myself, to name a few, can be recruited to help. Also, there is historical information, published in several new books that would be of invaluable assistance towards constructing such a course. Some examples include *An Unsettled Conquest, A Great and Nobel Scheme, Accounting for Genocide: Canada's Bureaucratic Assault on Aboriginal People,* and *We Were Not the Savages.*

I'll close with a quote from a report submitted to Nova Scotia's British Governor Cary in 1843 by Joseph Howe, who was the first Indian Commissioner appointed under the provisions of 1842 legislation, "An Act to Provide for the Instruction and Permanent Settlement of the Indians."

> *"I trust, however, that should your Excellency not be satisfied with the results of these first experiments, the blame may be laid upon the Commissioner, rather than be charged upon the capacity, or urged against the claims of a people, for whose many good qualities a more extended intercourse has only increased my respect, and who have, if not by Treaty, at least by all the ties of humanity, a claim upon the Government of the Country, which nothing but their entire extinction, or their elevation to a more permanent, and happy position in the scale of Society, can ever entirely discharge."*

My friends, you can be very instrumental in helping us to achieve, at long last, what Howe envisioned for our People one hundred and sixty four years ago in 1843: "their elevation to a more permanent, and happy position in the scale of Society."

Please consider doing so.

Respectfully Submitted,

Dr. Daniel N. Paul, C.M., O.N.S.
Chair of the Nova Scotia Council on Mi'kmaq Education

Dr. Daniel N. Paul, born in December 1938 in a small log cabin on Indian Brook Reserve, is a powerful and passionate advocate for social justice and the eradication of racial discrimination. As an author, journalist, consultant and volunteer, he has been an outspoken champion of First Nations communities across Nova Scotia for more than 30 years. The Nova Scotia Human Rights Commission, the Mi'kmaq Native Friendship Centre and the Confederacy of Mainland Mi'kmaq have all benefitted from his consensus-building skills and commitment to the community. Through his newspaper columns and his book, We Were Not the Savages, *he has helped to restore the proud heritage and history of the Mi'kmaq Nation.*

He is the recipient of numerous awards and honours, including a Doctor of Law Degree (Honorary) from Dalhousie University, Diploma in Recognition of lifetime of promoting Human Rights from Nova Scotia Community College, Grand Chief Donald Marshall Sr. Memorial Elder Award, MECNS Award, Order of Nova Scotia and Order of Canada. Other accolades include the City of Halifax Millennium Award, Honorary Doctor of Letters Degree from University of Sainte-Anne, City of Dartmouth Book and Writing Awards (co-winner of first prize for non-fiction, 1993 edition of We Were Not the Savages*) and District Chief Shubenacadie Mi'kmaq*

District: December 1988 to June 1990, an honorary title bestowed at the second annual meeting of the Confederacy of Mainland Micmacs.

He resides in Halifax in semi-retirement with his wife Patricia. They have two daughters, Lenore and Cerena. Lenore and husband Todd have made them grandparents twice, to Jenna and Julia. He also has a son Keith by a previous partner, whose children have made him a grandfather and great-grandfather many times over.

THE SUPERLATIVE ANNAPOLIS VALLEY

Allan Lynch

THERE IS A SPOT ON Highway 101 just beyond the Ben Jackson Road exit to the Glooscap First Nation's service area that, for those of us who grew up in the Annapolis Valley, screams "Home!" When we drive through the overpass on the Avonport Hill the Valley opens up before us.

Ahead and to the left are fields and marshes created by dykes built by the Acadians 350 years ago. Silver-tipped silos shimmer in the sunlight. Slightly to the right is the Minas Basin, either displaying its muddy brown bottom at low tide or the blue of high tide. Beyond the Basin is Blomidon, the mountain home of the Mi'kmaw creator, Glooscap. The belief is that Glooscap scooped out the land to create a place to rest, while he watched over his people. The earth he scooped out created the Minas Basin.

The Annapolis Valley starts in Windsor, Hants County and shadows the southern side of the Bay of Fundy to the town of Digby. Much of the history of Canada begins or relates to this 166-km-long fertile valley.

The Valley was and is a great place to grow up and live. In my generation, kids got to be kids. We were almost feral. After breakfast the door was opened and we were told to go play. Those with a dog got to take him/her/it along not so much for protection, but rather as a guide home in case we wandered too far. It was difficult to get lost or into too much trouble because of "The Mother Network." TMN were the eyes in the houses we passed. They knew where every kid was, who they were and when they needed to return home for dinner.

Mine is a somewhat bucolic memory of life here. The Valley is a place of plenty. It is one of the three primary agricultural areas in Canada, along with the Niagara region and Okanagan. I grew up in Kentville, which, like most Valley towns and villages is surrounded by rich, productive farmlands. When modern foodies speak of their adherence to *The Hundred Mile Diet* or rave of farmgate-to-plate restaurants, I shrug. That has always been Valley life. Until recently you could stand in the doorway of a Sobeys store and see an orchard that supplied some of the apples for sale inside. Otherwise, we went to farmer-owned markets to buy vegetables and fruits pulled from their fields and trees. A significant number of restaurants are either surrounded by or in sight of the fields, orchards and waters, which supply their menu.

For much of my life I have taken our abundance for granted. As I age, I appreciate how privileged we are. When others speak of "food security" it is an alien issue since the Valley has the soil, climate and ingenuity to always provide for us.

During Canada's sesquicentennial I learned that Kings County, where my father's family has lived since 1765 — my mother's family arrived in neighbouring Hants County in 1763 — is the most agriculturally diverse part of Canada, if not North America. A county planner told a group of us touring the county that when the federal government conducted a national agricultural inventory it found many parts of the country had two types of agriculture. Researchers were excited when they discovered areas with five types of farming because such a cluster was more sustainable and less susceptible to an economic roller coaster caused by bad weather or a single market upheaval. But when they arrived in Kings County, which has the same geographic footprint as Singapore (Singapore has six million people, Kings County has 60,000), they were shocked to find 11 types of agriculture. (The hog sector has declined, so now we say the county has 10 types of agriculture.)

This diversity in agriculture creates multiple, symbiotic relationships between farmers. One farmer sells his hay to the dairy farmer. The dairy guy sells manure to the vegetable grower and so forth.

The Annapolis Valley, like the Okanagan and Niagara region, is one of the top fruit-growing areas of Canada. That fruit heritage has spurred a new sector: wineries.

The first vineyards in North America were planted in Bear River by the French in 1611. Then over the centuries we focused more on less temperamental, easier to sell fruit crops and wine making was set aside. We returned to grape-growing and wine making in the 1970s. Those early wines were rough, often purchased as gifts — something bought out of loyalty to give away, but not drink yourself. Over time we learned which grapes grew best in our micro-climate (the Valley gets more sunshine and warmer weather than Halifax, an hour's drive away). Now, we have a delicious array of whites, reds, roses and sparkling (we-can't-call-it-champagne) wines. In essence we have become the new Napa.

The wine sector has sparked another evolution as a foodie destination. Cheese makers have come out of the closet. The Nova Scotia Community College in Kentville has a wine makers' course and a teaching vineyard. In summer a pink, double-decker Magic Wine Bus provides a hop-on, hop-off service to six wineries in the Wolfville area. There are organized cycling events to vineyards and if you're visiting Halifax, you can still join tasting tours to the Valley vineyards. Several, like that owned by celebrity grocer Pete Luckett, have great cafes and restaurants on-site.

Food has become the new recreation. Not that we ever shied away from eating. A *New York Times* writer said he had been to many places where people eat to live, but Nova Scotia was the first place he visited where people lived to eat.

Since people have to eat, the Valley became the breadbasket for Nova Scotia and quietly and persistently prospered. Valley people have lived comfortably. Most of us weren't rich, but since we lacked for nothing, we didn't grow up or live fixated on a need or a want. Our family, friends, neighbours all lived the same. We were privileged enough to take a lot for granted and not notice what we didn't have.

There was a time in my life when, influenced by television and movies, I urged my parents to get an apartment. People on TV and in movies always seemed to live in apartments, which to my small-town experience seemed glamorous compared to everyone I knew. We all lived in houses, with big yards. There were no elevators, no doormen, no parking attendants. Nor did anyone mow lawns or shovel snow.

Because my life was so happy, it took several decades to realize that not everyone lived as well as I did. In my early career, working for community papers in Kentville and Windsor I learned the Valley wasn't a happy bubble for everyone. But generally there was food, shelter and work. The pay might not have been great, but people got by, with help from those who knew they needed help.

My parents wanted me to know this place. Sunday drives were to parks, museums, an uncle's farm and Halls Harbour. At Halls Harbour I got to explore what tourism marketing now describes as "the ocean floor" — the beach at low tide. I also watched fishermen pick fish from the air. Because of the high tides in the Bay of Fundy, there was weir fishing. Nets were hung on large poles driven into the rocky beach. At high tide, fish swam into and got caught in the nets. At low tide fishermen harnessed their horses — occasionally a tractor — to a cart, which they stood on to harvest fish suspended in the air.

My father had a cab and tour business. As a kid I loved the reaction of American visitors he took to Halls Harbour. He always made two trips to show them the difference between high and low tide. The inner harbour has a 29-foot difference between tides. The visitors wouldn't believe it was the same place and often accused him of taking them to a duplicate village as part of an elaborate scam.

When we weren't playing with the perceptions of visitors, my parents ensured I knew about what was possible. Like most of my friends, I was raised with what might seem contradictory messages: don't draw attention to yourself, but know that anything is possible. With work. As I wrote in the dedication of my first book, *Sweat Equity: Atlantic Canada's New Entrepreneurs*, "To my parents, Marie and Harry, who never said no to the important things."

My parents knew the word "no," and employed it in relation to behavior and consumption, but it was never directed to ideas or dreams. They only ever asked, "Are you happy?" I was and am.

It took me a long time to grasp the concept that I came from a "have-not" province or region. This didn't and doesn't jive with the superlatives of this place. The Annapolis Valley is a place of quiet superlatives: first, oldest, biggest, highest, largest, greatest.

As I alluded to, we have the world's highest tides. Each tide that flows up the Bay of Fundy and into the Minas Basin is 160 billion tonnes of water. The volume of water is so great that it would twice fill the Grand Canyon and take 18 months to flow over Niagara Falls. It is equal to all the freshwater rivers in the world.

On land, we have more than 10,000 acres of apple orchards that, when in bloom, fill the Valley with their delicious, sweet, welcome-to-summer scent. We are home to The Habitation at Port Royal, which is the first permanent European settlement north of St. Augustine in Florida (it was first permanent European settlement in Canada, and pre-dates Jamestown). The Habitation was also home to North America's first dinner club, The Order of Good Cheer, and The Theatre of Neptune, the continent's first theatre. Even the First Nations people, the Mi'kmaq, seem to have been on this land long before other Indigenous people are recorded on theirs. For example, I've been told the Mi'kmaq were in Nova Scotia 14,000 years ago. In Banff, their history says the First Nations came there 10,000 years ago. In Saskatoon their people's history starts 6,000 years ago.

And from this small county we have had some big ideas and big thinkers emerge. Alfred Fuller, who created The Fuller Brush Company, came from Welsford, just outside of Berwick. Abraham Gesner, who invented the process for creating kerosene, and through this created the world's oil industry, grew up outside of my hometown. One of Canada's great industrialists, Roy Jodrey, grew up in Gaspereau, the little valley now dominated by wineries, behind Wolfville. Jodrey, who built the Minas Basin Pulp & Power and Canadian Keyes Fibre companies, held more corporate directorships — 56 — than any other Canadian. The day of his funeral, both the old Number 1 highway and TCH 101 from Windsor to Hantsport were bumper-to-bumper with limousines carrying mourners from corporate Canada to the small town from where he ran a hidden business empire. The Halifax International Airport was stretched to capacity as a fleet of corporate jets sat on the runways.

Grand Pré was also the birthplace of Prime Minister Sir Robert Borden. And curiously, Hall's Harbour was home to Ransford Buchanan. At age 18, Buchanan found employment with a Connecticut-based shipbuilder. Eventually he was ordered to deliver a ship to Constantinople. While there, Buchanan thwarted an assassination attempt on the Sultan. In thanks, the Sultan made Buchanan a Pasha, and provided him with a villa and harem. The harem didn't sit well with Buchanan's wife in New York, but it would have been rude to say no. Pasha Buchanan was eventually made Grand Admiral of the Ottoman Navy. With the outbreak of the First World War, Pasha Buchanan disappeared without a trace.

Valley residents also excel in the arts. Wolfville was the long-time home of the realist painter Alex Colville. In his lifetime, his paintings sold for many hundreds of thousands of dollars. After his death in 2013 his works moved up in price. In 2015, his painting *Harbour* sold for $1.88 million.

Sticking with the arts, the mostly widely read author of his time, Thomas Chandler Haliburton, lived in Windsor. His schoolboy diary recorded the first game of Hurley on Ice between members of the garrison and boys from Kings College (opened in 1788, it's Canada's first school and is still functioning) on Long Pond, Windsor in the winter of 1800. Hurley is an Irish game played with sticks and a ball. Hurley on ice became known as hockey so thanks to Haliburton's diary we know the first time hockey was played was in Windsor.

Haliburton lives with us today in all the expressions he gave the language. "It's raining cats and dogs." "Truth is stranger than fiction." "Quick as a wink." "Barking up the wrong tree." And many more.

The first Canadian woman to sell a million books was Margaret Marshall Saunders, who grew up in Berwick. The American writer Longfellow put the Valley on the map with his epic poem, *Evangeline*, about the 1755 expulsion of the Acadians. And Wolfville's John Frederic Herbin's writings increased knowledge about "his mother's people" the Acadians. His books provided the royalties which he used to compile the land for what became the Grand Pré National Historic Site. It is thanks to Herbin that Grand Pré exists and has double UNESCO World Heritage status: as the site of the deportation and as the longest continually farmed part of North America.

The Valley has had numerous agricultural innovators, from Charles Prescott, who launched the apple industry to a wave of Dutch immigrant farmers, who came after the Second World War and put their knowledge of how to profit from small spaces to good use. One of our more eccentric agricultural innovators was Windsor's Howard Dill. Dill created the giant pumpkin. It's thanks to Dill that the competitive craze for growing gigantic pumpkins and squash developed. From that we got Windsor's Giant Pumpkin Regatta, where hollowed out pumpkins are decorated and raced across Lake Pisiquid. It's sort of the ultimate way we play with our food. A current agricultural claim to fame is as home to North America's largest broccoli farm, just beyond Canning.

We have been leaders in medicine. My hometown was populated by pioneering doctors, like A.F. Miller, John Quinlan and Helen Holden, at the Nova Scotian Sanatorium. 'The San' had a store, radio station, fire department, heating plant, theatre, and accommodations for patients, nurses, and doctors on site. It needed to be self-contained since citizens shunned TB patients and sanatorium staff out of fear of catching this lethal disease. The San was so good at treating and curing TB that the actor Walter Pigeon and crusading physician Norman Bethune came to Kentville seeking a cure. Pigeon returned to acting and Bethune went to Spain for their civil war, then to China to provide medical care to Mao Zedong's forces, thereby having a major impact on the communist revolution and by extension the shaping of the 20th century.

The litany of highly accomplished people from here doesn't square with the concept of being a "have-not" place, nor do I recognize or accept former Prime Minister Stephen Harper's characterization of the region as having a "culture of defeatism."

We are successful; we have bred successful people and ideas, but have become a place Central Canada — and Ottawa — feels comfortable in overlooking or dismissing.

I love this province, but I hate how we have allowed others to define us, and with their definitions limit us. The national cliché is that successful people and businesses are created elsewhere. When I wrote *Sweat Equity*, Michael Donovan told me that when he and his brother Paul launched Salter Street Films (partly financed by Paul's *Globe and Mail* paper route) they couldn't get financing for their projects because decision makers in Toronto told them "the fact you chose to be in Halifax was evidence of non-seriousness."

The Donovans eventually sold Salter Street Films for $80 million and launched DHX Media, which is a billion-dollar entertainment powerhouse still based in Halifax.

Donovan maintains that the impediment to growth in Atlantic Canada is the lack of access to capital. Ironically, I overheard a former banker say his Kentville branch had more than $2 billion on deposit and they were the number three bank in town in terms of deposits. That money isn't invested in the Valley or province, but is siphoned to Central Canada to finance business there. It confirms Donovan's belief that Ontario-based bank decision makers are only prepared to grant Maritimers car loans and mortgages. Assets they can seize. Business investment is nearly impossible.

We are continually left out of any serious discussions or considerations on anything. For example, the Valley has some of the longest and bloodiest history on the continent, yet when the CBC produced a history series, *The Story of Us*, for Canada's sesquicentennial, it didn't mention The Habitation or Deportation of the Acadians. From a Valley perspective this series was *The Story Not of Us*. In 2011, when the CBC's Canada Reads panel considered Ami McKay's *The Birth House*, which went to international acclaim and seven weeks on *The New York Times'* bestseller list, it was dismissed by one panelist as a "regional book" because she lives in Scott's Bay, which was the location of the story.

Windsor-based Mermaid Theatre, which has the greatest audience numbers of any professional theatre company in Canada, is barely mentioned in Canadian media because of its small-town location, despite the fact that it plays to children around the world.

When the National History Museum in Ottawa (formerly the Museum of Civilization) produced an exhibition on hockey, it neglected any mention or reference to Long Pond and Windsor.

It seems that other books, movies, plays and programs about specific areas and other landscapes are celebrated, whereas a story from and/or about Atlantic Canada are reduced to "regional interest" with no larger message to convey.

I hate how we undervalue ourselves, which seems to allow others to devalue us, and how this complacency has allowed political operatives, whether elected to public office or a party insider rewarded with a government contract, to profit from the public purse with not much to show for their position beyond an out-of-date, generic website and photographs of cheque presentations and ribbon cuttings.

When I was in college I saw one of the seminal movies of my life. It was *Going Down the Road*. It was a bleak film about a couple of down-on-their-luck Cape Bretoners who left the island for the golden streets of Ontario hoping to pick up work as labourers or factory workers and live the good life. It didn't happen for them and I determined not to be one of those forced to leave the region — unless on my terms. Nova Scotia's unofficial anthem, "Farewell to Nova Scotia," has a line, "I grieve to leave my native land." That's how I and many I know who did go down the road felt.

When I and my generation launched our careers, because the population of the province is so small, there was basically one good local job in our field in any community. There was no job hopping to advance a career. If you quit a job you were viewed not as aggressive but potentially difficult to work with. That one good local job also helped depress pay scales.

Thirty years later, leaders in the business community in Nova Scotia and the region, supported by the publisher of a now-defunct business magazine, adopted the position that the lifestyle here was so desirable that our well-educated, healthy, hardworking young workforce would accept less pay to stay home. No doubt a lot of people were ready to take less to stay home, but we sort of made this an unofficial, self-perpetuating, harmful policy that cost us some of our brightest thinkers and doers.

Most of my classmates and friends had to move away for work. We were a golden generation, there was plenty of work around, but the pay was modest. Moving away meant more money, more career opportunity and advancement. But we are boomerang people. Those who left, left with the idea of building a bankroll and returning. In my early career I was always told I should be in Toronto. I didn't want to be in Toronto. But to be considered serious about our careers, we were expected to go because home wasn't seen as a place for success. I blame that on our modesty.

We have shortchanged ourselves and continue to do so by hiring economic development people and other "experts" based on an academic CV vs real world experience. I don't understand how someone with no business experience, who by their very career choices have shown themselves risk adverse, can be employed as business advisors. Yet they are hired for that very role. It seems equally curious that consultants focused on rural development are city-based and lack firsthand knowledge about rural or ex-urban life.

Our lack of self-knowledge and history is also limiting. For example, the 2014 Ivany Report, *Now or Never: An Urgent Call to Action for Nova Scotians* set a goal of doubling tourism revenues in a decade. The government and industry embraced the idea and goal as if it was revolutionary. But in 1993, the first year provincial tourism revenues hit $1 billion, the then Department of Tourism set a goal for doubling tourism revenues in a decade. It took almost two decades to reach $1.8 billion. So only through rounding off of figures did we sort of edge towards the target.

We brag about having the world's highest tides, but in the 1990s Nova Scotia tourism abandoned the Bay in its marketing and left it to New Brunswick to advertise. New Brunswick has convinced the world that it has the only access to Bay. At a dinner at the Jamison Distillery in Ireland, a colleague, who I consider one of the world's better travel writers, said, "Allan, your profile says you live near the Bay of Fundy. But you're in Nova Scotia and that's in New Brunswick!" I had to draw a map on the napkin to illustrate her error.

New Brunswick's Bay marketing is so persuasive that in three years, visitation to the Hopewell Rocks increased 71 percent, while Valley visitation grew 17 percent. In May 2018 I had a conversation with the editor of *National Geographic Traveler*. I was surprised that he didn't know we had the world's highest tides. I mentioned some of our other superlatives and he said, "You guys have a lot of stories to tell." We do and we haven't been telling them well, which is my frustration with the province and place I love.

Places become known for their successes. When I have tried to tell others about all the Valley superlatives they give me a patronizing look which suggests I am mentally feeble and unworldly. I have travelled to 35 countries on four continents and have seen how much lesser attractions are much better explained, positioned and marketed by their host destinations.

We have to work harder to be seen as a place where success can happen, where people with ideas can thrive and which is well worth visiting and paying attention to. We are not the poor man's Maine. The Ivany report found a number of impressive features and companies in Nova Scotia and directed that the focus now must be to increase the number of impressive companies as well as a renewal of traditional resource sectors.

We have so many stories to tell, so many ideas to contribute, so much success to build on, that I hope we find a way to employ them for the benefit of future generations, as well as visitors and potential investors. Our succeeding generations need to know they can live their dreams in this lush landscape. They can contemplate their future and enjoy the now over a plate of the fresh produce From land and sea - another culinary superlative comes from Digby which is home to the world's largest scallop fleet - washed down with a wide array of local spirits, craft beers, ciders, and wines good enough to be served in Michelin-starred restaurants in London and Paris.

Allan Lynch is a former newspaper publisher who chucked the office routine to return to his first love: writing. He contributes to magazines and newspapers from Singapore to Sweden. The author of four books and contributor to a dozen others, he is at work on his fifth and sixth books. Based near Nova Scotia's Bay of Fundy, research has had him crisscross North America and Europe and venture as far as South Africa, India and China. A ninth-generation Bluenoser, he is passionate for the province and region.

THE SAFE ZONE

Tareq Hadhad

I WAS ALMOST ON MY final stages of medical training.

My medical life started to be around my family — if anything happened, I can always be there for them. I was always sticking close to my family because they were very afraid about the war. Medical teams would be treating people who are opposing the government, or rebels would be afraid of medical teams who were treating the people who are opposing the rebels.

It was a very sensitive time to expose much of my medical identity in the street.

There were two things that happened. The first was when I was joining one of the classes at university and my mother, she called me and said, 'You have to leave now.' I said, 'Mom, why?' She said, 'I just don't feel right.' I said okay, but we have been living in this war for several months now and we just got used to it, so I can continue the class with the students and get back home. She said, 'No — you should leave now.'

I left at that time. It was the call that saved my life. Five minutes after that call, there were two mortar rockets that hit near the stage that we were in. Two of my friends were injured and other people actually died in that explosion at the university. It was very upsetting for everyone. It was definitely mother's instinct that saved my life.

A few weeks later, we started to move to another house in Damascus's safer zone. After finishing one of the shifts in the hospital, I was walking to the downtown house, a five minutes' walk. My nine-year-old brother Ahmed was in the car by our house. I went to him and we were doing a regular chat about how school went that day and should we bring anything to the house.

I was asking him if he'd made any new friends in the building we were in. A rocket hit near me and him. It was almost ten metres in front of me. He was very scared. The dust in the air was everywhere. We were on our backs on the sidewalk and I couldn't see anything. I thought that I am dead, but then I started moving and realizing what happened.

I couldn't hear anything. People were running all over the street, they were running to their houses, they were trying to leave the area. But I couldn't. I was in shock. I was trying to make sure that my brother was alive, that he didn't get injured, so I inspected him. He was fine, but he was very scared.

I carried Ahmed in my arms. He was opening his eyes, but not closing them. I was talking to him, but he didn't respond. I carried him into the house. My mother, after she heard the explosion, she went out on the balcony and she was saying, 'Come home! Come home!' I couldn't hear her. I was seeing her, she was waving her hands for us to rush into the house so she can make sure we are fine. She was crying on the balcony.

My mother opened the door and said, 'Are you OK?' She was doing the first aid for me and him. We were more in shock from the explosion, rather than being severely injured. The trauma that was caused to us by that explosion continued for several years and caused us nightmares. Every time we were talking together, we were always imagining that something was going to happen.

I was always telling my family: it's not time to do medicine, it's not time to do business; it's time to survive. I was trying to persuade my family that even though we had that belief that Syria is our homeland and we cannot leave it very easily, but we certainly also don't want to die. It's the human life that matters. Anything else can be rebuilt.

My cousin, who died in the war, he will not come back. But our house, or anything that was destroyed, it might come back when the war stops — even in ten, fifteen years. It doesn't matter. What matters is we should make sure everyone in the family is alive, is safe, is secure, and everything else will be fine.

We rushed to the border to Lebanon a few days after the explosion with only our clothes on our backs. We couldn't bring everything because we knew it would pose some challenges at the border. The Syrian border guards were telling us, 'Why are you going to Lebanon?' We were saying just tourism for one month. To Beirut, even though we didn't have anyone there. We didn't know anyone. All of our friends had left the country.

There was a conversation at the border that I can't forget. One of the officers from the Syrians, he was trying to send us back. He was saying, 'You can't leave the country. You should serve the military.'

There is a nightmare called the military book for every young Syrian man. It has all the records: if he served in the military or not; if not, why he didn't serve in the military. But you have to give a reason for why you didn't serve in the military, or why you are leaving the country.

The officer was saying, 'Oh, I see you are studying to be a physician. Physicians should serve in the military in this time where there is a universal war on Syria.' I said, 'You called it — it's universal. It's not my war.' He said, 'But you were born in Syria. You ate its fruits and vegetables, so how are you leaving it this way?' I told him I'm not leaving, I will be back.

All that time, my mind was going: all these Syrian people that are dying are the fuel of the war. If they all opposed continuing that war — on all the sides — the senior people, the aged people who are managing that war, will be thinking again about what the hell they are doing. Young people are really fed up to die in the war that was decided by people who are older than them. It's not their war. They have their entire lives in front of them.

After passing the border point, we arrived on the Lebanese land. That was my first visit to a country outside of Syria. We stopped the car. We were talking to each other as a family. We had our small car that was left working and were sitting on each other's laps — my father, mother, brother Ahmed and sister Taghrid. We were talking about where we should go now. What's next?

I remember there was no option for us. We just stopped in the middle of the road, trying to figure out if we knew anyone there we could call, but everyone we called was outside of the country. We were scared. It was a moment of uncertainty, a moment of despair. I started to see my father was for the first time in his life so concerned about the family. Even though we were at risk of dying in Syria, leaving the country was even harder for him than living in a place where rockets might hit our heads at any point. It was losing that sense of identity, losing your sense of your amazing history.

We started hearing the word 'refugee' more often and were always trying to avoid being registered as refugees. We were always thinking that being a refugee is really the hardest exercise that can be done on any human being. It tells him every time that he is a number and will not be considered a normal citizen at any point. It was very challenging for us to realize how hard it is to go to the United Nations and register as refugees. I definitely admire the work the UNHCR is doing, but it was not something that I wanted to do. I was forced to. I started realizing that I would become absolutely nobody if I don't register.

We were waiting in line to get our interviews with the UN. We were sitting on the benches in the hall and they were giving us numbers to pin like tags on our chests. They gave me a number and I really didn't look at it. They started calling my number, and I didn't realize they are calling me.

After three attempts, the UN officer came to me and looked at my number. He said, 'It's your number, sir. Why are you not replying?' I said, 'Because I am not a number. I don't want to remember these four or five digits my entire life. I have a name. You could have taken our names and called us by name.'

It was so sensitive to me. I was very upset, even though I know the UN is doing an amazing job. But it was not my world. I was forced to live in that world. Only a few weeks ago, we were in Syria. Before the factory exploded, we were an economically stable family. We were helping others, we were very active community members. Becoming refugees in Lebanon really dissolved all of our dreams, all of our history, and for sure the present that we were living in.

The next day I went to the same UN branch and volunteered to do anything that would take me out of the world they were always trying to put me in. A man said, 'You can come with us to a medical clinic we visit.'

I was there at 5 a.m. waiting for them, very excited to see how I can help. We went and were seeing sick children in the camps and trying to help them get the right medications. It was a very noble thing, exactly what I always imagined medicine would be. I was really honoured.

If a patient with a certain type of infection doesn't get treated, he can die within weeks. We managed to develop awareness programs against certain types of diseases so the refugees in the camps know the right ways to keep hygiene and their rights. I was not only a medical advocate, but a legal advocate. Even though I was spending nights away from my family, I was always trying to make sure they are fine and making some friends. We could only stay in Lebanon for six months and we had to sign a commitment saying we wouldn't work, wouldn't take a job from a Lebanese.

The type of life I was living in Lebanon, it was always a day-on-day basis. I didn't have the chance to plan for anything — only the next day. I couldn't see how my future would look like, whether I would stay in Lebanon or go back to Syria. Many Syrian families were leaving Lebanon for Turkey and then Greece, but I was trying to make sure my family was not thinking of doing this. I was trying to give them hope when I was very hopeless. I was trying to give them light, even though I didn't see any. I was making sure they didn't get with smugglers.

One of my far cousins came from Homs and stayed in Lebanon for two months and then the authorities arrested her with her children. They said she entered illegally. She decided to go to Turkey and from Turkey she was on the boat.

She texted me around 3 a.m. and said, 'I am on my way to Greece.' I said don't do it. Go back — just stay in Turkey. She said, 'I think Europe would give me a bigger opportunity in my life.' I wanted her to not risk the lives of her and her children. Every five minutes, she was sending a message saying we are fine. But it was 3:45 a.m. and I didn't hear from her. I was texting her, calling her, but no response. I was thinking maybe her phone wasn't charged enough. I didn't sleep.

I waited until 6 a.m. and then I was texting my friends — some in Greece, some in Turkey. They said no one arrived in Greece. We realized that Helena and the children and around 47 others drowned in the Mediterranean. The engine stopped and there were too many people onboard. Everyone died. That was the incident that changed my way of convincing my family to be patient, and everything will be fine. Life will give us another chance.

In early 2015, I was really trying to get my family out of Lebanon. I was seeing how my siblings are passing their years without a proper education. How my mother and sister were trying to be active, but really couldn't help. And my father was living in such frustration. He was depressed. My family was moving every second week, trying to find a place to hide from the checkpoints.

The idea of coming to Canada came in early 2015. It was January and I was in a taxi. The driver was telling me, 'Did you hear about scholarships from the Canadian embassy?' I hadn't. I went home and spent the whole night applying on the website. It was something I did and then forgot about. But I got that call from the embassy. It was from a senior immigration officer at the Canadian embassy. He was telling me he was very sorry he missed my application. He said it was excellent — they reviewed it a couple of times and really think not only me, but me and my family are going to do huge things in Canada.

I really thought it was a scam so I shut down the line. I was worried — how can I trust someone on the phone? I was always trying to make sure I don't fall into the scams because there were so many people that were trying to get some hope to the Syrians in Lebanon, Jordan, Turkey, that they would get them to the European countries, or Canada or the U.S., but they need everything they have. I was very cautious about that and opened my eyes very wide. As the oldest son in the family, I was always feeling that I don't only have the responsibility to get myself to the safe shore, but my family. Family is everything for me. Without my family, I would not have reached where I was.

After a few days, I get an e-mail from the embassy inviting me to an interview. I started realizing, it's getting serious. I didn't tell my family there is something real happening here. There were hundreds of thousands, if not millions, of Syrians they were trying to get resettled.

I went to the interview. It went very well. I went back home. I texted my family on the road and told them please don't sleep tonight — I have very sweet news for you. None of them slept. When I arrived, my father opened the door and everyone was waiting for me. He said, 'Are you fine? Is there anything that has happened today?' I said, 'Well, dad, we will travel.'

My family was applauding. My siblings were excited. My mother said, 'Where? To Germany?' I said no. My father said, 'Sweden?' I said no. My sister said, 'The United States?' I said no. They tried all the countries around the globe. After a moment of silence, I told them we would travel to Canada. Really, the first thing they replied — all at the same time, in Arabic — was, 'Canada is too cold! It's the coldest country on earth. How are we going to survive there? We need maybe ten jackets just to get warm.'

But I was seeing the excitement in their eyes. The warmth in their hearts. They were planning for their future after that moment. We were all seeing a great future being built in a country that respects human rights, respects the diversity, and welcomes people with their cultures. No one has to take off anything of their culture after they arrive — they are very welcome to keep their traditions. That's exactly what fascinated my entire family about this country. I read a lot about Canada. I was excited.

In early November, we started receiving the calls again for the full interviews with the Canadian consulate. So many Canadian officials were coming to Lebanon and booking full hotels for the interviews with tens of thousands of Syrians to bring them to Canada.

All of the families, they were shining hope from their eyes. They were very excited. It was the moment that would change everything, that would erase the suffering. They have all lived in refugee camps or slept nights in their cars after explosions destroyed their houses. It was something I had never seen — the happiness that these people, their suffering is coming to an end and they will be given a new life in a new country that will be their second home. My family was also living like that.

The consulate was asking us where we want to stay in Canada. I told him we are from the big city, we want to stay in one of the big cities. I was telling him we want to stay in one of the MTVs — Montreal, Toronto or Vancouver. He was laughing, and then he said, 'No. I think you should stay in a small town. In a small town, you will be welcomed to their family very quickly. You will find people around you. In small towns, everyone has time for you to rebuild your lives. It's the key recipe for success for families to arrive in small communities where people can take good care of you. If you arrive in a big city, you will become a number. You will become only the strange neighbour that everyone would not care about. Just arrive in a small town.'

It was very fascinating. We told him it doesn't matter — we can stay anywhere.

Everything was happening very quickly. We were receiving an e-mail every day from the embassy about the orientation for coming to Canada, how to live there. A few weeks after, I got the call that I should travel before my family. They promised my family would follow me. I was called in mid-December and they gave me less than 36 hours before my flight. I was really excited, but I was not really ready. I was expecting myself to arrive in Canada in 2017, 2018. But it was on December 16 that my flight would leave Beirut.

I packed up everything I could and was looking into the eyes of my family, promising them I would do everything possible for them to follow me as soon as possible.

When I was at the airport, I was trying to live these moments, because I knew I would be telling them to my children, my grandchildren, and all the generations in the family of the Hadhads that would be in Canada. I was trying to picture them. How promising everything was looking! All the Canadian officials were very welcoming to me at the airport with a big smile.

It was the first time I travelled on an airplane. It was such an excitement! I was really living the dream. I had some Syrian friends on the plane with me and they were worried about their life in Canada. They say they cannot learn the language. They were scared. They were seeing themselves stuck in a situation where they can't communicate and they don't have their cellphones and are lost in a new country. That's the nightmare they were having on the airplane.

I told one of the Syrian men to go on YouTube and learn some of the language from the tutors. He said on sentence: 'It's beautiful weather out there. It's beautiful weather out there.' He was repeating it again and again, just to tell it to the Canadians when he arrived so he can start the conversation in English.

When we arrived in Toronto on December 18, it was minus 22. We went to the airport — my Syrian friend was with me. He was looking at me and I was thinking: 'No! Don't say it.' We went to the official and he told him, 'It's beautiful weather out there.' The Canadian officer told him, 'Are you serious? It's minus 22 out there!' So my friend went outside and then came back. He was like a frozen chicken. He took my phone again and he rephrased the sentence. He said to the officer, 'It's a horrible weather out there.'

These were really some of the funniest moments I have ever lived. It was time of joy — of pure joy and unlimited happiness that everyone was arriving in Canada and knowing it would offer them all the chances to succeed.

The idea of coming to Antigonish was a completely different story. I didn't know I would travel to Halifax. I was always planning to stay somewhere around Toronto. They called me and said your flight is tomorrow. I said, 'Oh — to where?' They said somebody is waiting for you in Halifax. I said, 'What's Halifax? I want to stay in Canada!' They said, 'Halifax is just on the other side of the country. You will find people who have been waiting for you a long time. They will be very pleased to see you.'

I went to the gate and there was somebody telling me to go to the backseat. I went to the backseat and was sitting by the window. All I was seeing was the eyes of my family members in the window. I really didn't see anything else. It was the second time I had flown and it was very memorable. The airplane was swinging in the air, flying within windy weather. It's only one hour to Halifax. I saw on the other side of the aisle on the plane was another Syrian family. There was a man, there was a woman and their kid. They looked very exhausted. They didn't know where they are going.

I was telling them, 'You will arrive safe. Everything will be fine. This is your new country and I'm pretty sure there are people in Halifax waiting for you as there would be for me too.' I didn't know that, but I was very confident that as a young man in his mid-20s, I would find a way. I am in a much luckier situation than millions of people who are arriving in Europe around midnight and they have no one there. They always start from exactly scratch.

My entire flight to Halifax, my thoughts were around what I'm going to do in Canada. I absolutely imagined everything. I imagined continuing my medical studies, or starting something new, working in a not-for-profit organization, NGOs, or start my studies from zero.

When we arrived in Halifax, I was the last to land, with the Syrian family. We arrived at the gate and the airport officials said. 'Sit down for now and we will call the group that came for you so they're ready to welcome you.' I had no idea what they are talking about. I know no one, so how would a group come to welcome me?

After everybody had left, I went down to meet the people who did everything to bring me to Canada. Everything was going on in my mind. In each step, I was imagining, who can these people be? Are they going to support me? How am I going to be treated? Am I going to be lost in the country? But there was a sense of comfort. I started to be less nervous.

I was looking through the glass and seeing tens of people waiting there, carrying signs, carrying flags and flowers. I was staying in my place. The people were trying to come to me! They were trying to enter the luggage area, even though it's illegal. They were that excited to see me. I went out and everyone said, 'Are you Tareq?' I said, 'Yes, I am Tareq, but I am sure I am not the Tareq you are looking for.' They said, 'We are sure you are the Tareq we are looking for. Tareq Hadhad, is that right?' I said, 'Oh! You know my last name too. That's exciting!'

I read the signs — they were in Arabic and English. They had brought translators. It was such a moment. This group of people, they didn't know me before. They didn't care about who I am, how do I look. They didn't care about my religion, my ethnicity. They just came to the airport to meet someone who had travelled 7,000 kilometres from the Middle East because he lost everything and is seeking safety and opportunity again. And peace.

I would say the community of Antigonish has done something that is one of the noblest things on earth. When you are helping people without knowing them, when you are spending your time and efforts and money and sweat and tears on things you believe in — helping humanity, wherever people are suffering, just bring them to a safe zone. And not to end that warm-hearted welcome and support on the first handshake, but to walk that road with them.

Within a few seconds, I was thinking that. How great that is. How inspiring. Not only for me, but also for our family for generations to come. We would have a hand when we arrived in Canada and it would be our responsibility in the next few years to offer hands to help others survive and escape suffering.

Everyone was crying. They were looking at me like I was a gift for them. I felt like I was the prime minister. We drove to Antigonish.

Tareq Hadhad, the founder and CEO of Peace by Chocolate and one of the Top 25 Immigrants to the Maritimes, came to Canada in December 2015 as a Syrian newcomer. He studied medicine at Damascus University and proceeded to join the medical relief efforts for the Syrian refugees with UNHCR and WHO through a local organization when he arrived to Lebanon in 2013 as a refugee himself.

Passionate about peace and youth entrepreneurship, and just after arriving in Cananda, he and his family started their company "Peace by chocolate" in Antigonish, NS, to sponsor peace building projects and support the local economy by offering jobs. The company later turned into a phenomenon that inspired so many people around the world and was mentioned in a speech by Prime Minister Hon. Justin Trudeau at the UN summit in September 2016 in New York as a remarkable example for the contributions of the newcomers in their communities.

After a series of media interviews with 500 media agencies including BBC, CNN, PRI, CBC and much more, Tareq and his family won the Newcomers Entrepreneur Award and was chosen by Google as the National Hero Case in Canada in 2018. He is also challenging being physician in Canada. He is now serving on the board of director for Invest NS and is grateful for the encouragement and support from his new community. He is now also a public speaker and engages in media campaigns to support youth entrepreneurial skills as well as linking the Syrian youth and helping the Syrian refugees all around the world.

The Hadhad family operated a large chocolate business in Damascus, Syria, until the war started. A tank shelled the family home in 2012, forcing them to flee internally. Airplanes bombed the factory later that year. Tareq Hadhad, the eldest son, recounts the terrifying events that forced them to leave Syria for Canada, where they would start Peace by Chocolate in Antigonish, Nova Scotia. This account is adapted from the forthcoming book, Peace by Chocolate, *by Jon Tattrie.*

WELL GROUNDED

Clara Dugas

GENEALOGISTS AGREE THAT ALL THE people with the family name Dugas in the Maritime Provinces and in Quebec are descendants of Abraham Dugas, who settled in Nova Scotia in the 1630s.

My story begins with Joseph Dugas. He was born in 1738 in Cobequid near what is now Masstown. By the time he was born, the British had captured Acadie and changed the name to Nova Scotia. Tensions between France and Great Britain were growing. What had been a hundred years of peace for the Acadians was changing. In 1755, the Acadians were deported and shipped to the British Colonies along the Eastern seacoast. Their houses, barns and crops were burnt. A few lucky families, however, managed to escape. Between 10,000 and 18,000 Acadians were displaced, expelled from their lands.

Joseph was 17 years old in 1755. When he had turned 16, obviously ingenious and adventuresome, he had joined the militia. At some point he was injured then brought to the hospital in Louisbourg. By then Louisbourg had been captured by the British. He managed to escape. From there he travelled to Camp d'Espérance on the Miramichi River where Acadians gathered for protection. These were deplorable conditions. The Acadians often resorted to chewing on beaver pelts for nutrition.

It was there that Joseph met Marie-Josephte Robichaud, who was at the camp with her parents and sister. She was three years younger than Joseph. She had been born in Annapolis Royal. Joseph and Marie-Josephte fell in love but their time together was short lived. The British soon attacked the area and many Acadians were captured. Marie-Josephte and her father ended up in

Nova Scotia. Her mother and sister died along the way but she and her father were eventually imprisoned at Fort Edward in Windsor.

During this time, there is no trace of Joseph Dugas. Marie-Josephte and her father were finally released from prison after the treaty of Paris was signed in 1763. Eventually, they found their way back to Annapolis Royal. By then, most of the land that the Acadians had once lived on had been granted to English Planters from New England. Life was not as they had left it. It was not long after before Joseph arrived in Annapolis and found Marie-Josephte. This must have been a joyous reunion for they were married within months. I like to think of them as our own Evangeline and Gabriel, fictitious characters created by Henry Wadsworth Longfellow in his poem *Evangeline*. Isabelle, the first of their seven children, was born in the spring of 1764

While the Acadians were in exile, Colonel Charles Lawrence, Governor of Nova Scotia, the mastermind for the deportation, had died. His successors were more sympathetic towards the Acadians. In 1768, land was set aside specifically for Acadians along Saint Mary's Bay in southwestern Nova Scotia and called the township of Clare. Joseph had heard of this. In the summer of 1768 he and Marie-Josephte, now eight months pregnant, along with their daughter, Isabelle, made the 115 km trek from Annapolis to Saint Mary's Bay with their horse. They crossed the Bear River, the Joggins and the Sissiboo River. It took them a month to reach the area now known as Belliveau's Cove. Along the way, they took refuge in Mi'kmaw settlements. Twenty-one days after their arrival, Marie-Josephte gave birth to their son, Joseph, the first Acadian born on the shores of St. Mary's Bay.

The first winter they suffered tremendously from isolation and hunger. They survived mostly on wildlife such as pheasants, deer and shellfish. The next spring, more Acadians came from Annapolis to settle the area and St. Mary's Bay soon became the most populated Acadian settlement in Nova Scotia. Joseph died in 1821. Marie-Josephte lived into her 90s. They are both buried in St. Mary's cemetery. A monument in memory of this couple was erected in front of Joseph Dugas School in Church Point. The inscription, written by the historian Alphonse Deveau, reads:

> *Le courage de ce couple seul, en face de grandes difficultés de survie, a inspiré un sentiment de fierté à tous les colons qui les ont suivis.* (The courage of this one couple, in the face of great difficulties to survive, gave a sense of pride to all the other settlers who followed them.)

Those are my ancestors. Those are my roots planted in the very soil of Nova Scotia. Church Point is where I was born and raised. It is my home. Not far away is another place, a magnificent place I would like to call home but I cannot. History got in the way. Within the glorious Annapolis Valley is the little village of Grand Pré. There is a hill in Grand Pré overlooking what is now part of the UNESCO World Heritage Site and where a small stone church stands, a replica of an earlier church from the 1600s. I love visiting this site, especially in the summertime when the blossoms and flowers are in bloom. On the grounds, not far from the statue of Evangeline, are old, gnarled and crooked French willow trees, unsightly but strong. The French willows were planted by my ancestors in the 1680s.

Those are the roots of my past. Like our ancestry, the roots of these ancient willows have stood the test of time. Our ancestors have spread throughout Nova Scotia, struggled and survived. If only those willows could talk. They have seen and heard so much. They are reminders that our history is one of tragedy, yet also one of faith, strength, happiness and hard work. My culture and my Acadian heritage are all well rooted.

My grandmother, Isabelle Comeau-Dugas was born in 1870; a little over 100 years after the Deportation began. In other words, she was only separated by about three generations from this historical tragedy. You would have thought she had heard about the Great Upheaval but one day, I asked: *Grand'mère, qu'est-ce que vous pouvez me dire de la déportation des Acadiens en 1755?* (Grand'mère, what can you tell me about the Deportation of the Acadians?). She said she remembered hearing of the great fire of 1820; four miles of fields, houses and barns were burnt along the coastline she told me. That was not what I meant. In the final analysis, she did not know.

My grandmother was a strong woman. She valued her Acadian heritage, in spite of a lack of historical facts, based on the values of the Catholic church and handed down orally from generation to generation. Living on the edge of poverty with seven children, she was strong and determined. Like her predecessors, she was not just determined to survive physically but determined to make sure our language and religion would survive. In order to do that, our parents and grandparents tried hard to keep us within the confines of our own community. Socializing with others our age from adjacent English speaking communities like Yarmouth and Digby was shunned. The railway was our main connection to an outside world with which we rarely associated because it was English and predominantly Protestant. This was their way of protecting us.

It took me years to realize that this was a form of survival for a people that knew fear, disconnection and oppression. This was a people who had lost everything except their own religion, their own culture and their own language. And yet they were happy when we, their children, began learning English, thanks first to the radio, then to television in the 1950s and even our Primer readers in school like *Tom, Betty and Susan*.

Once, during a summer visit, an American relative said to my mother, "The children seem to be picking up some English." She replied in her broken English, "Yes, yes! I make dem watch le télévision as much as I can."

During my first trip to France in 2004, I stayed in three different hotels in five days. At the first hotel, I went to the desk and asked for towels. I didn't need towels. I simply wanted to speak French. The clerk answered me in English with a strong French accent. It puzzled me. At the second hotel on our itinerary, I did the same thing. I received the same reaction. By the time we arrived at the third hotel in Lyon, France, I wondered if the clerks thought I was English. So I said, in French, in my own Acadian accent, *Je vais vous parler en français. Croyez-le, croyez-le pas, je suis francophone. C'est ma langue maternelle. J'aimerais bien que vous vous me parleriez en français. Merci.* (I will speak to you in French. Believe it or not, I am French. I would appreciate being answered in French, thank you.) The gentleman replied, *Ah oui Madame, certainement. Vous parlez un très beau français du dix-septième siècle.* (Ah yes, Madam, certainly. You speak a very good seventeenth century French.) I was elated.

Ours is not standard French. During the time when the *Académie Française* was busy normalizing or standardizing words and pronunciation in France, we were isolated in far off Nova Scotia. We knew nothing. We simply kept our ancestors' accents and their limited vocabulary. In our own community, we were constantly reminded that there were those who spoke well, in other words, the clergy, the nuns and our teachers. And there were those who did not speak well such as our parents, our friends and our neighbours.

We did, and still do, speak a seventeenth century dialect, but it was our mother tongue. We owned it. The French Academy in Paris could not change that. We were and are still proud of our language. We could speak so-called standard French with the priest, the nuns, the college students who came to Collège Sainte Anne from Quebec, but once we were in our homes, our own French came back to us. We may have been made to be ashamed of it; we may have been told that we were lazy in not using standard French but ours is *la langue de Molière*. It's French borne from hardship, perseverance and pride.

There is no denying that we have come a long way but in hindsight my greatest vexation about being an Acadian in Nova Scotia, besides the tormented lives my ancestors endured, was the education system during my high school years. Because of the provincial government's lack of recognition of the Acadian people of Nova Scotia, we were denied what we should have been given: a right to education in our language. The education system for French Acadians in this province has been a thorn in my side.

I remember well in the 1960s, my eighth grade history book was entitled *The History of Nova Scotia*. One — only one — sentence within the whole text, mentioned the Acadians. That one sentence read (and I know it from memory): "And then the Acadians were deported." That was it; just that sentence and absolutely nothing about where they lived or their great contribution to our province.

Henry Wadsworth Longfellow intrigues me. Since I've graduated and learned more about Longfellow's epic poem *Evangeline: A Tale of Acadie*, an epic poem which placed our history in its rightful place and made it known around the world, I've wondered why it is that an American who never even visited Nova Scotia could write such a compassionate poem in 1847, almost a century after the Deportation. How could he have placed our people on the map and yet our own government could not include a chapter in the textbooks of our schools? Nova Scotia, our own home, chose to ignore or erase the history of the dispersed Acadian communities. Or as Sally Ross and Alphonse Deveau state in their book *The Acadians of Nova Scotia*, "according to textbooks used in the 1960s and 1970s, Acadians did not exist in the present and three centuries of their history remained untold."

Acadians, born in Nova Scotia before the 1970s, went through a school system that disregarded their language. We never really learned to read and write in French. In the public schools in the Acadian regions of Nova Scotia, teachers often taught in French but textbooks were in English or bilingual. I remember classes of over forty in high school with classmates who chose never to answer in class so they would not have to speak in English and be made fun of or corrected by the teacher. I was always eager to speak out, but only if I sat up front, close to the teacher's desk so everyone in the back would not hear me. In that way, I could also avoid scornful looks from my classmates.

We were lucky enough to have a French grammar and literature program from Quebec until Grade 10. But from 1893 to 1972, there were compulsory provincial examinations at the end of Grade 11 and Grade 12. All the exams were in English, putting Acadian students at a disadvantage. In Grade 11, we were forced to give up a rich French program and settle for the provincial program designed for English speaking students in order to prepare us for the end-of-the-year provincial examinations.

Those of us who chose a college or a university outside our Acadian communities regressed in both reading and writing French. I wanted to become a teacher. I could have gone to Collège Sainte Anne, now Université Sainte Anne in Church Point, a francophone institution. But in the 1960s I would only have received a Bachelor of Arts, which meant I would have had to go on to another university to receive a Bachelor of Education. This would have been costly for my family who could ill afford to pay university tuition. I decided to go to Nova Scotia Teachers' College in Truro, an all-English college. It was affordable because at the time, tuition was paid for by the provincial government. It did not financially burden my parents.

I remember well my first day in French class at Nova Scotia Teachers' College. There were two classes of first-year students. Our professor was English speaking. On the first day he pompously made the following announcement: "All the French speaking students in class will never have a mark on a test or an exam any higher than 75 per cent. It would not be fair to the English-speaking students. So I will stop marking your papers once you reach a mark of 75 per cent."

I was shocked. French had been my favourite subject. Next to my mark in religion, it was usually my highest mark in high school. I felt belittled, insignificant, bullied and penalized because I was French. I still remember my great disappointment. I wanted to go home, tell my parents what this school was like. I wanted them to help us argue and defend our rights to be proud of our language. But I couldn't. I wouldn't be going home for months and besides, it wouldn't make any difference. And going to the principal of the college was unheard of. How could we express ourselves? We were just out of our own French communities. Who would listen anyway? Would we be penalized for objecting? We kept quiet. Our parents had taught us well.

There were two French classes for first-year students. Monsieur Edwards from Isle Madame, Cape Breton, was the professor in the other class. His mother was Acadian and he was francophone. Friends of mine in his class were marked according to their ability to speak, read and write French. They, unlike me and my classmates, were even able to get a 100 on tests and exams. And this discrepancy was accepted, tolerated. It was obvious that our heritage was valued by some and not by others. We were victims of discrimination.

Ironically, at the beginning of the first semester, the college had regular tests of English grammar and comprehension for new students. After all, we were to become teachers in Nova Scotia for the most part; we were expected to excel in English. You were allowed to write the tests three times. If you failed two of the three times, you were expelled. Out of the 10 students from Argyle and Clare (the Acadian regions in southwest Nova Scotia) and as many from Cape Breton, no one was expelled. Many English-speaking students were. Some of us came close, but every one of us stayed on. We knew our English literature and grammar. At the end of the weeks of tests, we were jubilant.

Things did not really start to change in Nova Scotia until the mid 1970s. It is not because of the provincial government that things changed but, rather, because of Pierre Trudeau and the arrival of the Official Languages Act passed by the federal government in 1969.

When all is said and done and I look back, I know many people made mistakes. Many have wronged the French Acadians here in Nova Scotia but nevertheless, I feel privileged for so many reasons. My pride in living in Nova Scotia as an Acadian is many fold especially when I am represented with my people in books, in the Legislature, in the House of Commons and other public institutions.

I remember with fondness the first *Festival Acadien de Clare* in 1955. I was six years old. My mother and I were on a float in that first parade. Mother instilled in me a love of our heritage. She was as strong an Acadian as I have known. The summer she was nominated Honourary President of the festival was one of the happiest of her life. The joy of taking part over the years in the *Festival Acadien de Clare* was rich and rewarding as any celebration. Parades, picnics, social gatherings, concerts were all festivities in which we took part and still do.

The first festival was so popular that the chamber of commerce decided to continue it. Every summer the festival is a week filled with celebrations, family reunions and tourists. Since 2006, not only do artists and musicians from

Clare participate, but also groups from other Francophone regions such as New Brunswick, Quebec and Louisiana. I feel privileged whenever I prepare to attend or work for an Acadian Festival. All the hard work our ancestors put into saving our heritage is like a good soup, a delicious *fricot* — without stirring it, without adding salted shallots and fresh potatoes, fresh meat, the soup is bland. Our soup is rich. Our heritage is rich.

Two weeks before Mother passed away in 1997, in spite of being weak and not well, she wanted to go to the festival. We helped her get dressed in her Acadian costume. She proudly sat in the car as we headed to the parade. With the window down on this hot August day, she waved her Acadian flag and smiled the same Acadian pride that dominated our home.

In 2004, Acadians in Nova Scotia hosted the third *Congrès Mondial des Acadiens*, World Acadian Congress. The family reunions, meeting new cousins, hearing talks from genealogists seems to have made us thirsty for more knowledge regarding our ancestors. Since then, more Acadians have become interested in their own genealogy. Tours are organized to visit places in the Unites States, France, Quebec and Saint Pierre-Miquelon, where Acadians were deported in the 1700s and there is an Acadian Congrès every five years somewhere in the Maritimes.

From 2005 until 2011, Clare had its own International Storytelling Festival, *Festival de la Parole de la Baie St Marie*, bringing into the region French storytellers from Quebec, France and Belgium. Being a storyteller, I greatly benefitted from this. Since then, I have had the chance to travel as a bilingual storyteller. This has helped me immensely with my spoken French. It was not easy at first. I was reluctant to speak my dialect with francophones outside Nova Scotia. At first I'd confess that maybe the public would not understand my accent. The answer was always the same: *Nous t'invitons parce que ton accent est différent*. (We invite you because your accent is different). Many francophone storytelling friends tell me they like to listen to my accent. They say it has a rhythm not found in standard French.

I love so many things about my province — the varied landscapes, the mountains of Cape Breton, the sea coast, the wilderness, the fishing boats, the beautiful beaches and the valleys. But most of all, I am proud of what *Acadie* has become thanks to its people who made it possible. Since 1937, the Acadians have had their own French newspaper, Le *Courrier de la Nouvelle Écosse* created by Acadians for the Acadians of southwestern Nova Scotia in response to the lack of opportunities to read in French. Now it is available to all Acadians across the province. As early as the 1830s, there was an Acadian in the Senate. Now we have a Minister of Acadian Affairs. As of 2016, our Lieutenant Governor is Acadian. Since 1996 we have had a French provincial school board, *Conseil scolaire acadien provincial* (CSAP).

Unfortunately, the population in some Acadian rural areas is diminishing. More and more young people are leaving the smaller communities to go work elsewhere. The decrease in church attendance is also a factor as it was the pillar of Acadian culture. English is spoken more frequently among the Acadian youth. However, Halifax Regional Municipality has French schools that are overcrowded. There is hope.

We have a French radio station, Radio Canada. That helps me with my own French and keeps me up to date with world news *en français*. We even have a French community radio station in Halifax. There are other community radio stations elsewhere in the province.

I recall my mother longing to hear French spoken on the radio or the television in the 1950s and 1960s. There was no such luxury except for a TV program on Friday evenings called *The Plouffe Family*. It was an English program but the actors spoke with a very strong French accent and that pleased mother. It was better than nothing. In the 1980s, some of her favourite soap operas were dubbed in French. She'd say to me, *Écoute donc ces acteurs. Sont-ils pas savants? Ils peuvent parler anglais et français.* (Listen to these actors. Aren't they clever? They can speak English and French.) I didn't have the heart to explain to her that they were dubbed. Now I have the pleasure of watching several TV programs all in French, some from Quebec, some from France. Mother would have enjoyed that.

There are over 10,000 francophones in the regional municipality of Halifax, many of whom are Acadians. I am a member of *Regroupement de Aînés de la Nouvelle-Écosse*, francophone seniors. We celebrate and socialize together. Some of us volunteer in the French schools to read and tell stories to the elementary children, *en français*. Whether we are in Acadian communities or in towns or the city of Halifax, we can all profit from the varied opportunities to maintain our heritage and our language. However, these accomplishments did not arrive like manna from heaven. They were the results of hard work and advocacy especially as a result of the Official Languages Act and the *Canadian Charter of Rights and Freedoms*.

I am proud of what Acadians from Nova Scotia have achieved as individuals, as groups, as companies and corporations. Musicians such as Grand Dérangement, La Baie en Joie, Cy, Blou, Ronald Bourgeois, to name but a few, have all made it on the international stage. Industries such as *Comeau's Seafoods* and *Acadian Seaplants* are known worldwide. Phil Comeau, a cinematographer, has brought his documentaries about Acadians all over the world. These talented people showcase our people and our culture to the world.

People of Acadian descent living outside Nova Scotia in places like the Eastern United States, France, Martinique, St. Pierre-Miquelon and especially Louisiana call Nova Scotia *Le Berceau de l'Acadie* (the Cradle of Acadie), their Homeland. Whenever I see an Acadian flag I am proud to be an Acadian living in Nova Scotia and I am reminded that after 400 years we are still here. Like the French willow trees, we are well rooted.

Clara Dugas is from the village of Little Brook Station, overlooking St. Mary's Bay, Clare, Nova Scotia, also known as The French Shore. *Presently she lives in Halifax County. Her childhood dream of becoming a schoolteacher came true in 1969. In the late 1980s, within the confines of her Grade 1 classroom, she began telling short stories of her own childhood. She was first inspired to be a storyteller by her mother who was a storyteller herself.*

In the early 1990s she joined the Storytellers/Raconteurs du Canada. *In order to be exposed to some of the best storytellers in the country, in 1995 she studied at the Toronto School of Storytelling. She has told stories at Grand Pré, at the Clare Acadian Festival, at many festivals in Quebec, France, North Carolina and in Clare.*

Clara retired from teaching after 35 years of dedication to the profession. Now, when she is not travelling to storytelling festivals, she spends time doing what she loves best — rug hooking, reading, writing and telling stories in schools, in French and English.

MAKING NOVA SCOTIA HOME:
A MATTER OF CHOICE AND RESISTANCE

John J. Guiney Yallop, PhD

Off To Home

We are at the Look Off,
looking off
over the Valley
towards Wolfville.
"I feel like I've died and gone to heaven,"
my partner says
inhaling the salty breeze
that wipes away his allergies.
A bald eagle,
our daughter's Spirit Animal,
circles above her head.
This place will,
eventually,
be(come) home.

I WROTE THIS POEM TEN years after our move to Nova Scotia. I had written a similar prose piece some years ago and sent it in to CBC's *Information Morning*; it was read on the show by host Don Connolly. A former student from the Bachelor of Education program I teach in sent me an e-mail afterwards saying that he had heard my story on his way to work as a new elementary school teacher and that it had made him smile. In the story sent to CBC, I had countered my partner's comment about dying and going to heaven with, "It has not been heaven, but it is home." I guess that is what I had been looking for — home, not heaven.

Before our move to Nova Scotia in late June of 2008, we drove from Ontario in May so that I could show my partner and our daughter what we had said yes to in my acceptance of an appointment to the faculty in the School of Education at Acadia University. Not knowing the Acadia University yearly schedule, we arrived the week of convocation and had been lucky to find accommodations in the town. Our daughter celebrated her ninth birthday in Wolfville and we went to the Look Off, just outside Canning, a place I had visited when I first came to the campus for the interview and presentation. Standing at the Look Off we looked back over the place we had said yes to. That yes would be revisited, and tested, more than once over the next decade.

I was born in Newfoundland. With the exception of a year in an Irish seminary right after high school, Newfoundland was home for me until I was 23 years old; like many Newfoundlanders, of course, it would remain home even when I left the island. With a B.A. from Memorial University of Newfoundland, I left home for work. That work was in Nova Scotia. The interview/selection process had been very competitive, but I landed what I have sometimes called a dream job and I turned all my attention to the challenges of my new work, surpassing the expected targets of performance in my first weeks.

But it was not enough. Six weeks into that dream job I was fired because I was an out gay man and, according to my supervisors, that was not going to work in this position. Technically, I was not fired; I agreed to a termination settlement that, at twenty-three years of age without the advice of any counsel except for an old feminist friend back in St. John's whose advice was "get in touch with your anger," certainly seemed like less of a choice than an ultimatum. I left Nova Scotia for Toronto; Ontario would be home for the next twenty-six years of my life.

For years I managed to forget the painful ending of those first six weeks in Nova Scotia until one summer, two decades later, while driving back home to Newfoundland, I stopped in to see an old friend in Nova Scotia who knew me during those first thrilling and then, almost, devastating weeks. We talked about the experience. She confirmed for me my memories that the decision had been less than equitable, less than what would be considered legal by today's standards. I was able to acknowledge the strength of the young man who survived discrimination and what is often identified as the narrow regionalism in and within Nova Scotia.

Coming Back

Yes is not a first and only;
it can be repeated
when pain has passed through memory,
settled in the body
like history.

When I defended my doctoral dissertation in 2008, I travelled to five universities for interviews and presentations; the latter are sometimes called job talks. My partner often jokes about my small suitcase standing in the hallway of our home ready for the next drive or flight.

Acadia was one of the universities I visited. As the driver turned the limousine onto Highway 101, carrying me towards Wolfville, he said, "You won't see much after this; it's mostly just trees." "This is just fine with me," I replied as I kept my gaze out the window at the inviting tranquility as winter passed and spring offered new possibilities. Even before I left Wolfville after the interview, meetings and presentation, to head back home, I knew that this was my first choice; I was glad when a short time later I received the offer of employment from Acadia University.

The first year was a mixture of wonderful and painful; less like heaven, it was more like hell. My youngest of three sisters, just a few years my elder, died on Winter Solstice after her four-year battle with colorectal cancer that had metastasized to her lungs. I was diagnosed with prostate cancer early in 2009, shortly after my 50th birthday. This was not the new life I had expected, or hoped for; the new dream was becoming a nightmare. The c-word made me think of the d-word. I had moved my family here and now I was going to die and leave them. Fuck!

But! There is always a but! My colleagues at Acadia University were among the best I could ever have asked for, or expected. They covered my classes when I needed to go to Newfoundland to spend time with my dying sister. They were there to support me and my family through my own cancer diagnosis and treatment. They either dropped off prepared meals when I was recovering or they stayed with those meals they had prepared and sat at the table with me and my family. My students were also wonderfully incredible. They understood my absences from class. They received warmly colleagues who covered classes for me. They sent me their assignments electronically when necessary. They also reminded me to slay the dragon in my fairy tale.

The community was also caring. When my partner, a usually very private person who, having grown up in Toronto, liked his anonymity, would go downtown for groceries or to pick up our daughter at school, he would be greeted by hugs and expressions of concern for me, for him and for our daughter. And our daughter, who had earlier in the school year joined a community theatre group — Women of Wolfville (WOW) — was supported by those wonderful women and another wonderful woman, her vice-principal at Wolfville School. We had not died, and I was not actually dying, but maybe we had gone to heaven.

Poetry has often been for me a way to process experiences. I got my appointment to Acadia University after defending a dissertation that was, in part, a book of poetry. My book, *OUT of Place*, contains the poetry of that journey. Through another journey, the diagnosis, treatment and recovery from cancer, I also wrote poetry. I put together in a chapbook I called *Notes To My Prostate* twenty-five of those poems. I sometimes joke about the fact that, while I did not actually write poetry during my surgery, as I was being wheeled into the room where it would happen, I said to myself that this would make a good poem; I think it did.

Note To My Prostate #15

Arrival at the hospital.
The waits.
The tests.
The wheelchair.
The funny slippers.
The gown.
The pill.
The blanket.
The porter.
The chart — a binder.
The anaesthetist.
The nurse.
The door.
The entrance — grand.
The theatre.
The lights.
The thought — this is where I'll die.
The touch.
The needles.
The sleep.
The awakening.
The pain.
The relief.
The joy.
The grief.
Life.

In the years that followed, my partner, formerly the city hall gardener in Brampton, Ontario, started a gardening business. It was not particularly successful, so he went back to school at Nova Scotia Community College taking the Continuing Care Assistant Program. As I write this he is out caring for others like he cared for me following my surgery for prostate cancer and like he cared for his aging and dying grandmother. His gardening skills are now focussed on the gardens around the house we call home.

It's Not Always Easy

It's not always easy
to make a home
in your 50th year of life,
but you reached past pain,
loss,
hurt,
into a garden waiting
for your hands.

We (re)created home
together
stripping away injustice.
Paint is more than a covering;
colours are choices,
responses to life
and ways forward.

Growing A Girl in Nova Scotia

I watch you growing
making home
in a place that both embraces
and enfolds
you;
hesitation is one response to difference.

You walk into circles
some expanding,
some contracting/controlling.
We throw you lifesavers —
other circles;
sometimes you grasp,
other times you swim away
towards the wave.

We trust you,
but not those who hide
behind waves.
You are at your best
swimming above the waves
revelling in moments
and revealing who
you really are.

Perhaps the most frightening thing about our move to Nova Scotia was raising our daughter here; perhaps it would have been the most frightening experience anywhere. It has also been the most wonderful. Watching someone grow into their own identity is incredibly rewarding … particularly when you have been part of that growth. For more than a decade — for more than half her life — Nova Scotia has been home to Brittany. While Ontario, the place where she was born, still has a strong connection for her, and while Newfoundland is where most of her family lives, Nova Scotia is, at least for now, our daughter's home. I think, in many ways, it always will be.

Looking Forward

I remember yesterdays
like whispered gossip,
transformed invitations into being.

Trauma is a word that is used quite widely these days, sometimes to refer to any unfortunate incident or behaviour that upsets. The shock and pain, however, of losing that first significant job in Nova Scotia was probably more than being upset. Maybe it was traumatic and left me with …. With what?

I moved through the processes academics are presented with … renewal, tenure, promotion. Even with success, each one presented a reminder of betrayal. I write stories and poems about my life in order to understand better how to live my life. I write stories and poems about home in order to discover and claim home. Discovery and claiming are mutual experiences when we want to feel at home. When I want to feel at home, I find that I must let a place and its people discover and claim me; I become part of that place and one of its people.

Home is a Place

Home is a place
we return to,
coming back
we find our bodies reaching
over the landscape.

Longing is not enough
when we need the soil
against our feet
and behind our fingernails.

But, some days,
like today,
longing needs to be enough
as I sit in another hotel room
writing myself home.

Now, whether I am driving south to the beginning of Highway 104, or arriving by train towards Amherst, or sailing west on the Cabot Strait towards North Sydney, or flying into Halifax Stanfield International Airport, I feel that I am coming home. Nova Scotia was not my first home, and I do not know if it will be my last home, but home it is today. As I write these words in one of Wolfville's many cafés, I know that I am home.

John J. Guiney Yallop is a parent, a partner and a poet. He is also a professor in the School of Education at Acadia University. John lives in Wolfville, Nova Scotia, with his partner, Gary, their daughter, Brittany, and their pets.

CFA VS. HBC VS. BRH

Vernon Oickle

I CRINGE WHENEVER I HEAR the term CFA, meaning Come From Away. I hate the phrase because I hate the implied, negative connotation that often comes with its usage.

While the label does adequately describe people who move to our region from elsewhere in the world or from another part of our great country, most times when it's used the undertones are often very clear — you're not from our community so please don't bother us with your opinions, suggestions or ideas.

However, anyone with such a negative and pervasive attitude obviously fails to recognize the opportunity that comes when new people move into our communities. We ought to embrace such individuals, not push them away. We ought to welcome them with open arms and invite them into our inner circles, not shun them or attach labels to them. We ought to become their friends, not see them as foreigner invaders intent to undo everything we have built up.

I appreciate that in some cases the phrase is used to accurately describe people who have relocated to our piece of paradise for whatever reason, be it family, retirement, health, business, or employment opportunity but I also feel that in other incidences it's used in a derogatory manner to assign blame or even to ridicule others.

Most of the times, I find its usage to be offensive and even confrontational, used to ostracize rather than to include. This is especially true in a group setting when ideas and information are being exchanged. I've seen this happen in public forums and functions when it's thrown out to the gathering as a verbal form of finger pointing when someone doesn't agree with an idea or suggestion.

How often have you heard: "What do you know? You're a CFA." or "That's not how we do things around here. If you were born here, you would know that." or "We've never done it like that before." or "You may have done it like where you're from, but around here, we do it our way."

What exactly does CFA mean anyway? In this case it's used to describe people who have relocated here but what exactly is the cut-off date when you are no longer considered a CFA? Is it five years? Is it 10? Maybe 25 or 50? My point is, aren't we all essentially CFAs?

Yes, some of us may be second, or third, or fourth or even fifth generation Nova Scotians, and that makes us a BRH (Born Right Here) but the fact remains that the only people who are essentially native Nova Scotians are First Nations people. Technically, everyone else is a CFA. Instead, then, as a good friend of mind suggests, let's call them HBCs, meaning they are "Here By Choice?"

The point is, at some juncture in history, the ancestors of those who consider ourselves to be "real" Nova Scotians essentially came from away, but when it comes to the use of that phrase the bottom line for me is that it really doesn't matter how long you've lived here because as soon as you move to the province you should consider yourself to be a Nova Scotian, as should others around you. That's how everyone should see you.

It shouldn't matter where anyone came from or even why he or she relocated here unless they're a master criminal or have some other nefarious background. What matters most is that someone was so impressed with the beauty and the positive attributes of our area that they choose to move here and we should be happy about that as it means others recognize the potential. With these new people come new ideas, new energy, new vision and a new insight that, in most cases, they are willing and anxious to share with their new neighbours. It's up to us to embrace these individuals and to welcome them into the fold.

My experience over the years has been that we can learn a great deal from these individuals if we let them into our communities and make them feel as though we appreciate their contributions. In fact, in many cases, the ideas from these individuals have often breathed new life into local events and into the community itself. They often come with new and innovative ideas and they are willing to invest their time, energy and, in some cases, their money into improving their new home.

There are many positives about this arrangement as people who have relocated to our neighbourhoods often see things from a new and different perspective. Many of us who have lived here our entire lives may lack the ability to see new angles and as such our ideas may become stale and out dated. We also have a tendency to look inward and with blinders so sometimes an infusion of new ideas can breathe new life into our events and the community.

This isn't to say that all our local ideas are bad ones nor is it to suggest that all the ideas from people who move here are all good ones, because that is not the case. However, it does mean that we should meet in the middle and find ways to cooperate. Above all, we should keep an open mind and we should be understanding and supportive of each other. After all, the end result is to produce success in whatever we do. The key is to end up with the best ideas regardless of where they came from or who suggested them. In that way, we all benefit.

That having been said, the onus of this cooperation does not rest solely with those of us who grew up here. In fact, it's a two-way street and I too get irritated when new people arrive with an attitude that suggests that they believe they know what's best for us and the communities we've called home for many years. That is not the way to make friends nor is it a good way to encourage cooperation.

It's also off-putting when these individuals suggest that they may have moved here because they were attracted to the romanticized image of a small, rural community that seems so appealing. As such, they sometimes resent change because it goes against their vision. But by the same token, we don't appreciate anyone telling us that they know what's best for us. Open and honest dialogue is the best approach as we work toward a solution that benefits everyone.

Most of us "locals" will agree that change is sometimes necessary for the survival of our communities and we know that if we don't grow and evolve with new ideas and unique initiatives, then we run the risk of growing stagnant and perhaps even regressing. Instead, these individuals should be encouraged to express their views and we should welcome the input with open minds, but in the end, regardless of where the idea originated, we must do whatever is best for our communities.

Those of us who have been fortunate enough to grow up in this wonderful part of the world take a great deal for granted, but the fact that we are attracting many new people to our province is something to embrace as it's proof that Nova Scotia has lots to offer. That being said, we must be willing to share and accept new ideas regardless where they originated.

Vernon Oickle is an international award-winning journalist, newspaper columnist and author of 29 non-fiction and fiction books. His previous works include Ghost Stories of Nova Scotia; I'm Movin' On: The Life and Legacy of Hank Snow; Strange Nova Scotia; Bluenoser's Book of Slang; *the bestselling* 'Crow' series; *the* Nova Scotia Outstanding Outhouse Reader *and* The Nova Scotia Book of Lists. *He is currently the managing editor at MacIntyre Purcell Publishing Inc. Liverpool is Vernon's Nova Scotian home. It's where he was born and raised, and where he and his wife Nancy raised their two sons.*

In 2012, Vernon received the Queen Elizabeth II Diamond Jubilee Medal and, in 2015, he received a Distinguished Alumni Award for Community Leadership from Lethbridge College, where he studied journalism. He was deeply honoured when, in 2014, South Queens Middle School, in Liverpool, announced the creation of the first annual Vernon Oickle Writer's Award to be given to a student who excels in the art of writing, either fiction or non-fiction.

SETTLING IN

Glenna Jenkins

"MOM! GRANNY TOOK HER TEETH out at the table!"

We were seven seated in the kitchen — Blair, Gary, Mark, Robbie, Janet, Granny, and I. Baby David was upstairs, asleep in his crib. We were just tucking into dinner, when Granny dug a thumb and a forefinger into her gob, yanked out her dentures, and plunked them down beside her plate.

"There now, that's better," she said, licking her gums. According to Granny, Mom's spaghetti sauce and noodles didn't call for a full set of teeth.

We sat there, sauce dripping down chins, noodles slithering off forks, while Granny gummed down her own spaghetti. Younger brother Robbie turned a sickly shade of green and threatened to spew all over the place.

"Blaahk, Mom, look what Granny did!"

Mom was standing by the stove, serving up her meal. She turned and sucked in a breath, "Mom, put your teeth back in!"

My mother's relationship with her own mother had never been an easy one. But after my parents bought our first home and Granny decided to help us settle in, Mom sprang for her plane fare. Then she and I picked her up at the airport.

In those days, at Halifax Airport, you could go upstairs in the passenger terminal, without buying a plane ticket or passing through security (there wasn't any), stand at the large windows that faced the tarmac, and watch planes take off and land. Mom and I stood at a window and watched for the Eastern Provincial Airways flight from Sydney. The sky was clear blue. But the gathering cumulus clouds and a windsock that blew in a north-easterly direction meant Granny would be having a bumpy ride. Soon, we heard the roar of engines and watched her plane touch down, bounce, and touch down again, and then taxi toward the terminal. When its propellers shut down, a mobile staircase was rolled up to the door and passengers began to disembark. But, we didn't see Granny.

"Maybe she changed her mind." Mom sounded hopeful. "Maybe she decided to take the bus." She looked at me and shrugged. "Your grandmother is full of surprises."

Finally, there she was, peering out the door, preparing to take a tentative step. She slid her purse into the crook of her arm and grabbed the railing. The stairs shook as she lumbered down. Her purse swayed; her flowered cotton dress blew in the early evening breeze. She reached the tarmac and looked around, then practically heaved herself toward the building, lumbering side-to-side and somehow trundling forward all at the same time. Mom and I rushed downstairs to meet her in the baggage area.

Granny hobbled through the single glass door, sheet-white and shaking. The instant she saw us, she began to blurt out the details of her ordeal. "We went way up into the sky, high above the clouds. We smashed and bumped all over the place, but somehow we all landed safe and sound. It was a miracle, I tell you — there were eighty of us aboard that plane and nobody died."

We would hear that story over and over, during her short stay at our new home.

Granny's visit survived the episode at the kitchen table. It lasted through her destroying Mom's brand new ceramic teapot: she had tossed in a fistful of tea bags, filled it with water, carefully placed in on the stove and turned the burner on high. She then sauntered away and promptly forgot about it. But, when she almost blew up the kitchen and set the house on fire, Mom decided she'd had enough.

Our family had just returned to Halifax after several years of living a pillar-to-post whirlwind of arriving in one temporary home and departing for another. When my parents got married, Dad had been completing a medical internship at Dalhousie University. They soon moved to Greenwood, in the Annapolis Valley, where he worked for the Royal Canadian Air Force in return for the Canadian Armed Forces having helped pay his way through medical school. That was the deal, those days: the Forces helped finance aspiring physicians' medical education in return for their working for them after graduation. Dad's obligations amounted to a three-year stint in Greenwood, Nova Scotia.

Those early years were lean ones. Mom had insisted on living in the town of Middleton, instead of on the air force base. "There's too much drinking there," was all she said. She also told me about the odd sleeping arrangements in the first house they rented: she placed one child in a dresser drawer, another one in a crib, and another in the bathtub when it wasn't being used for bathing or hand washing the laundry with a scrub board.

After Dad finished his job in Greenwood, our family moved to Toronto, where he resumed his medical studies and Mom became a master chef of fried baloney and Niblets corn. And picked up the garbage the neighbours in the apartment block behind us threw into our back yard, thereby adding to her already long list of chores.

From Toronto, we travelled to London, England, on the Empress of Britain, an ocean liner that was more like a floating hotel: it had two dining rooms, a movie theatre, a games room, and a swimming pool. And every family took a turn sitting at the captain's table for dinner. We spent Christmas somewhere in the middle of the North Atlantic and docked in Liverpool in the dead of winter. From there, we travelled by train to a tiny township on the outskirts of London.

UK winters aren't as harsh as they are in Canada. Nevertheless, Mom made sure we were prepared. On our first day at our new school, my brothers wore long woollen trousers and winter jackets, while the British boys sported woollen shorts and blazers. I wore a helmet-shaped woollen hat, a beige woollen coat and matching jodhpur-style leggings — no doubt all the rage among seven-year-olds in Toronto — and buckled overshoes (as equally sensible as the woollens). I must have looked like I was heading out on an Arctic expedition as I no sooner entered the classroom than my new teacher trotted me out in front of the other year-two pupils (grade one, in Canada).

"Look everyone, this is how Canadians dress for winter."

The class gawked in silence as Miss Jones made a spectacle of me on my first day there. I was immediately shunned and didn't make a single friend the whole year. Neither did my brothers. Years later, my mother recounted how much this had bothered her. But, my brothers and I didn't notice. We had each other and we knew we could count on Mom's ready smile and Dad barrelling in through the front door sometime after six o'clock.

Mom worked hard to make a home for us in the tiny duplex they rented that year. She always had a pan of warm brownies waiting on the counter after we returned from school. And when we came home, one afternoon, and asked why we didn't have tea like all of the other children did, she also catered to this new demand. My younger sister was born in July. So, on top of tending to a newborn and all of her other tasks, Mom served tea at precisely four o'clock and then turned around and prepared dinner for a family of eight, two hours later, when Dad was expected home.

There were also excursions, like the time Mom piled us onto a double-decker bus for a trip to the British Museum. Four-year-old Mark wandered out the front doors and got lost in downtown London that afternoon. Mom recounted how she had to leave the rest of us with complete strangers and go on a frantic search. She found Mark at a nearby police station, where a London bobby was trying to find out where he lived.

"What's your name?" he asked.

"Muck."
"What's your mother's name?"
"Mom."
"Where do you live?"
"Home."

Even at that young age, Mark could form a concept of home. It wasn't "Canada," the response my parents used when queried in London, or "We're Bluenosers," which was what Dad usually said in Toronto. For them, the houses we lived in, in all of those places, were transient arrangements, found at reasonable rates, close to public transit so Dad could travel to the hospital or the university and leave the car with Mom. Mark spoke for all of us kids when he alluded to the fact home was the place our parents were; it wasn't a physical structure or a civic address. It was somewhere we felt safe, welcome, and secure — it was somewhere we knew we belonged.

Dad described the year in London as being the *feather in his cap* that catapulted him toward a successful career. For Mom, however, it was hard slogging and a complete letdown. After six months there, she wanted to return home to Nova Scotia.

"That would have meant spending the next six months living with Granny," she later told me. "I didn't see that as a choice; I had to stick it out."

Mom did more than *stick it out*. She created a home for us in a draughty duplex, with no central heating, situated in a rough township where we were shunned for our religion, the size of our brood, and our Irish last name — Landrigan. There were no play dates, no birthday party invites, and few visitors. I don't remember a single overture being made to welcome our family or help us fit in. We were *come-from-aways* before we even knew what the term meant.

Mom was stoic through all of this. Each time we moved, she was left alone with three, five, and then six children, in more-distant places, with no car most days, no laundry facilities, and no family support. Years later, I asked my mother why we hadn't stayed in London. I had a romantic notion of what it would have been like to grow up in the UK. Mom recalled the cold reactions to her Canadian accent and the even chillier responses to our family name. She also reminded me of our poor reception at the local school.

"We would never have been accepted. We would never have fit in." She pursed her lips into a thin-lipped grin. "We were happy to come home to Nova Scotia."

My parents bought our first permanent home in Halifax. They chose a big white house, on Robie Street, in an area close to Dad's work, good schools and a Catholic church. They wanted to settle into a quiet neighbourhood and live a normal life. How they figured on doing this with four and then five boys and two girls all under the age of twelve is anybody's guess. Seven children and a big side yard meant our home became a magnet for every other child in the neighbourhood. This all put the kibosh on my parents' notion of living a quiet life. When Granny came to visit, the 'normal' part of their plans nearly went up in smoke. And if Mom had let her stick around longer, the Landrigans would have won first prize for being the loopiest family in Halifax's uppity south end.

After we moved in, my parents began the arduous task of turning the new house into a home. Mom painted rooms, refinished furniture and sewed slipcovers. Then she had the kitchen renovated. Out went the old appliances, the plywood cabinets, the faded counters and the cracked linoleum. In went new appliances, light oak cupboards, bright new counters and tile flooring. Mom loved her new kitchen. She spent hours in it, testing Julia Child recipes for boeuf bourguignon and braised ribs. And lobster thermidor and crème brûlée when she and Dad entertained. Meanwhile, Dad directed operations outside. He, my elder brothers and I cleared rocks from the yard and loaded them onto a trailer. Then Dad hauled them to the dump. Next, he dug a trench around three sides of the yard and planted a boxwood hedge. He ordered topsoil, raked it over the hard, barren ground, and planted trees and sowed grass. Then he built a picket fence, a task that took weeks and the fence remained unpainted. That is, until Granny noticed.

When the landscaping was finished, the boys and I proceeded to scrape a makeshift baseball diamond through the green shoots of Dad's newly sown lawn. Granny found a paintbrush and some white paint and announced that she was going to spiff up Dad's new fence. For this particular task, she wore her old housedress inside out, in case it got splattered with paint. She donned a floppy sunhat to provide some shade. She grabbed the paint and a brush and hobbled out the front door and down the sidewalk, toward the fence. Mom followed with a wooden chair for Granny to sit on and a jug of lemonade to keep her hydrated in the hot mid-July heat.

Granny spent hours, each day, painting the fence and splattering even more paint over her face, hat, dress, and bare arms. She also chatted up every passer by.

"Who would you be, now?" she asked. Her jowls flapped, her pale-blue eyes sunk into a wrinkled face that soon turned beet red under the hot afternoon sun. "Do you know my son-in-law, Dr. Paul? He built this here fence." Granny was proud to be helping him out.

By mid-day, sweat dripped down her face; her thin cotton dress clung to an ample girth that spilled over the edges of the hard wooden chair. She put down the brush, unclipped her garters and rolled down her stockings. They looked like donuts over bare ankles that practically oozed over the tops of her black lace-up shoes.

By the end of the week, Granny had applied two coats of paint to both sides of the fence and become acquainted with everyone in the neighbourhood. Satisfied with a job well done, she put the lid on the paint and carried it and the brush into the house. Being a frugal Cape Bretoner, she decided to save the paintbrush for a later task. So, she took the can, still dripping with paint, down to the basement, rummaged around for a tin of turpentine, found one, and returned upstairs. She entered the kitchen, found an aluminum pot, poured in the turpentine, put the pot on the stove, and plunked in the brush. Then she turned the stove on high and sauntered out of the kitchen.

Maybe Granny thought the turpentine would take longer to heat up. Maybe she simply forgot about it and turned her attention to another task. In any case, a sharp, distinct chemical odour soon permeated the house. Then, I heard the scurrying of feet and Mom's high-pitched shriek.

"Oh, dear God!!!"

I had been sitting in the dark shade of the living room, engrossed in a book. I rushed into the kitchen to find Mom shoving her hands into oven mitts and easing the pot of boiling turpentine off the stove. She had already turned off the burner.

"What's the matter?" I asked.

"Granny could have blown up the whole kitchen! She could have burned the house down!" Mom was breathing heavily, now. Her mouth hung open, her eyes were ablaze. If I had ever seen my mother in a state of shock, this would have been it.

Later, Dad gritted his teeth when he said, "She could have killed someone."

"I was only trying to help," Granny said, looking confused.

"Marie!" Dad said.

Mom stood there, holding back tears. "I can't do this anymore. She has to go home." She couldn't even look at Granny.

"I'm not flying," Granny said, her lips scrunched up into a tight frown. "I'm not getting on that plane — I'll die up there!"

"Fine, then," Dad said. "You can take the bus."

Mom helped her pack; Dad drove her to the depot.

We didn't see Granny for a long time after that. I suspect Mom had not been forthcoming with the bus fare. Nobody dared ask.

Glenna Jenkins writes novels and short stories that are gleaned from real-life events. Her stories have appeared in Jilted Angels, A Collection of Short Stories, *Broad Street Press;* Riptides, New Island Fiction, *Acorn Press Canada;* Snow Softly Falling: Holiday Stories from Prince Edward Island, *Acorn Press Canada; and* Where Evil Dwells: The Nova Scotia Anthology of Horror, *MacIntyre Purcell Publishing. Glenna's first novel,* Somewhere I Belong, *is based on a true story and was released on November 1, 2014, also by Acorn Press Canada. The Canadian Children's Book Centre selected this YA novel for its 2015 list of Best Books for Kids and Teens, and gave it a red-star rating, which signifies "titles of exceptional* calibre." This novel was also short-listed for a 2016 Prince Edward Island book award. Glenna lives with her husband, John, and their two dogs, in Lunenburg, Nova Scotia, where they enjoy visits from their four children and their significant others and their new granddaughter Danica. Glenna also works as an editor and is presently writing the sequel to Somewhere I Belong.

RETURNING TO MY NOVA SCOTIA HOME

Dr. Peter J. Ricketts

I REMEMBER MY FIRST BREATH of Nova Scotia air as if it were yesterday. As I stepped out of the plane I inhaled deeply and the smell and taste of salt and fresh ocean air filled my mouth, nostrils, and lungs. After seven months living in Windsor (the Ontario one) and breathing the less than healthy air that was being spewed out by the smelters just across the river in Detroit (thank goodness that the air has been cleaned up considerably since), the clean, salty ocean air of a foggy Nova Scotia "spring" afternoon assaulted my senses like a rescuing party liberating my lungs from months of captivity. Having grown up in the resort town of Bournemouth on the south coast of England, I had missed the sea air and the fresh, salty winds that come with living by the sea. It was April 1979, I had arrived in Nova Scotia, and I had no intention of staying.

I had come to Canada in September of 1978 to take up a short-term lectureship in geography at the University of Windsor, with the intent of spending nine months and then going home to England. During my time at Windsor, Saint Mary's University advertised for a nine-month position in its fledgling Department of Geography, teaching not only what I had been doing at Windsor but also a new course in Coastal Zone Management.

This was exactly what my unfinished doctoral thesis was about, and I was excited at the opportunity to create a new course in this emerging field of interest. And so it was that I found myself landing in Halifax in the mist for the interview at Saint Mary's. I was offered the position and in late August, 1979 I made the long trip from Windsor, Ontario to Halifax, Nova Scotia in my 1976 Volvo 242 (brown with red and beige racing stripes) taking the route through New England and the overnight ferry from Portland, Maine to Yarmouth, and then the scenic drive along the Lighthouse Route, catching glimpses of the ocean, coastal inlets and small towns and villages along the south shore on the way to Halifax.

I still had no intention of staying, and as far as I was concerned at the time, Halifax was a stop on the way back home and a useful opportunity to strengthen my teaching experience, and complete my doctoral thesis in preparation for a career as a university professor in England. There was no way that this Nova Scotia would become my Nova Scotia home.

I was warmly welcomed into the Geography Department at Saint Mary's and I got on extremely well with my departmental colleagues, and I am proud to say that we are still good friends almost 40 years later. I started to explore the incredible coastline and landscapes of Nova Scotia, and developed a number of field trips for my students in physical geography, coastal geomorphology and coastal management.

I remember my first visit to the Annapolis Valley and my first glimpse of the imposing white building that graced the campus of Acadia University in Wolfville. I remember thinking what an astonishingly beautiful campus it was, but if anyone had suggested that I would return in later years as President of that university, I would have laughed in their face. First, it had no geography department; second it was Baptist and I was Catholic; and third, I was never getting into university administration! Besides, I was not going to be staying in Nova Scotia.

Well, my nine-month lectureship was followed by a one-year professorial appointment, and then a tenure-track appointment, and before long I found myself committed to staying in Nova Scotia at least for a decent period of time. This is not to say that I was unhappy with my situation, far from it. I had started to fall for Nova Scotia from the moment I breathed its air for the first time, and I had formed strong friendships that remain so to this day.

I was happy that I had landed in the career that I had long sought — even if it wasn't in the country of my birth. I completed my PhD in 1982 and in 1984 two important milestones occurred — first, I got married to Maryann (née Worobetz) whom I had met while in Windsor during my first year in Canada, and secondly, I became a Canadian citizen. These two events firmly cemented my relationship to my newly adopted country and province.

Over the coming years I grew to love Nova Scotia as I discovered more about its geography, its history and its people. The physical geography of Nova Scotia is incredible and what I love most is the variety of inland and coastal scenery in a relatively small area, small at least for Canada. In many provinces you can drive for hours and hours, covering enormous distances and seeing relatively little change in the landscape.

Don't get me wrong, I am not knocking the enormity and beauty of the rest of Canada, but you can drive the length and breadth of Nova Scotia in a few hours and you will cover an incredible diversity of landscapes. This diversity is created by the complex geology of our province, where so many different rock formations make up the landmass, and where ice sheets and glaciers have deposited, eroded and shaped the surface sediments, where rivers have carved out valleys, where sublime lakes scatter the landscape, and where ocean waves, currents and tides have produced an amazing variety of coastal features.

Fundamentally, my Nova Scotia home is defined by its coastline, which is truly spectacular. From the huge tides of the Fundy shore; to the capes and bays of the Gulf of Maine; to the wild bays, beaches and rocky shores of the Atlantic coast; to the sheltered beaches and coves of the Northumberland shore; to the majestic cliffs and headlands of Cape Breton; Nova Scotia has it all. It was wonderful to teach courses like coastal geomorphology and coastal management and be able to take students on local fields trips to see for themselves how our coastlines are being shaped and how human activity is so intricately entwined with the physical development of the coast. It is like having a living laboratory right outside the doors of the university.

One of my favourite field trips was to the Minas Basin, where I could show my students the wonders of the immense tides of the Bay of Fundy, and where they could see how the coastal features of the area have been and continue to be shaped by the enormous force of the water that ebbs and floods twice daily. I was fascinated to see the dykes that had been built by the Acadian settlers and how they had allowed so much land to be reclaimed for agriculture, and how they were still functioning in essentially the same way as when they were designed and built hundreds of years ago.

The contrast with the Atlantic coast is huge, where geological diversity and exposure to the high wave energy of the North Atlantic has produced incredible beaches and spectacular rocky shorelines with so many bays, coves, inlets and islands. This is the unique beauty of Nova Scotia, and what makes the moniker "Canada's ocean playground" so appropriate. Of course, Nova Scotia is so much more than a playground and the numerous communities that are scattered along its complex and diverse shorelines reflect the degree to which the history of the province has been dependent upon and shaped by reaping the harvests of the resources that were abundantly provided by the ocean and the land. The coastal communities of Nova Scotia are as varied as the coastline itself, and the relationship between Nova Scotians and the ocean continues to define the essence of what makes the province so special.

The 1980s saw Halifax develop as one of the most livable cities in Canada, and certainly as one of the most student-friendly cities. One of my best memories from that time is 1984, the first year that Halifax hosted the Tall Ships, and the city was buzzing with life. The weather was great, the crowds were large, and the ships created an amazing spectacle as they paraded into the harbour. There was a real feeling that Halifax had come of age not only as a place to visit but also a place to live; with street events, buskers, and sidewalk cafés giving the sense of a city come alive. It was the first time that the restored Historic Properties and the redevelopment of the wharves and boardwalks (which at that time were nowhere near as extensive as they are today) demonstrated what an incredible attraction the harbourfront could be for city tourism and business, and how farsighted it had been stop the planned extension of Cogswell Street that would have lost them forever — and how interesting that the Cogswell interchange is still very much an issue in 2019!

The first Tall Ships event showed the way for how Halifax could capitalize on its historic harbourfront and maritime history. That same year also marked the visit of Pope John Paul II, when the Halifax Commons was transformed into an enormous outdoor church, packed with people of all ages, but especially young people who were inspired by the message of peace, hope, and freedom that the Pope brought at that time of great concern about global survival.

Another milestone year for me was 1992, the year that the federal Minister of Fisheries and Oceans, John Crosbie, declared a moratorium on the Northern Cod fishery. Initially intended to last only two years, the moratorium was a necessary response to a collapse of the cod stocks that would eventually extend to the offshore fisheries in general, and the impacts on coastal communities and the economy of the Atlantic Provinces were profound and long-lasting. I was part of a small group of academics and government scientists and policy analysts who created the Coastal Zone Canada Association (CZCA) in 1993, and the first Coastal Zone Canada (CZC) Conference was held in Halifax World Trade and Convention Centre in September 1994, with its focus on building sustainable coastal communities.

Over 700 people attended, and I remember Brian Tobin, who was then the Minister of Fisheries and Oceans (and known as "Captain Canada" for his role in the famous "Turbot War") in the new Liberal government of Jean Chrétien, giving the opening keynote address and declaring that the stocks were not recovering and that we could be looking at a very long recovery. Unfortunately his forecast has proven to be more accurate than even he would have thought at the time, and today in 2019 we are still a long way from recovery of those stocks, and the impacts on the coastal communities of the region continue to be felt. I am pleased to say that the CZCA continues to exist, holding CZC conferences every two years. I was honoured to be the President of the Association when we held the 2014 conference in Halifax for the second time to celebrate the 20th anniversary of that first momentous meeting.

In July 1995, after 16 very happy and successful years at Saint Mary's, I joined Dalhousie University as Dean of Graduate Studies. At the time I was told that I was the first person to move from SMU to Dal as a senior administrator. I don't know if that is true, but it certainly was unusual. A few weeks earlier in June 1995, I had driven to the Dalhousie campus to meet with my soon to be new staff at the Faculty of Graduate Studies. This was the time when Halifax hosted the G7 summit (what Prime Minister Jean Chrétien called the "Chevrolet Summit") and we had experienced a number of exciting days in which leaders of the

G7 countries arrived, including President Clinton and President Boris Yeltsin who attended as an "unofficial" G8 representative of the Russian Federation.

It so happened that the day I was to visit my new office and meet the staff was the day that Bill Clinton and Boris Yeltsin were to have a one-on-one meeting in Dal's Arts and Administration Building (now called the Henry Hicks Building), to be followed by a speech by President Clinton in the quad. As I approached the campus by car, all of the entrances were blocked off and so I turned into the Dalplex site off South Street in search of a spot. As I entered the lower parking lot, I found myself faced with an army of security forces wearing full riot gear and armed to the teeth. I smiled sweetly and gingerly backed up and got out of there as quickly as I could. When I finally made it to the Dal campus, the entire A&A Building was cordoned off and the mass of people in the quad prevented me from getting anywhere close to the building that day. I did, however, get the opportunity to hear Bill Clinton from afar as he gave his speech to the crowd, watched over by snipers who were on every tower and rooftop of the graceful buildings that surrounded us. Needless to say, I had to wait for another day to visit my new office and staff.

At this time, the provincial government wanted to do something about rationalizing universities in Nova Scotia, and Dalhousie had been pushing to take on the lead role through an amalgamation of the Halifax universities. The reaction to this proposal from the other universities was visceral, and while the government backed off from supporting that position, it did float the idea of some kind of "rationalization", and identified a number of program areas (including Engineering, Education, and Computer Science) where the government felt that there was "unnecessary" duplication; meaning that they could be merged into being offered at a single institution.

As a result of this process, Education programs at Saint Mary's and Dalhousie were closed and merged under a single Halifax-based Education department at Mount Saint Vincent University. My starting day at Dalhousie coincided with the first day that the School of Education was closed, accompanied by the closure of the master's and doctoral programs. Not long afterwards, the government announced the amalgamation of TUNS and Dalhousie, and as Dean of Graduate Studies I had the responsibility to negotiate the incorporation of the graduate programs at TUNS into Dalhousie's Faculty of Graduate Studies. Computer Science, Architecture and Planning were relatively straightforward, but Engineering was a different story.

Given the level of independence that the Faculty of Engineering had enjoyed under the TUNS structure and the disparity between the relatively high level of scholarship funding at Dal compared to that of TUNS, it was no easy task to bring those graduate programs into the Graduate Studies structure at Dalhousie. Major institutional change is never easy, especially when you have a merger of a smaller institution into a much larger one and the smaller one wants to retain as much independence as possible, and so the process was fraught with challenges and difficulties. Looking back on it, I think we did a good job in a situation where it was impossible to please everyone and meet all of the expectations. However, difficult decisions were made and the groundwork was set for what would turn out in time to be a successful merger of not only the graduate programs, but of the two institutions themselves.

In 2000, the opportunity to take on a new role enticed me to leave Nova Scotia and head west for Kelowna, British Columbia, where I became Vice-President Academic at Okanagan University College (OUC). This was a big move for the family, which had grown to include two young children, and while we were excited to be heading to new experiences out west, we were sad to leave Nova Scotia and our many friends and colleagues.

I had spent 21 years in Halifax after what was supposed to be just nine months, and now I was headed for what was initially to be a two-year secondment to BC. As before, it turned out to be for a much longer time, and we ended up living in Kelowna for six years. Little did I know that my experiences in dealing with the Dal/TUNS merger would come in very handy when faced with a much larger and more complex situation when the BC government decided to split OUC and move most of the university programs under the University of British Columbia. But that is a story for another time and another place.

In 2006 we moved to North Bay, Ontario when I was appointed Vice-President Academic and Research at Nipissing University, and then to Ottawa in 2009 when I took up the position of Provost and Vice-President Academic at Carleton University. Sometime in the late fall of 2016, I met with an executive search consultant in a hotel coffee bar in Toronto, where he suggested that I look at the opportunity to apply for the Presidency at Acadia University, and so it was that in July 2017, my family and I returned to Nova Scotia after an absence of seventeen years.

During that time, I had kept in touch with friends and colleagues, had visited NS many times and had tried to keep up with what was happening with universities in the province. Now I was returning as a President of one of those universities, Acadia; but after so many years away, what changes would I find and how much would still be the same? Well, it is certainly true that some things remain the same — tight finances, relatively high and seasonal unemployment, stagnant demographics with an aging population, challenges in delivering health and education services, plus the difficulties of sustaining many small and remote communities that once flourished when ocean and land resources were rich and plentiful. And of course, the warmth and generosity of the people and the beauty and wonder of Nova Scotia haven't changed either. But other things have changed, and some important ones for the better.

When I left NS in 2000, the government mantra was that Nova Scotia's universities were an economic liability — we had too many of them and they cost too much. Today that thinking has changed 180 degrees, with the NS government proclaiming as often as it can that the universities are a huge asset and essential to the province's economic, social and cultural prosperity. The relationship between the Presidents of the universities is extremely good, and the level of collaboration and cooperation through the Council of Nova Scotia Universities (CONSUP) and with the provincial government is better than it has ever been, especially compared with the often adversarial one that existed back in the 1980s and 90s.

The result is that our universities and the NS Community College are recognized as critical to the economic and social growth of the province. On their own, universities are now a major sector of Nova Scotia's economy, with a recent Gardner Pinfold study showing universities as Nova Scotia's third largest exporting industry after tire manufacturing and seafood processing — more than fishing and well above forestry, lumber and paper combined. Our universities are major sources of attracting out-of-province and international students to NS, many of whom choose to stay and many more who would stay if they could.

On the college side of the post-secondary spectrum, the NS Community College has been transformed into one of Canada's leading community colleges. While funding remains tight and inadequate, the days of annual budget cuts and double digit tuition increases are gone, and hopefully never to return. I am delighted to be back in my Nova Scotia home where the diversity and quality of its universities are now celebrated as one of the major strengths of our province, where education is viewed as an investment in the province's prosperity, and where the role of universities in community and regional development is recognized, valued, and supported.

Another turnaround has been in the area of Indigenous relations. I think it is fair to say that in 2000, relations between the NS government and the Mi'kmaq were mostly played out in the courts. When I arrived in Kelowna, I was so impressed at how the Okanagan First Nations communities were working to improve their standards of living while at the same time preserving and enhancing their culture, language and education. The relationship with the university was well developed, whereas during my entire time in Nova Scotia I had never really encountered any Mi'kmaq except in the context of my research in coastal and ocean management.

While in Ontario and influenced by my experience in BC, I had worked hard to develop better relations with Indigenous peoples, and at Carleton we implemented a whole new strategy with the Algonquin and Mohawk First Nations, as well as with the Inuit and Métis communities in Ottawa. The impetus provided by the report of the Truth and Reconciliation Commission has galvanized universities across Canada to do better, and I was pleased that a process to look at decolonization at Acadia had been started by my predecessor, Ray Ivany.

In September 2017, I attended a meeting of the Mi'kmaq-Nova Scotia-Canada Tripartite Forum at Membertou in Sydney, NS at which I saw what a change had occurred over the past 17 years. The biggest revelation to me was to witness the NS Minister of Justice, Mark Furey, receive a standing ovation following his speech at the main banquet. In 2000, the Minister of Justice wouldn't have got past door let alone be the guest speaker and get a standing ovation at the end. Times had clearly changed, and for the better. The fact that the governments of Canada and Nova Scotia were working collaboratively with the Mi'kmaq on so many important areas of life was a eye opener to me, and it inspires me to believe that we can do something special at Acadia as we seek to play our part in the reconciliation process.

Another area where things seem to be going in the right direction is on climate change and coastal management. In the mid-1990s I was involved in the development of the Coastal 2000 report, which laid out a framework for integrated coastal management in Nova Scotia. It was partly driven by concerns over climate change but in reality it was more to do with addressing the sustainability of Nova Scotia's many coastal communities that were suffering from the decline of the fisheries industry.

Unfortunately, Coastal 2000 was dropped when the government changed, and so climate change and coastal management were not really on the government's radar when I left in 2000. Today there is a clear recognition that climate change is a major and growing concern for Nova Scotia, and indeed the entire planet. Some of this is no doubt due to the fact that we are experiencing on a regular basis the increased vulnerability of Nova Scotia's coastal communities and infrastructure to the impacts of sea-level rise and increased storminess. However, it is also something that the provincial government understands and they are recognizing the need to rely on science-based evidence and develop appropriate policies. The current consultation on developing coastal protection legislation is a welcome initiative, and perhaps will actually result in action this time around.

A great deal of good work was done on the Coastal 2000 report and subsequent efforts, and it will be important to incorporate that work into the new policy framework. Oceans play an enormously important role in climate change, being a major component of both the global carbon cycle and the global climate system. Oceans are also being greatly affected by climate change, through such impacts as warming, acidification, changes in currents, sea-level rise, and increased impacts of ocean and coastal storms. We need to be taking this very seriously indeed, and Nova Scotia's approach is welcome and gratifying. There is still a long way to go, but the fact is that the necessity to deal effectively with the impacts of climate change is creating major new opportunities for ocean economic and resource development.

This takes us to another important change and that is in the recognition of the importance of oceans to the Nova Scotia economy and the growing collaboration between ocean and coastal industries, government, universities, and communities. I was involved, albeit in a small way, with earlier initiatives in the late 80s and 90s to get something moving around ocean industrial capacity. Bob Fournier was Associate Vice-President, Research at Dal when I was Dean of

Graduate Studies, and he attempted to get more recognition of the importance of oceans through what was called the Nova Scotia Oceans Initiative (NSOI). However, despite these best efforts, industry was not ready to collaborate and governments were still focused on the negative side of the things, especially the collapse of the commercial fisheries. Attempts to get people to think about other ways by which the province could build on its ocean location and expertise fell on deaf ears at the time. The time was not right to get buy-in for the notion that we needed to collaborate with as well as compete against each other in order to expand the capacity and value of the oceans sector in Nova Scotia.

Today, I am delighted to see how this has changed and the extent to which the major players, including important industrial, business and investment interests, are working together to build this important sector of our economy and life, such as through the recently funded Oceans Supercluster. Furthermore, the growing challenges of dealing with climate change are generating new opportunities for the sustainable use of ocean resources for economic growth, improved ocean ecosystem health, increased economic diversity, and better prospects for livelihoods and employment — the so-called "Blue Economy" approach.

A recent OECD report on the ocean economy estimates that the value of ocean-based industries worldwide will double in value to over $3 trillion US by 2030. Growth areas within ocean-based industries include marine aquaculture, offshore wind and wave energy, fish and seafood processing, ports and shipping, maritime safety and surveillance, marine supplies and equipment, marine and coastal tourism, and marine biotechnology. Nova Scotia is well positioned in these areas, and of course we have the added potential of tidal power due to the immense tidal range in the Bay of Fundy.

The oceans industry is not the only economic sector that has changed. Wine has changed too! When I left Nova Scotia in 2000, there were only two wineries in the province; and only one of those, Grand Pré, was located in the Valley region. Today there are some 23 producers in the vicinity of Wolfville alone, and they are producing some outstanding wines. It reminds me of when I arrived in Kelowna to discover how superb the Okanagan wines were, and how the development of a wine industry based upon quality rather than quantity could generate a high value tourism industry, through the pairing of local and regional wines and foods.

I am delighted to find that upon returning to Nova Scotia and settling in Wolfville, I am once again surrounded by a burgeoning wine industry that is putting the region and the province on the wine and food tourism map. Add to that the expanding production of local craft beer, cider and liquor, plus the increasing demand for produce from sustainable and organic farming operations, you have the ingredients for a major source of economic and social development in the region. It is also an area where collaboration between Acadia and local industry is paying dividends, and where the presence of university level expertise and facilities allows for an industry to develop and flourish more than it could without such critical support. Wine is not the only sector where there is growing potential for economic development through university-industry collaboration.

The agri-food and beverage industry has long been an established strength of the Valley region, and the development of bio-technology and pharmaceutical industries, some utilizing the accessibility to marine biological resources, is on the move. Furthermore, over the next few decades, the expansion of automation and artificial intelligence will completely change how we work and live. New technologies and digital analytical capabilities are providing the capability for small and medium-sized enterprises, sometimes even just individuals, to engage in global economic activity from anywhere. Again, this are areas of the new economy and society where universities like Acadia are capable of stimulating and sustaining economic, social and cultural growth in our region. I am very impressed by the spirit of entrepreneurship and innovation that is so evident in Nova Scotia today, something with which Acadia has been engaged for over 35 years when these were not words commonly associated with universities. I see so much great potential for the Windsor-Gaspereau-Wolfville-Kentville-Annapolis corridor to flourish in the new and developing sustainable economies of the 21st century.

I truly believe that we have the opportunity to transform this province over the next 10 years, and that is what I see as so exciting about being back in this province after a 17-year absence. Nova Scotia has a real opportunity to promote itself as Canada's most sustainable province and as Canada's most livable province. In a world that seems to be going crazy at times, such a place will be very attractive to those who seek out a more balanced and enjoyable lifestyle. We need to do this in partnership with our Indigenous communities, who are one of the few domestic populations that are growing, and where the potential for economic and social growth is significant. The barriers which are preventing Indigenous youth, as well as youth from communities that have traditionally been marginalized in our society, from succeeding in education must be eliminated so that a greater proportion of our own domestic population can benefit from and contribute to the prosperity of our province.

Just as I remember that first breath of Nova Scotia air, I also remember the first time I drove over the crest of Highway 101 near Avonport to see the majestic profile of Cape Blomidon set against the red and blue waters of the Minas Basin. That iconic view is etched on the memories of everyone who travels to the Valley and is part of the folklore of Acadia's alumni. From the first time I saw it back in 1979, I have always thought that Acadia's campus and its location was the most beautiful in Canada, and one of the most beautiful in the world. I feel privileged to have been chosen as Acadia's 16th President and Vice-Chancellor. Established in 1838 as an act of social justice to provide university education to those who were excluded from the existing institutions at the time, the creation and survival of Acadia is a testament to the resilience and foresight of Nova Scotians in general.

I am excited by the opportunity to play a role in helping Nova Scotia become more successful and prosperous. If my Nova Scotia home commits to becoming the most environmentally, economically and socially sustainable province in Canada, then perhaps a lot more people will want to make it their home as well.

Dr. Peter J. Ricketts commenced his six-year term as Acadia's 16th President and Vice-Chancellor in July 2017. Born in Harrogate, Yorkshire and raised in Bournemouth on the south coast of England, Dr. Ricketts earned his BA (Honours) degree in Geography at the University of Nottingham in 1974 and his PhD from the University of Southampton in 1982. In addition to serving as President, Dr. Ricketts also has an academic appointment at Acadia, as Professor of Earth and Environmental Science.

Dr. Ricketts' appointment at Acadia brings him back to Nova Scotia, where he began his full-time academic career as an Assistant Professor of Geography at Saint Mary's University in Halifax in 1979. Before his appointment at Acadia, Dr. Ricketts served as Provost and Vice-President (Academic) at Carleton University in Ottawa from 2009 to 2017 and has over 20 years of experience as a senior university administrator in Nova Scotia, British Columbia and Ontario, including a term as Dean of Graduate Studies at Dalhousie University in Halifax.

Dr. Ricketts is internationally-recognized for his expertise in coastal zones and ocean management and has published extensively in these subjects. He co-founded the Coastal Zone Canada Association and served as its president from 2002 to 2008, and again from 2012 to 2016. In June 2016, Dr. Ricketts was awarded the H. B. Nicholls Award by the CZCA in recognition of his leadership and significant contribution to integrated coastal and ocean management in Canada.

He is currently a member of the Global Oceans Forum, which works to develop ocean and coastal policy options within the implementation of the UN climate change framework. He is a passionate advocate for the internationalization of university education and has also published in areas related to higher education and international education. He served as the inaugural Chair of the Internationalization Leaders Network of the Canadian Bureau for International Education (CBIE) and also served for five years as Director of Ontario Universities International.

Dr. Ricketts lives in Wolfville with his wife, two children, and poodle, and is an avid soccer fan, still supporting his home team of Bournemouth.

MY BEAUTIFUL NOVA SCOTIA HOME

Neville MacKay

WELL, I'VE GOT TO SAY that when I stopped and had a think about "Neville" and all the stories, events, and nuances that go into the making of this man, I found myself at one moment laughing, another shuddering in embarrassment, then sobbing tears of joy, and then of utter sadness.

I hope you enjoy the journey as I tell you about my life in my Beautiful Nova Scotia Home.

I'll get the basics looked after first: I was born in Shelburne in the spring of 1963 to Bruce and Joyce MacKay. I was the fourth, and youngest, son to them. I don't remember my two oldest brothers ever living at home with us because of the age differences. In fact, my oldest brother was married when I was a toddler and I hear I was held in my mother's arms at the service. So, it was my brother, John, and I who shared our childhood together.

Growing up in Middle Ohio (miles out of town on a dirt road!), I had a really wonderful upbringing, filled with love, laughter, and kindness, which as a combination, washed away the pain, upset, anger, and fear that comes with having an active alcoholic as a father, the fact that we were apparently not that well off, and coming to the realization that I was "different."

We had a humble home, with flower and vegetable gardens, fruit trees (the peach trees were grown from pits Mum had planted), various cats and dogs, ducks, chickens, rabbits, a pig at one point, and although I can't remember, I hear we had a cow or two as well! We didn't have an indoor toilet, we heated our home with a wood stove and furnace, and we filled the "tub" (in the kitchen next to the stove) with water heated from the stove for years. We grew what we could, hunted for what we could, and lived a humble life in the country.

In the winter, my brother and I would keep an eye out for when Dad came from the toilet, so we could be next — that way the seat would still be warm! Over the years, improvements were made; the biggest being the indoor toilet, sadly installed after my Dad had passed.

DAD

Dad was in the Second World War, as was Mum. He served in the Canadian Army, and although he spoke little of his experiences overseas, the scars he carried internally plagued him his whole life. He was a farmer, a woodsman, and a man who cared deeply for this world. He worked as a fire spotter, climbing the tower daily to keep watch. In fact, I remember the first time I climbed the tower with him and called Mum at home (I think I was four) and she was a little less than happy that this had happened. He had a beautiful garden at the base of the tower, and I learned how deep his love was for Mum when he would bring her flowers home from this garden, or his lunchbox would be filled with wild strawberries. He was a man who split wood, hunted, and used a power saw, but knew this was nothing I would ever excel at so he never pushed me. I am forever grateful for his understanding and compassion.

My Dad was an active alcoholic when I was younger and was sent to detox and rehab when I was about 12. When he went into recovery, it was such a positive turning point for all of us. He never touched a drop again. After a time, he and Mum started square dancing weekly, sometimes two or more times a week, played cards together, and even held hands. He joined the Lions Club, and for the remainder of his life he was a happy and a healthy (mentally at least) man. I learned a lot from this: determination, compassion, and love of life.

I remember one day when I was 11 or 12 and we were in the truck together. He stopped and wanted to show me a lady's slipper orchid that had grown around a fallen tree and still managed to bloom. He told me in his kind way that although there will be many things in this life that will try and knock you down, stop you, or get in your way, there is always a way to get around these obstacles and still shine and bloom. I live by these words to this day. He taught me ways to grow vegetables and the importance of moving your crops around and composting. From him I learned what could be harvested from nature to use as medicine and food, to gauge the weather to come from the trees, clouds, and animal activity, and that every being is here for a reason and deserves respect.

MUM

Mum was also active during the Second World War; she was in the British Army. My parents met, fell in love, and married in England. She immigrated to Canada towards the end of the war and settled with Dad to make their lives together. She didn't really know how to bake at all, and did not like the idea the first time when a dead rabbit, fur and all, was given to her to "clean." But over time she learned the ways, and became a great baker. She sold baked goods she made to so many. Those who knew me then know I never looked like I'd missed a meal. Let's just say we never went hungry!

Mum taught me so much about love, respect, and life. I learned to bake, cook, and garden from my mum. She and I spent countless hours in the kitchen (apparently I was small enough to sit on the kitchen table while she made cookies), lots of time in the garden and going for walks picking berries. Like I said earlier, I was not a woodsman, although I did go fishing with Dad, opting to learn other gifts from Mum. In fact, I learned colours and to count long before I was of school age because of her.

Next to the back door we had morning glories that bloomed all summer. These flowers lasted only a day, and Mum would have me go out in the morning to count all the pink and blue ones for her. I remarked later in life how wonderful that was, that she counted these flowers and got me to do so too. Well, she NEVER counted a bloom herself! In fact, she said she could have a second cup of tea by the time I was done! Good for her, right?

A LOVE OF PLANTS

Both my parents taught me a lot about nature and instilled my love of plants. My father would dig up strawberry plants in January and we'd have them in the house; my Mum showed us how to pollinate them with a paintbrush so we would have berries. I got to take a calla lily to school for show and tell once.

We used to keep a fat tick in a jar so we could see how many babies can come from one insect. Mum and Dad would also plant the odd seed in with their houseplants so we could be surprised when a petunia or nasturtium would pop into bloom in February. Gosh, we even had to get up in the night when the cactus was blooming. (Mum had a cactus that bloomed only for one night, and not very often, so it was a huge deal to see it!) This was the same too, when the northern lights appeared; up we would get to witness the wonder.

One late November, Mum asked me to go out with her, as there was something she wanted me to see. It was a little jolly jumper (a type of mini-pansy) that was blooming next to the house. It had but three petals left and they were chewed and torn. She reminded me that although these little petals were pretty much gone, they were still beautiful and that we needed to enjoy them now, as we'd not see them again for months to come.

I will be forever thankful to both my parents for all they did to make me the man I am today.

THE SAME BUT DIFFERENT

Growing up in rural Nova Scotia was both challenging and rewarding. We had little but didn't need much. I was bussed to school, where I met many wonderful people (and a few assholes) and tried to do the best I could. When I started school, I had a bit of an accent, because of my mum being British, my dad not always being present, and several of our neighbours who helped with my upbringing also being British. (There are still words I am uncomfortable with like "tomato" and "fork".)

Well, I guess children didn't like too many obvious differences, so I learned quickly that a different accent was not an asset. I was also led to believe at first that being left handed wasn't a good thing. In fact, my teacher put me in a right-handed desk and disappointedly said, "Another leftie MacKay." Impressions are made at a young age, and this was one I decided to address as soon as possible.

Of ALL the things one would think I needed to keep "in the closet," being left-handed wouldn't be one of them. Well, it was. I did not want to write with that backwards slant, have my ink smudge on the paper and my hand, and refused to write with my hand contorted so weirdly. So I asked my father, who had brilliant handwriting, and was right handed, for help. He said to sit across from him and write what he does, but pretend I am looking in a mirror. Well, it worked! You'd never guess I was a leftie, unless you see me write (I turn the paper almost upside down!)

I did well in elementary school and into high school. It was in the high school days when I developed as a gay man, although it never was a big "coming out" event like you hear. Sorry!

I do recall the time one summer when my cousins came to visit from Boston. They stayed next door at their mother's, our aunt's. I can still hear my Dad looking out the window and saying, "Here come the fruits!" and me looking out to see how they walked, etc... so I would know! (They were both gay, older and out.)

I never got in with the "wrong crowd" in school, but did have a little fun now and then, experimenting with different substances, cigarettes, and even a girl! (I have never slept with a woman though, so her dignity and mine were upheld.) I LOVED the drama group and couldn't wait to be on stage! I also was one of the first boys taking home economics rather than woodworking and shop. I excelled with my skills of sewing and baking. I even made a dress for Mum, a jacket and a pair of pants for Dad.

I was a member of the local 4-H club. What an incredible experience that was, one I would strongly recommend to anyone, especially rural folks. I am not into a lot of farm animals, so cows and horses are not my thing, but there is so much more. I learned to speak publicly from being in 4-H. I got to present either a speech or demonstration in front of our club (with about eight to 12 members). If I won, and I often did, I went on to the county, regional, and provincial competitions. Not only did I learn to speak publicly, I got to travel across not only Nova Scotia but Canada (first time on a plane), learned the importance of teamwork and of course team spirit. We did projects together, raised money for our trips, and learned so much. I met so many incredible people, many of whom I remain in contact with.

MY MOTHER'S BLOOMERS

I graduated high school, and rather than going off to university like the rest of the world (I had the grades!), I decided to go to Alberta and stay with my brother for a time to see what that would be like. Good, bad, and otherwise, I learned a lot from it all and am thankful I went.

I got a job as a delivery driver at a florist shop, which I hated, but I was determined to continue my path towards being a florist. I remember going to a floral show and seeing the designer on stage, regaling us all with their wisdom and talent. I thought and decided then and there that I would one day be up there, sharing love through the beauty of flowers, with the world. I lived and worked in Alberta for many years, absorbing all the knowledge I could from some of the most talented in the business, until in the late 80s when my father died suddenly.

The weight of my grief was relentless, both because of our loss and because of the distance I was from Mum and home. So, I packed it in and moved back to my beautiful Nova Scotia to start all over. Although it took a time to get back into the swing of things, I settled with my partner at the time in Halifax, where I got a job with a local florist. It was here when things started to improve for me.

The thing about going forward and upward is that there is often a snag that pulls you sideways or a block you've either got to chip your way through or get around, and I had a few of those. I split with my boyfriend, which after a few months I understood how much of a blessing that, indeed, was. Halifax is and has been for years, to me anyway, a city filled with a lot of understanding and acceptance and a spirit of "live and let live." I have embraced this my whole life. I know there are bad people here too and if you look for them or open yourself to this energy, they/it will find you. I choose not to.

In 1992 I opened, with two business partners, my store on Spring Garden Road and called it My Mother's Bloomers. We didn't know a lot about business really, but determination was on our side (and a bit of blind faith). I had two business partners who believed in my talent and I am forever thankful to them.

Let me tell you why I would ever think of calling any store My Mother's Bloomers! When we were children, we would help Mum out in the garden and she would call us her "little blossoms", "blooms" or "petals." See where I'm going with this? Now, this is not a name many would forget, let me tell you, and I have great fun when I ask a gentleman in an audience if he has ever been in "My Mother's Bloomers!"

It was tough starting a business, getting my name out there and building trust in the community, but now after 26 years the business is doing great. We've been on the brink of bankruptcy more than once, have made and lost a lot of money, allowed many people to build a future, and most importantly have provided flowers to countless people who have used them to console, celebrate, love, and enjoy. In fact, just recently a gentleman stopped me at a conference I was speaking at to tell me of when his father passed, 26 years ago, and how I took the time to create a piece for them using flowers they picked, etc. I am honoured and humbled every day that I get to do what I do. We've moved the shop a couple times in those years, settling in our cozy corner of Creighton and Falkland streets in North End Halifax.

My business did so well because of being here in Nova Scotia. I know this to be true. I have been told to go to Toronto where I can make more money, or that people don't appreciate you here. Well, none of that is even close to true. Since opening My Mother's Bloomers, my personal profile and business has grown worldwide. I started being a guest on CTV's *Breakfast Television* (Now called *Morning Live*) shortly after we opened shop, and I am still a regular on the show. I've been on many national television shows, as well as in the USA. I write for several publications, have a book out with two more on the go, and speak internationally. It's quite something for a kid from Shelburne.

THEN COMES MARRIAGE

I met my husband at my shop. David would come in and buy a rose for his then partner every couple weeks or so and whenever I would help him I would suggest he try something different. One day I was out and saw David and asked why I hadn't seen him in a time. Well, he had split with his boyfriend. Happy days … for me, anyway! I then explained to him that when I suggested he try something "different" I didn't mean a flower!!! (I have been told I have more nerve than a sore tooth). Anyway, we've been together over 20 years and married for seven.

"Gay marriage" seemed, to David and I, as crazy as the first telephone was to many, but it happened and is now not a big deal here in Canada. (Like cannabis will be soon enough I believe). When we got engaged, we thought it best to keep it quiet, as we are quite well known. But after a little fun I had one morning on air with the Breakfast Club on C100, all was out in the open! We are both so very thankful things happened this way. Our wedding was attended by all sorts of folks, from the Lt. Governor to singers, artists, and many other wonderful friends and family. I should mention too that it was broadcast LIVE on the radio. Oh, and CTV also taped it to show on air for the world to see, with many live feeds on social media as well.

That sort of "Kardashian" attention was not what we wanted at first, but because of it a lot of boundaries were broken, many people got to hear and see happiness, love, and laughter through our lives, and people spoke of love and how many different types of love there are in this world after witnessing this for themselves, knowing who we are already. It was an incredible thing.

When I was in our store the next week, a lady called to tell me that she and her daughter watched our wedding, after which her daughter came out to her. This lady cried as she thanked me for opening this dialogue with her daughter. She said she will always be grateful. David, who is a master hair stylist, had a client (a phycologist) tell him that one of her clients told her that after hearing of our marriage, they felt normal. You can only imagine how those things have made us feel; the gratitude we have for so many people is beyond words.

David and I co-own the store now. Although he still is a hairdresser, guitarist/singer, and tour guide, he is always there for me and the business.

GRATITUDE

I am so thankful for all the people in my life, both now and in the past, because I have been guided throughout my journey by them all. I have worked and continue to work with the best in the floral industry, surrounding myself with the best energy and spirits around. (Thank you, Ricky, for reminding me of this power.) Because of this energy around me and the love of the people here in Nova Scotia, I have allowed myself to try and succeed at things I never thought possible.

I am a member of the Canadian Academy of Floral Art and get to represent Canadian floral artists whenever I travel the world. I am also a member of Professional Floral Communicators International, which is an elite group of floral presenters, and am a proud member of the World Flower Council, which is a group of international florists that promotes world peace through flowers. When I present internationally, I often have a map with Nova Scotia circled so they can see where I live. It is wonderful to hear how many have either visited or would love to visit our province!

I've had the honour of being parade marshal at Halifax Pride, raising the Rainbow Flag not only in Grand Parade Square, but also at a senior's home and in my hometown. I've gotten to speak, emcee, and present at countless charitable events, and have been recognized with several awards for my philanthropy work. (I even got a commendation from the Lt. Governor!) I speak not only as an emcee, but also as a keynote and motivational speaker for many groups and organizations all over, which is both unbelievable to me at times and also so very humbling. I have an incredible team —Stephanie and Danielle — at VOX, who believe in me, as well as countless others!

I am on the design and education team of North America Smithers Oasis (and am the only Canadian on this team by the way) and travel all over Canada and the US presenting and teaching the latest in floral design and trends. I also get to judge international competitions because I am a certified judge through the World Flower Council. I write for two magazines in my spare time (whatever that is!) and have done so for years, which is so much fun, especially when I am somewhere far away and get recognized for my work. I recently wrote my first book, so now I can say I am an author! It's called, "Neville on the Level" (available at Amazon.com) and now that I've done it, I am working on two more, a children's book and one all about flower stories.

My father told me that my big mouth would get me in trouble and will take me a long way too. He was right. I am not afraid of speaking, and if you ask for my opinion, you'll get an honest one, not always one you would like to hear though. My big mouth has gotten me on stages all over the world as well as television (and one tiny part in a movie). I get to host, on occasion, some of the stars from the television show, *Coronation Street*, when they come to Canada, and have befriended several. (Imagine that, right? ME? From Shelburne?) Not only that, but I take groups annually to the set to see a taping of a scene and to walk the cobbles. There'll be more to come and other tours too, so keep up with what I am doing ... if you can!

I've done floral work for many well-known folks including two prime ministers, several mayors, and premiers and Lt. Governors, delegates from the G-7 Summit, Sir Elton John, Cher, Sir Paul McCartney, Celine Dion, and members of the British Royal Family. In fact, when Harry and Megan were wed, I got to do a bit of live commentating on CBC about it.

Legacies are important for many of us, and I am thankful to have made a difference already. I was given the honour of having a day lily named after my store a few years ago, and it's proudly growing at the Halifax Public Gardens. In the summer of 2018 the Nova Scotia Dahlia Society named a new dahlia that they propagated in my honour. Now there is a dahlia in this world called "Neville MacKay." They did this because of my work at the Public Gardens promoting and sharing the beauty of these incredible blooms over the years. I was, and still am, really astonished and a bit overwhelmed by this gesture.

Growing up here in Nova Scotia and being involved with so many people has been an incredible journey. It's been tough at times and really beautiful as well. I learned at an early age that I am no better than anyone else; I just know different things. I know people who truly believe they are actually better than I am and I really do feel for them. I am just as (often more so) comfortable in a trailer in the middle of nowhere as I am in a fancy house, and that is simply because of my upbringing. I appreciate the simple things, as many of us do here in Nova Scotia, and after travelling and living in other places, I know the beauty that is all around us, and never ever will I take it for granted. We are NEVER more than 10 minutes away from a postcard here in Nova Scotia, and I take every opportunity to enjoy them all.

I'm just Neville, and everyone knows that. I love this province, and the people here. We are an incredible, diverse, and interesting bunch, and it's no wonder people from around the world flock here to absorb our friendly energy. I hope to continue to "push petals" for many years and look forward to the opportunities that come my way. My wish for all is to "share love through the beauty of flowers!" and I will work every day to see this happen, as flowers celebrate love and life from the womb to the tomb. I am and will always be grateful to be a Nova Scotian.

I LOVE my Beautiful Nova Scotian Home!

Neville MacKay is a talented retailer and floral designer who is well known throughout the floral Industry and beyond for his creative flare, quality workmanship and entertaining personality. He's affectionately referred to as "That Bloomin' Neville!" (among other things!)

Neville appears as an expert and entertainer on many national and local TV and radio shows across Canada, and is sought-after internationally as an expert presenter. He also owns and operates a cutting-edge floral and retail gift shop in Halifax, My Mother's Bloomers, with his partner of 25 years.

Besides running the shop, Neville also hosts tours to the UK, and has taken the stage across Canada and beyond as emcee, auctioneer, host and keynote speaker, artfully telling his story along with the magic of making those in his presence feel inspired, connected and entertained. His philanthropy work has led to him receiving many awards, including a commendation from the Nova Scotia Lt. Governor. He's designed floral arrangements for celebrities and Heads of State, including Rod Stewart, Glenn Close, Sirs Elton John and Paul McCartney and members of the British Royal Family.

His work has been featured in many publications internationally, and has also written a book. Mostly, Neville LOVES flowers, and loves to share their power and beauty with everyone he can.

HOME IS WHERE THE HEART IS

Starr Cunningham

I'M 51 YEARS OLD AND have lived in Halifax for more than half my life. Despite that fact, I still call Pictou County home. I've tried to stop, but I find it next to impossible. My children say it's strange because the only home they know is in our Nova Scotia capital. Not so, for me.

I was born in New Glasgow on Groundhog Day 1968. Former Premier, Dr. John Hamm, was there to catch me. It's funny that I ended-up interviewing him some 35 years later in my role as a CTV reporter. My friend and former colleague, Steve Murphy, likes to joke that Premier Hamm was the first man to see me naked!

My ties to Pictou County run deep. Both of my parents were born and raised there. One grandfather worked the Foord seam in Stellarton. The other built a rural grocery store in the small community of Alma.

My parents lived in a small trailer next to the store for the first few years of their married life and then moved our ever-growing family to Six Mile Brook — a community deep in the rural lands of the county. My paternal grandmother maintained a family home there that she would lend to her children when needed. My mom and dad moved us into the "County House" for a few years while they saved enough money to build a home of their own in Alma.

During that time, our family of two girls expanded to a family of three — Starr, Stacey, and Shannon. Three girls born in four years. We also had a dog, a turtle, and for those who really know my story, a goat named Gertrude who lived in the house!

There are many things I could write about my Nova Scotia home. I could rave about its natural and rustic beauty. Its coastal shorelines that sometimes seem to call my name. Its fresh and delicious seafood that makes other mussels, clams, and scallops look pithy in comparison. Its four glorious seasons; each full of beauty in its own way. Its penchant for bagpipes, lighthouses, and a seemingly never-ending flow of delicious and thirst-quenching ales. I could but I won't. Instead, I'd like to focus on something far more meaningful and far less tangible.

My sister Stacey is just ten months younger than me. She arrived, two months early, on Christmas Day 1968. While we're close in age, we couldn't be more different if we tried. I'm blonde. Stacey has jet-black hair. I'm 5'8" tall. Stacey is a foot shorter at 4'8". She excels at team sports. I'm a solo sports fan. I lead the Mental Health Foundation of Nova Scotia. Stacey resides in a supervised living program and has a part-time job. I write books. She sometimes struggles to read them. I have two children. She has none. I worry about things like money, my mortgage, and future university bills. She doesn't. And, *she* is my Nova Scotia home.

So how can a person be a home? It's not so much about her *being*, but rather about what she creates around her. Her community is an open, caring circle of family and friends who love her as much as she loves them.

Stacey exudes happiness unfiltered. She brings smiles to the faces of strangers. She laughs from the soles of her feet to the top of her head. She inspires goodness in others. She finds it incredibly difficult to curse (even when I egg her on!). She never speaks badly of anyone. She celebrates every birth she hears on *East Coast FM* and feels genuine sadness when she receives news of a death. She loves all animals (with the exception of cats!). She adores cuddling babies. She savours every bite of food like it's the best thing she has ever tasted.

The essence of Stacey is what makes me proud to be a Nova Scotian. The way she is encouraged to flourish *in* her community, *by* her community. The way she is supported and protected yet permitted to live her own life. Nothing about Stacey's experience has been straightforward, but it has been made better, even gentler, by the people in and around Pictou County.

Many former viewers ask me why I chose to leave my successful career in television to work at a not-for-profit organization. In fact, I get asked about it so often that I've written a talk entitled "From the Newsroom to the Nova Scotia Hospital." I like to joke that it had absolutely nothing to do with Bruce Frisko!

All kidding aside, I loved my job at CTV. For 23 years I was invited into the living rooms of Maritimers to share stories, interview experts, talk politics, experience unique and exciting opportunities, and provide context for breaking news. I had the pleasure of interviewing celebrities such as Morgan Freeman, Joan Rivers, and Jamie Lee Curtis. I enjoyed conversations with sports heroes such as Paul Henderson, Theo Fleury, and Catriona Le May Doan. I shared a cup of tea with the *Outlander* series author Diana Gabaldon, had time alone in the green room with Canadian novelist Timothy Findley, and poured back a pint of beer with the ever-charming and talented Frank McCourt. I drove a monster truck called the Virginia Giant. I took the controls of a Cormorant helicopter over the Atlantic Ocean and I had the honour of running in the Rick Hansen 25th Anniversary Relay as a representative of Nova Scotia. I held an enviable position that allowed me to engage, connect with, and experience adventure. Few know it was Stacey, and her community of support, who pointed me away from my career in journalism.

As a fan of Special Olympics Nova Scotia, I emceed the organization's annual gala fundraiser for 15 years. Stacey was (and still is) an athlete. I served on the board of directors. In January of 2013, Stacey and I delivered the gala's keynote address. In all honesty, it scared the hell out of me. For the first time in more than two decades, I was sharing my own story rather than talking about someone else's. The result was (please excuse the high drama!) life-changing.

After watching the audience's reaction, I realized I had a compelling story to share and, more importantly, people were interested in hearing it. The profile *CTV Atlantic* had allowed me to build was significant. It provided me with a voice that could educate, entertain, and perhaps even motivate. There was no turning back.

If it weren't for Stacey and our involvement with Special Olympics, I wouldn't have been compelled to make a change. Having Stacey in my life has, in many ways, led me to my career in mental health. It has also made me, and my entire family, more aware of what it means to lean into a community of support.

Stacey's life is rich for many reasons. She is connected to Summer Street Industries. Summer Street is an organization that's very well known and loved in Pictou County. It works with people who have intellectual challenges by making the community aware of the skills, talents, and gifts that everyone has to offer. It has more than 5,000 customers, 2,000 donors, 200 clients and a large network of friends and partners. It offers programs that focus on employment, education, independence, and accomplishment. It provides Stacey with support, guidance and vital peer connections

Stacey also volunteers in the childcare program at the local YMCA once a week. She has a boyfriend of 15 years, tonnes of friends, a housemate she enjoys spending time with, and the constant attention of a full-time counsellor through Highland Community Residential Services. HCRS is dedicated to the creation and growth of homes, programs, and support networks for people who have intellectual challenges or mental health concerns. Its mission is to foster personal growth, independent living, and a high quality of life. It has done that, and more, not just for my sister, but also for countless other families in Pictou County. And Stacey isn't just a client of HCRS, she also works for the organization. Four days a week, Stacey does short shifts at the HCRS head office where she interacts with staff, answers phones and greets visitors.

Stacey goes to the movies, bowls, attends just about every parade and festival that happens, and has a far busier social life than I do. She works with her counsellor and roommate to prepare weekly meal plans, chore schedules, and exercise goals. She takes pride in her home and loves to have friends and family drop by for a cup of coffee that's often strong enough to keep you awake for weeks! She also loves to walk and go to Tim's for tea. She does so freely and confidently, sometimes with friends and sometimes just on her own. She loves soap opera magazines, keeping a daily journal, and spending time at the cottage. She flies (on her own) to Toronto at least once a year to spend time with Shannon. She also has no problem hopping on the bus to come to the city to stay with me for a long weekend with very little notice. She visits our parents quite regularly as well. Simply put, Stacey has a full and satisfying life. She understands the importance of hard work and the reward of vacation. She feels supported and loved. Independent and happy. Safe and valued.

Stacey *is* my Nova Scotia home. She symbolizes everything that makes our province strong and remarkable. She thrives thanks to family, friends, innovative programs, overall societal acceptance, and the support of a county that truly cares. Would Stacey flourish elsewhere in our country? I really can't say for sure and I'll never know. Stacey belongs in and to Nova Scotia. Her community loves her, lifts her up, and holds her dear. Her sincere and beautiful spirit sparks kindness and joy in others. She makes people smile and exudes a never-ending attitude of gratitude. To me, Stacey and her circle of support epitomize our province at its very best. I guess that's why I will forever call Pictou County home …

Starr Cunningham is the President & CEO of the Mental Health Foundation of Nova Scotia. An acclaimed journalist, best-selling children's author and dedicated community volunteer, Starr holds an Honours Journalism Degree from the University of King's College.

Starr is a National Recipient of a Difference Makers – 150 Canadians Leading for Mental Health Award *from CAMH – Centre for Addiction and Mental Health, Toronto. She is the 2017 Halifax Business Awards* Business Person of the Year Silver Recipient *and the Northwood Foundation 2017* Live More Advocacy Award Winner. *She was also named the Rising Star Award Winner at the 2015* Maritime Philanthropy Awards.

Starr serves on the Bell Let's Talk Community Fund Advisory Committee – Atlantic Region *and the Nova Scotia / Prince Edward Island St. John Ambulance Board of Directors.*

Starr writes a monthly column for Senior Living and is a regular contributor to Our Children *magazine. Starr will be invested into the Order of St. John in 2019 at Government House.*

THE BOOK

Robert Hirtle

FOR SOME REASON, MY SISTER christened it Idleburg. I think it was from some German castle near where our forefathers came from, but I couldn't find it on the Internet. It may certainly have had those overtones to her in her youth, but for some reason that name never caught on.

For me, and pretty much everyone else who ever visited or spent the night there, it was, and is, known simply as "The Camp."

Not what the prim and proper folks from Ontario might call their lavish retreats in what is colloquially known as "Cottage Country," although many have moved eastward, to our lake and others, for cheaper, but just as enjoyable recreational venues.

No, this place was, and is, far from that, and that is what makes it so special.

My dad and mom, Doug and Noreen, had the camp built in 1958, ostensibly as a dry place to go to if it happened to start raining while they were out on the lake fishing. In reality, it was meant to be far more than that. The camp was, essentially, an escape. Although we were a very tight-knit family, home wasn't always where the heart wanted to be.

The matriarch of the house, Jessie Florinda Ann Caroline Hirtle, or "Aunt Flo" as she was affectionately known, ruled the roost. She and her half-brother, Harvey Joudrey, who built the house in Dayspring in 1909, collectively raised my father after their brother, Dad's father Foster, divorced my grandmother when Dad was a youngster.

Foster, Harvey, and Flo had a fourth sibling, Gladys, who was a spinster school teacher and often came on the weekends to "visit," and that, unfortunately, always sparked what conservatively could be described as a two-day argument.

It is not an exaggeration to say that Gladys and Flo hated each other more than anyone else on the planet and as a result they fought constantly, from the moment the former walked through the door until she left two days later, or on some occasions earlier if the arguing became too intense.

The cause of the deep-rooted hatred was primarily jealousy, Flo being envious of her sister because she had to stay home and look after their parents in their old age while Gladys saw the world, or at least a few other parts of Nova Scotia, in her capacity as a teacher.

In fact, Flo's distaste for her sibling was so acute that after Gladys died in 1976 and was buried in the family plot, she made Dad buy a separate cemetery lot for her, Mom, and Dad, just because she didn't want to be in the same space with her sister, even in death.

And so the idea of building a camp that would allow us to collectively escape those weekends of mayhem was born.

For a site for his retreat, Dad settled on a 104-foot by 102-foot piece of waterfront property on Keddy Cove, at the foot of Molega Lake, a sprawling body of water that spans both Lunenburg and Queens County, although most of its seven miles rests in the latter district.

The cost of buying the land and hiring two men to construct the 14-foot by 18-foot building was the paltry sum of $400. That included the lumber, roof, and side shingles, and everything else — except the outhouse. Dad built that himself.

Originally, the camp was equipped with a pair of old iron army cots which, once upon a time, were bunk beds, and another single cot where myself and my two siblings slept, as well as a double bed where Mom and Dad lay their heads at night.

Because there was no electricity until 1974, we cooked on a wood-fired stove and kept our food preserved in a 1930s vintage icebox, which contained a couple of ice packs brought from home that usually lasted no longer than a day or two. Light in the evenings was supplied by a pair of oil-powered hurricane lamps and a Coleman gas lantern, which Dad had to take down and "pump up" every so often to keep it from going out.

The advent of electric power changed everything. We now have a refrigerator — a vintage 1948 Crossley model — a more modern microwave oven, electric kettle, toaster, and other creature comforts. We've also had to replace the doorstep a few times, re-shingle the roof and do a major renovation to the outhouse a few years ago, which was carried out primarily with the help of our dear friends, John and Kim Berkeley. Thanks to their help, the privy has been re-named "Berkeley Manor," and now boasts all the usual accouterments of the typical, outdoor toilet, including the half-moon in the door. But through all the years and various changes, one thing at the camp has remained a constant, and that is "The Book."

It started out innocuously enough on April 20, 1962, when Mom decided to pen the first journal entry on one of the back pages of the wooden-bound guest log, which contains the names and comments of various visitors who have passed through the door over the years.

> *"Good Friday,"* that first post began. *"Back all day with the children. It was a beautiful day, but no fish. (Who cares.)"*

With those words, a tradition was born, and it became a steadfast rule that whenever anyone visited the camp, for whatever reason, they had to write something — *anything* — in The Book.

In the ensuing 55 years no less than seven volumes of entries have accumulated, documenting a variety of interesting family information and sometimes just general facts about things such as the weather, who was suffering from what illness or had what surgery, who recently died in the community, and a whole lot more.

I can, for example, tell you that on May 4, 1965, yours truly landed his first ever trout, which measured a whopping 10-and-a-half inches. It was a momentous occasion for a nine year old, one that Mom dutifully recorded, adding that Dad caught one, as well, "but I got skunked."

March 12, 1966, there was about "16 inches of good, hard ice" in the lake, a fact that was confirmed by my dad who cut a hole through it in order to obtain enough water to make coffee that day.

Of course, through the years, while there were many of those, perhaps, "mundane" moments, which were well documented, there were also many "classic" entries, stuff that you might see on television but never expect to experience in real life.

One of those happened in July 1984 when my brother, Leonard, and then-brother-in-law Albert went back to spend the night on what the former described in the book as a "perfect" evening.

It didn't stay perfect for long.

Things started to go downhill when the bottom fell out of the metal barbecue we had lit to cook our steaks, sending glowing hot coals bouncing around the deck and the three of us scrambling to get water from the lake to put them out before we burned the camp, and the surrounding forest, to the ground.

Averting that potential tragedy and able to engage our limited ingenuity before we were too overcome by adult beverages, the three of us jury-rigged a new barbecue using an old stove-pipe cap that we found in the outhouse and the grill off the old barbecue.

With supper behind us, I decided to make the best of the warm summer evening by taking a dip in the lake before the sun went down.

I was out there happily bobbing around when suddenly, the force of nature came calling — and unfortunately not of the number one variety. I had to do a number two and quickly.

Having little time to think and even less time to get out of the water and run to the outhouse, I made a snap decision — I'd let her go ... right in the lake. Shouldn't be a problem, I thought. Albert and Leonard were sitting on the deck having a brew, so I was the only one in the water. My little ball of excrement should float to the top and eventually find its way to shore in a location between our camp and the next-door neighbours'. There, it would become fish food or eventually waste away to nothing, just as Mother Nature intended. ... That's what I thought. I really did.

Unfortunately, things sometimes are dependent, not on one's own actions, but on those of others. Within minutes of me releasing my little jewel to the devices of the elements, Leonard appeared on the shore clad in his swimsuit and asking me how the water was.

It wasn't long before he came wading out on a direct collision course with my recent defecation.

I waited in anticipation and as he approached it he paused for a moment, and cupping his hand underneath the excrement and lifting it in the air to better see it, said in a loud voice, "Hey, what's this?"

It was probably the longest second I've ever experienced, the period from when Leonard scooped up the little brown nugget until he realized exactly what he held in his hand.

"Holy fuck!" he bellowed. "Somebody shit in the lake!"

Then, with a throw that would make a baseball hall of famer envious, he propelled the turd mightily towards the shoreline and began vigorously washing his hands.

The evening was so memorable that Leonard couldn't wait to document it in the book:

> Robert has (in a most undignified manner), turned a beautiful, clean lake into a stinking shit heap," he wrote later that evening. "Actually, outside of a religious barbecue (read holey) and a lake littered with smelly brown bananas, the evening has been little more than mildly exciting.

The next day, after a night's rest and reflection, he continued with a second entry:

> It just occurred to me that we are using drinking water out of the same lake that brother pooped in last night. I knew the coffee tasted funny," he wrote. "Robert must like the coffee. He's on his 'turd' cup.

He continued on, saying the Environmental Protection Agency should be notified about the "poo-lution" in the lake.

> *Who knows, maybe it's 'ass-id' rain. Robert says 'A guy shits in the lake and can't live it down. Alas, we must keep reminding him of this grave injustice to Mother Nature.*

While *The Book* served to preserve so many happy, humorous, and treasured memories, within it also came sadness:

> *July 9-10, 1977*
>
> *This will be the last entry in this journal. Douglas died on June 21st after being sick with a brain tumour for two months. I feel closer to him back here than anywhere else as he loved it and I know he is here with us.*
>
> *I came back with Robert, Heather, Andrew and Mary Jane yesterday. It was a nice weekend. God bless the young people. I don't know what I would do without them. It was very hard to come back, but now I hate to leave.*
>
> *Bye Old Camp*
> *Noreen.*

When Dad died I was 20 and was just getting my feet wet, having recently been hired by the Bank of Nova Scotia. Mom, on the other hand, had never driven a car, never paid a bill, had never gone grocery shopping. She was a typical 50s-60s stay-home wife.

That all changed for both of us on June 21, 1977.

We, my Mom and I, grew up together, basically, because we had to. And Mom went on to evolve. Thankfully, Dad had enough investments and such to allow her a comfortable, if not extravagant life, so she didn't have to work. Widowed at 45, she never remarried (although I am told she had suitors).

But after she got her driver's license, she certainly made regular trips to the camp, with Aunt Flo and whatever was her current dog in tow. She would spend the weekend, go down by the shore and sit on her chair, smoking cigarettes, and fish, loving every minute of it.

Her camp trips continued until the early 2000s when tide and time, who we know wait for no one, stepped to the forefront, and she physically couldn't go there alone any more.

> *July 16, 2006 ... I cannot believe I am back here. It has been a long time and I really do not expect it to happen again. But who knows? Any way, Heather & Robert invited me to come back over night. It really was great. We played Trivial Pursuit, Robert and I both trying for the middle. Robert won of course. I let him win. But don't tell him.*
>
> *They are busy cleaning up to go home. I am going to adopt them. They work so well. It's been great, and God willing, I may get back again.*

> Bye Ole Camp
> Noreen.

Just over a year later, Mom again went to camp, unknowingly for the last time.

> *September 3, 2007 ... Dear Old Camp — Surprise, everyone. Barbie [my cousin] is down for a week's visit so she, Robert, Victoria [my daughter] and I came back for a short visit. It is a beautiful day, nice and sunny with a cool breeze blowing. We played trivia; Victoria and Robert whipped our asses off. Then the others went in for a swim.*
>
> *I have really been happy to be back here. God willing it happen again. Lots of great memories.*
>
> *They are packing up to go home so I will say,*
>
> *Bye Old Camp*
> *Noreen.*

It was, sadly, her last good-bye.

Three years later it was my turn to write in *The Book*. On September 20, Mom's birthday, I went to the camp to write her eulogy. Alone. I just figured there, with The Book, would be the place to be, so I wrote, ironically, the last page in that particular edition:

> *It is with heavy heart that I write what will be the last entry in this journal. Mom died on Friday, September 17 after a courageous battle with cancer.*
>
> *Despite the recurrence of her pneumonia and another trip to the hospital, she seemed to be doing okay up until Tuesday evening, but sometime between then and Wednesday afternoon she took a dramatic turn for the worse and the decision was made not to seek a more aggressive treatment for her pneumonia as the prognosis would likely not improve.*
>
> *I find it ironic that I write in the camp journal about Mom's death on the day, which would have been her 79th birthday. This is the place that was closest to her heart and I can almost feel her and Dad's presence as I listen to the tick of the clock and the breeze whispering through the leaves in the trees.*
>
> *Although Mom hadn't been here for three years, she never stopped thinking about the camp and all the memories it holds. Memories that we all hold dearly in our hearts forever.*

Whenever I want to get close to you Mom, I will come back here and I know you'll either be down on the shore with a fishing rod in your hand or up in the camp, sitting by a warm fire, waiting to play cards.

Thanks for everything Mom. You are the best Mom a person could ask for.

With Mom's passing, the camp fell to me. However, although my name is on the deed, it really belongs to the whole family, like it always has, and hopefully will continue to be.

It is part of our roots, our family tradition — our little piece of Nova Scotia heaven.

Robert Hirtle was born in Bridgewater and has lived in Lunenburg County his entire life. A self-described jack-of-all-trades-and master-of-none, he has worked for two department stores, a construction company, two banks, as a guard in the county jail, as a car salesman, and finally as a journalist for Lighthouse Media Group out of their Lunenburg office for nearly 14 years. In that latter career he was recognized both regionally and nationally for his writing and photography, but was unfortunately forced to retire due to health issues in 2015. He was awarded the Queen's Diamond Jubilee award in 2012 for his journalistic efforts as well as his volunteer work in the community over the years. He has lived in Mahone Bay since 1979 with his wife Heather, where they raised their son Patrick and daughter Victoria.

THE KEEPERS OF THE LIGHT

Janice Landry

BACKSTORY:
ON GREY AND STORMY DAYS, the salty spray of the Atlantic would pound against our kitchen window, which faced Point Pleasant Park, across Halifax's North West Arm. I would stand on our worn, black and white checkered linoleum floor, rapt with attention. There is nothing like a good storm — if you are careful not to venture too close — which tragically some still do and end up making news headlines.

I have a deep respect for the power of the water. That respect started with my late father.

As far back as I can remember, Capt. Basil (Baz) Landry, M.B., who was a veteran Halifax firefighter, would constantly remind me to be careful near the ocean, or any body of water, for that matter. "Wet, black rocks are slippery," is a warning he constantly gave me. It's something I have said to our daughter, Laura, so many times I have lost count. On visits to Peggy's Cove, I am hyper-vigilant, to the point that it can become irritating for whoever is with me. As beautiful as the iconic Nova Scotia landmark is, the potential danger of a rogue wave means I am never totally relaxed when exploring those rocks. We never venture too close.

Not on my watch.

That's because, in 2019, 13 years after his passing, I can still hear Baz inside my head warning me, and therefore, Laura, to never get too close.

Baz is the person who taught me to respect the Atlantic, to not take its strength for granted, and to have a controlled, but low-level fear of its unpredictability. Dad had witnessed plenty of trauma and death over the course of his 31 years of service with the former Halifax Fire Department. He knew what water could do to a body. As a veteran journalist, who now has as many years on the job as my father did when he retired, I have covered countless emergency scenes. I have also witnessed the results of drowning and accidents involving water.

The ocean is memorizing; it's not always merciful.

Growing up in Purcell's Cove, about a half-hour drive outside of downtown Halifax, on those stormiest of days, I loved to watch the ocean water splatter and pour down the kitchen window pane, leaving behind streaks and odd shapes.

I was hooked.

The proximity of the ocean to my childhood home never scared me. I found it fascinating, soothing, and invigorating. Our first house in the Cove was surrounded by ocean on three sides. During those formative years, I was just steps away from the most intriguing and educational playground a young person could imagine.

I am grateful for my childhood.

I now live farther away from the water, in a wooded area. The forest is also memorizing. Deer regularly visit our backyard. The sound of a storm ripping through our tall trees can be deafening, even frightening. I now also have a deep respect for the power of the wind — after storms like Hurricane Juan pounded our province.

Near the end of his life, Baz told me, while in hospital for the final time, that it appeared that I had a happy childhood because of the way I live my life as an adult. I found that comment poignant and observant. This is the first time I have shared it publicly.

Dad was right.

Baz also grew up in Purcell's Cove. The Landry homestead was on Keefe Drive, about two houses down from where we lived when I was a child. I would climb down over our small embankment, which was protected by a short white fence, to skip stones, walk on a nearby reef at low tide, look for beach glass and shells, and go swimming. I learned how to swim in that coastal community.

Being in or near water still makes me happiest.

I remember my late father being on the shoreline protectively watching over me as I floated, and eventually swam for the first time, in a shallow inlet. I was elated. The memory of that moment still makes me smile. As much as dad was always warning me about the water, he always let me go near it — once I had proven to him I was responsible enough. I am sure he was watching over me more times than I realized.

I am sure he still does.

I started writing as a youth while living in Purcell's Cove.

I would sit at an old wooden desk in our spare bedroom and look out at the water. I still sit at a desk facing a window today. I don't like to write unless there is a window near where I am working.

Baz Landry was 100 percent right: my childhood near the Atlantic Ocean has helped define my work and who I am today. My love of the water has followed me into adulthood. It also led me to apply for an unusual creative opportunity, in 2017.

CHANCE-OF-A-LIFETIME

I am part of a Facebook group called "Nova Scotia Writers." Its administrator posted about a chance for Atlantic Canadian artists, across different genres, to apply for a two-week Artist in Residency. It would be taken at the lightkeeper's cottage on the grounds of the Port Bickerton Lighthouse, on Nova Scotia's Eastern Shore, during the summer of 2017.

I applied but never thought I would be chosen.

One of the photos I used in my detailed residency application was of a lighthouse model Baz Landry made in 2001, five years before his death. The name of the piece, which depicts a lighthouse, wooden dock, and seaside community, is called "Lighthouse Keeper: A way of life in the past." It sits on a shelf in my family room, along with another model Dad made of the Landry homestead on Keefe Drive.

Dad started making models after he retired from firefighting in 1988. He liked to stay busy. And, he did — he kept creating until he entered the hospital for the last time. I have his final unfinished model; a reminder to keep trying until I can no longer.

On the underside of the lighthouse model, my father wrote a short passage, in cursive handwriting, on a small piece of lined stationary. It's taped to the bottom with heavy, wide clear tape. "This model was made by Basil Landry, 2001. There were a few people from my home village of Purcell's Cove who kept lighthouses for many years."

I love that Dad was part of my Artist in Residency application 11 years after his death.

My childhood home on Keefe Drive, like my father's homestead, looked out at a lighthouse — this one on the tip of McNab's Island — at the mouth of Halifax Harbour. We both grew up listening to a foghorn and seeing a beacon off in the distance. The chance to live and work right next to one, all alone for two weeks, was both exhilarating and a tad frightening. I had not lived alone for two decades, since before our daughter was born, in 1999, and before I had married, in 1995. I lived next door to the ocean from approximately 1970 to 1984. It had been 33 years since I had left Purcell's Cove.

What a gift the residency has been for me personally and creatively. The Port Bickerton Artist in Residency program entered its fifth year in 2018. I was the program's fourth recipient, and the first writer from Atlantic Canada to be invited to live and work on site.

I am eternally grateful. It's probably the closest I've ever come, since the early 1980s, to being that kid again.

The first night in Port Bickerton wasn't what I was expecting, and at the time, it felt unnerving.

That day was July 29, 2017.

THE LIGHT OF SOLITUDE

It was a foggy Friday afternoon on Nova Scotia's Eastern Shore. It's about a 226-kilometre drive from Halifax, along several roadways, to reach the lighthouse. The last two kilometres, you leave the paved road, in the small community of Port Bickerton, and drive down a narrow gravel and dirt laneway to the property. The entire site is called the Port Bickerton Lighthouse Beach Park. There are nearly four kilometres of hiking trails and several beaches to explore.

The afternoon of my arrival, the fog was so thick I had no clue the ocean was only a few metres away as I drove down the road towards the lighthouse. I could not see the Port Bickerton harbour, shoreline, or anything else, except the road immediately in front of my car. I later learned the lighthouse is situated on the "western extremity of Barachois Head" and marks the entrance to Port Bickerton Harbour.

The rugged shoreline and a few small beaches are on the immediate right driving into the site. The dense woods and a few bogs and ponds are on the opposite. There are no houses on the road into the lighthouse. In the summer and early fall, when the park buildings are open, and after the site volunteers go home for the day, you are completely alone, surrounded by woods, down a pitch-black road, two kilometres from the nearest human being. Even then, if you backtrack out, you are only met by a few houses where the Lighthouse Road begins. Have you ever lived in an isolated home in the woods — for two weeks — by yourself? Could you?

It was a little unnerving in the dead of night with no traffic, conversation, or television. There is a DVD player in the cottage. At night, I would read or watch old movies like the *Pink Panther* series, starring the late comedic genius, Peter Sellers.

They were a childhood favourite. My father and I would laugh until we cried watching Inspector Clouseau, the bumbling police inspector, played by Sellers. I know I watched those movies while at Port Bickerton so that Dad was somehow there with me, and so that I wouldn't feel alone.

LIGHTHOUSE ORIGINS

When you arrive at the end of the Lighthouse Road, there are three buildings on the site. The lightkeeper's cottage, which was built in the late 1950s, is situated on the left. It is available for rent by the week during high season, and whenever the artist in residence is not on site.

At the very end of the cul-de-sac is the automated lighthouse. "The most recent lighthouse, (circa 1960), the third in the series, was de-staffed and automated in 1988. Fisheries and Oceans Canada identified the Port Bickerton

Lighthouse site as surplus to its needs and no longer required in the mid-1990s. Ownership of the property was subsequently transferred to the Municipality of the District of St. Mary's in October 2012," according to the lighthouse website.

Just before the automated lighthouse, also on the ocean side of the road, sits the Nova Scotia Lighthouse Interpretive Centre, which was founded and opened in 1997. It is on the exact footprint of the original lighthouse. "The very first lighthouse, the contract went out in 1900. The contract was given to a man by the name of Emery Taylor from Stillwater…it was [for] five-hundred dollars," said Dale Kaiser, a senior guide at the Interpretive Centre during the 2017 season.

Dale's uncle, Harvey Taylor, was the Port Bickerton Lighthouse keeper from 1937 to 1940. Dale said he grew up next door to Harvey. He now lives in his late uncle's former home. Both men served in the Canadian military.

"My father got involved in volunteering there (at the lighthouse). I just carried on. I always had an interest in this place. I can see it from my bedroom window. Ever since I was a little kid, I always wanted to be the lighthouse keeper. That was my dream. By the time I got out of the military, there was no such thing as a lighthouse keeper," said Dale.

The senior guide said construction of the first lighthouse took approximately one year. Historical documents indicate the first beacon shone on the property in 1902.

It was a kerosene lamp.

"Someone would physically have to light it every night. At the time, there were no residents here. The first lighthouse keeper had to row out or walk along the beach to get down here. There were no working parts to the lighthouse. It was run by a single, one wick kerosene lamp. It could be seen for seven miles [on a clear night]," Dale said.

The original lighthouse was destroyed by fire in the 1920s. "That was here until 1924, when it became unstable, toppled over, and burnt. The kerosene lamp tipped over and caused a fire…there was some sort of temporary light put here until 1930. In 1930, they built this particular building right here," explained Dale, while sitting in the second lighthouse, now the home of the interpretive centre.

The second lighthouse beacon also operated via kerosene from 1930 to 1962. A major improvement had occurred with the introduction of a Fresnel lens in the tower, to help magnify the light as far as possible.

A second fire swept near the area in 1947.

Dale said a forest fire, which started in Fishermans Harbour, burned its way up to the lighthouse. "So, the fishermen, they had to get together with the bucket brigade and start pouring water on the roof. There was no electricity at the time, no pumps…It was such an intense fire, sparks would keep lighting the roof on fire."

The men from the community saved the second lighthouse. One of the hiking trails on the lighthouse grounds is called "The Fire Barren," where visitors can view the long-term effects of a decades-old forest fire.

In 1962, Dale said a third fire occurred, in the foghorn building next to the lighthouse. "The lightkeeper was peeling paint with a blow torch and some kerosene had seeped down…they managed to save the foghorn itself. The only thing they lost were the fuel tanks. That building burned down, but the lighthouse was untouched… As the result of that fire, the government recommended that there be no more kerosene-operated lighthouses, so in 1962, they built the cement lighthouse next door and [it] was completely run by electricity and automated, including the foghorn. Up until 1962, the foghorn [also] ran off oil," Dale explained.

That lighthouse is still operational today. "Everything was fully automated by 1987, and that's the year the last lighthouse keepers left this station," he said.

The rugged, mysterious, and isolated property is managed and preserved by the Port Bickerton and Area Planning Association, a group of dedicated volunteers, and their supporters, who outshine the pristine scenery. The hospitality I was shown during my two-week stay was truly heartwarming and typical of the people of the East Coast.

I could not have been made to feel more at ease by the husband and wife team of Wilda Kaiser and Bruce George, my welcoming committee. Wilda is the director of the Port Bickerton Artist in Residence program. Bruce is on the property's board of directors. Wilda, who is a painter, was also the Artist in Residence during the summer of 2017 at the nearby historic Sherbrooke Village, about a 30-minute drive from the lighthouse and Port Bickerton, in the town of Sherbrooke, Nova Scotia.

A group of concerned community members saved the lighthouse property from what would have been a disastrous fate. "In response to plans by the federal government in the mid-1990s to transform the lighthouse site into a toxic waste dump, concerned citizens in Port Bickerton formed the non-profit, all-volunteer Port Bickerton And Area Planning Association (PBAPA) to ensure the continued existence and protection of the lighthouse and the surrounding property," according to lighthouse website.

It is a gift to all Nova Scotians, and to the site's many visitors from around the world, that it has been rescued.

The evening of my first night, after Wilda, Bruce, and the two guides had left for the day, I was alone.

IN APPRECIATION OF ISOLATION

It was night one.

I sat on a small sofa inside the living room and could see the beacon revolving in the lighthouse. The foghorn sounded. I could not see beyond the parking lot. I thought to myself, "What the hell have you gotten yourself into?"

Despite the fact I was slightly on edge, I wanted to explore the grounds near the cottage, lighthouse, and interpretive centre. A foghorn is remarkably loud when you are standing near a working lighthouse. There is a sign posted on the building's exterior warning people to wear ear protection.

While walking in the fog, not far from the lighthouse, I turned to look back towards the cottage.

I was not alone.

In the short brush, near the edge of a grassy field, stood a massive deer. It looked startled to see me. I was certainly frightened for a second by it. People who follow me on social media know I have many deer who visit our Halifax area home on a regular basis. I always feel like my late parents send them along as a sign.

I watched it watching me.

Eventually it wandered away into the woods. I never saw it again. I found it comforting to have seen it that first night, when I wasn't so sure how I felt about being alone and isolated for two weeks straight.

The isolation is part of the gift of the experience.

"A lot of people would say to me, 'Why do you come down here? There's nothing down here.' Then I'd say, 'Now you're starting to get it, right?'" said Dale, who, as an amateur historian, speaks reverently about the area's history.

I came to appreciate the isolation — but it took days. In all honesty, it took about a week.

I wrote. I read. I edited.

Repeat.

I was highly productive during my residency.

I walked and hiked every day. I took photos and explored trails. I searched for beach glass on the property's shoreline and on the beaches that dot the Lighthouse Road. I walked the road to its end and back, four kilometres, hoping to catch a glimpse of otters or beavers in one of the ponds. There were plenty of butterflies, sea gulls, terns, and fishing boats. I listened to the waves and surf. I never listened to music outside of the cottage.

The terns were a draw for one important guest at the lightkeeper's cottage in the weeks leading up to my stay. According to my hosts, Canada's first female astronaut, Dr. Roberta Bondar, stayed in the small home while studying the roseate tern, a species of seabird found only in a handful of places in Canada, including an area near the lighthouse. An autographed photo of Dr. Bondar lay on a table in the cottage when I arrived. I kept it near my workspace as a source of inspiration.

MYSTERIES ABOUND

The people I met during my residency were also an inspiration; they and their stories. The tales they told are mesmerizing.

Eileen Beiswanger said she saw odd lights on the beach and shoreline near the lighthouse before there was even a road into the property. She cannot explain exactly what she saw, heard, or experienced — on numerous occasions — in or around the Port Bickerton Lighthouse, when her family were the lightkeepers from 1956 to 1961.

Eileen said they would see the lights and think that visitors were coming. They would tidy up and go outside to greet their guests, only to find no one there. Eileen said she also saw lights while walking on the shoreline, both heading into town, and while heading back to the lighthouse. "Different times before we had a road, I'd go up the beach before dark and start back after dark and I'd meet lights coming on the beach. And, I never ever met anybody. It was creepy, I'll tell ya."

Eileen and her late husband, Harold, were the keepers of the light, before automation, when kerosene lamps at Port Bickerton still lit the night sky. Eileen is one of the few remaining original Port Bickerton lightkeepers still alive, as of this writing in February 2018.

Harold's father, Irvin Beiswanger, was also a lighthouse keeper, with his wife Catherine, from 1940 to 1956. Eileen and Harold took over from them. The younger couple eventually had four children: Elaine, Michael, Clark, and Wynn. All six of them lived inside the lighthouse. According to a document hanging in the interpretive centre, there were eight families who were lightkeepers at Port Bickerton, for 87 years, from 1901 to 1988.

Eileen and Harold were the fifth family who lived there, when travel was very challenging. "There was a path partially through the woods and partially on the beach. But normally, everybody who wanted to walk to or from the lighthouse here usually waited until low tide."

Eileen, who worked at the nearby fish plant, said her late husband saw a need for a road when they started to have children — so he built one himself. "We decided to buy an old car and cut the back off it, so we could haul gravel in it. I could use it to drive to the fish plant, and he could use it to carry gravel in… and [we used it to] travel up and down the beach because our good car, the car we used to go into town and everything, we wouldn't [want] to destroy it over the rocks."

Eileen said her husband literally floated the car over from the community on oil barrels. He wanted to use the reassigned car as a makeshift truck, with a homemade box on the back, during the road construction. Harold was a determined man with great ingenuity and work ethic.

Eileen said it was strangely commonplace for framed pictures to fall from the lighthouse walls for no apparent reason. They were never damaged. The family would pick them up and re-hang them. This would happen in varying rooms, and on different occasions.

Dale Kaiser said he experienced the same thing.

Dale said he was talking to Keith Horton, who is one of the directors, while the two were sitting in the two rocking chairs in the Beiswanger's former bedroom. A picture of the original lighthouse, which hangs near the entrance, suddenly fell off the wall and the glass shattered. A large nail that held it there was still firmly in place. There was no obvious reason for the picture to come crashing down. Dale said this happened about a year before my visit, in September 2016, after the student guides had left for the season and had gone back to school.

The senior guide also said there were occasions that items on display in the gift shop would be moved off the shelves and swept across the floor into a corner near a doorway. The staff would find the unbroken items once they came back to re-open the lighthouse the next day. Dale showed me the area where the gifts were moved. There is no vent or windows which would have allowed a breeze or gust of wind to move them during the night. The storm door was firmly closed. It's a tiny room with a few shelves and a cash register. Most of the items for sale are locally produced products.

> DK: "I don't believe in ghosts."
> JL: "That (movement of displays) doesn't really phase you?"
> DK: "No, but I have no explanation for it either."

Another senior lighthouse guide and volunteer, Donna Blackie, said she would turn on small battery-operated lanterns and place them on an old organ, which sits near the two rocking chairs in the former bedroom. Donna said when she would leave the room, and later come back, the lanterns had somehow been turned off. There was no one else near, or with, her. She checked the batteries and they were fine. This happened several times, and without explanation.

Eileen and I sat in those same rocking chairs for our interview. Nothing unusual happened during it, or at any point during my residency. I found it slightly disappointing, as the unexplainable is fascinating. I did take what they told me to heart. I did not wander around alone at night.

Why push your luck?

Eileen also spoke of loud noises her family would hear up on the top floor of the lighthouse. "We could be sitting here, and remember, we had no television, and things would be quiet, and all of a sudden, it would sound like an airplane, or maybe, say horses, upstairs in the tower, or cows, or anything, making this noise up in the tower. And, you'd go to the tower and there wouldn't be a sight of anything."

They never heard the noises in the daytime.

Dale said he has also experienced the auditory mystery while working on site in 2015 and 2016: "…it sounded like people walking around [up] there, but there was no one there."

> JL: "And your immediate reaction was — what?"
> DK: "What am I doing down here? (laughs). I've never been here by myself."

> JL: *"Would you stay here overnight by yourself?"*
> DK: *"I think so."*
> JL: *"You're not so sure."*
> DK: *"No."*

In another odd occurrence, Eileen said when her family lived there, she was upstairs emptying the bedpans, as there was no indoor plumbing. She placed the waste into a pot to take it downstairs to empty into the outhouse. She said she lost her footing at the top of a steep staircase. There are several sets of stairs inside the lighthouse leading up to the tower. This first set is on the main floor, near the entrance, and the last one she would have had to manoeuvre before heading outside.

There are 15 steps. Donna Blackie counted them for us while Eileen told me her stories.

"I had my boots on, they were wet on the bottom." Eileen said. She slid down the entire set of stairs, without spilling a drop from the full waste bucket. "I just went airborne and I went off the top step and landed on my feet at the bottom and never spilled a drop. I didn't fall. I was still on my feet at the bottom," said Eileen.

> JL: *"You don't associate anything happening [in the lighthouse] with something frightening. You associate it with something caring?"*
> EB: *"Protective; I think something was protecting me."*

DAILY LIFE AT THE LIGHTHOUSE

Eileen had another much more serious incident during childbirth, a close call inside of the lighthouse. A doctor was called to the scene. "Before there was any road, I hemorrhaged after one of my children. The doctor had to be brought in a boat, the doctor from Moser River. Our local doctor in Sherbrooke was gone off fishing or something."

Eileen was transported off the site via boat.

She said they never owned a phone the entire time they lived and worked at the lighthouse. Their only means of communication was a ship-to-shore radio. Eileen and her husband, as part of their duties, had to report twice a day to Camperdown, Nova Scotia radio to report the weather conditions. The radio was kept in the kitchen. It was their only method of communication until the 1960s. Eileen was usually the one who did the weather reports because, "They always asked for me because I had the best voice," she said, laughing.

Not long after Eileen's medical emergency, her husband started the road construction. "He was determined. We talked about it. Because after I hemorrhaged, we had children to go to school and everything...The men from the community helped him."

The kitchen, where radio traffic was background sound, was the epicenter of life at the lighthouse. "We mostly lived in the kitchen. We had good food, always."

They kept ducks, chickens, and hens, "So we had our own eggs," she said. They had a cow to milk, which was one of Eileen's many chores and responsibilities. They also typically owned a pig. When it was foggy, she couldn't dry their laundry outdoors, so she ran cables or a line inside the lighthouse to hang their clothes. She used cloth diapers for all four children. They had no electricity, so they used a gas washer, and a combination wood and coal stove to cook. There was a coal furnace. The coal came in bags via boat and was stored in the basement. They worked by kerosene lamps and had one Coleman lantern. Electricity was not hooked up until 1966.

It was hard, relentless work; a job that never ended. Eileen and her family were dedicated to keeping souls safe, and, in return, they never had serious injury befall them, despite the odd occurrences and close calls.

"I love the water. I like the ocean. I love it here," she said.

Eileen and her husband would take their coffee in the morning at breakfast. Tea was reserved for afternoons. She also made homemade spirits, and one crock of fermenting dandelion wine almost scared an assistant lighthouse to death.

Manning the lighthouse meant a 24-hour watch, requiring her husband, as the primary keeper of the light, to have an assistant, who also lived with them. Eileen said she was fermenting the dandelion wine in a crock behind the fridge, where no one could see it. It was very quiet in the lighthouse. The wine was making a "plopping" noise as it aged. The pressure inside the container would force the oranges and other ingredients to bang up against the sides of the pot. Eileen said the unexplained sounds frightened the assistant lightkeeper. "We got up one morning and the old guy said, 'I'm not staying here any damn longer. This place is haunted. I'm not coming back tonight. I'm getting outta here!'"

The batch of wine was potent in more ways than one. "It was good. It had lots of kick to it. We didn't drink much, but we were always very generous with the company," Eileen said.

> JL: "Your assistant lightkeeper thought this place is haunted. Do you think it's haunted?"
> EB: "No. The only thing I think is haunted are the lights we saw on the beach. I think there may be some ghosts between the main community and here. But this building, I don't think is haunted…Pictures fell of the walls all kinds of times. Those are very good ghosts. It's harmless ghosts."
> JL: "So you definitely think there are ghosts here?"
> EB: "Oh, definitely. Those type of ghosts aren't going to harm anyone. They're protective ghosts."
> JL: "Why do you think they are here?"
> EB: "Because of the different things that have happened; the shipwrecks."

Historical accounts of shipwrecks are found in logs inside the interpretive centre. One discusses a large schooner, *The Erby*, running aground in dense fog on a nearby island.

All 41 men were spared.

"I don't know if I believe in ghosts. Stuff you don't understand, you can't dismiss it. Maybe there's a lot of things you don't want an explanation for," concluded Dale Kaiser.

POSTSCRIPT:

My two-week residency was unforgettable because of the efforts of Wilda Kaiser, Bruce George, Don and Ardeth Dodge, Dale Kaiser, Donna Blackie, and Eileen Beiswanger. I would also like to thank the other members of the Port Bickerton and Area Planning Association/Board of Directors, the student guides, lighthouse grounds crew, and community members who I met during my stay and community author event.

It was a career highlight to live among you and to learn about your community's riveting history.

There is something truly compelling about Port Bickerton, its lighthouses, stunning park grounds, and the volunteers. These Nova Scotians have become our modern-day *keepers of the light* — by collectively helping to preserve an important and fascinating chapter of our Maritime history.

They, and their predecessors, are an integral part of what I consider to be *My Nova Scotia Home*.

Janice Landry is an award-winning writer, journalist, and author who has been a life-long storyteller. Janice's fifth book is slated for potential release during fall 2019. Silver Linings *is partially dedicated to her late mother, Theresa Landry, who died during its writing, in late summer 2018.*

A dedicated wife, mother, and daughter, Janice's late father was a veteran Halifax firefighter of 31 years. A Canadian Medal of Bravery recipient, Capt. Basil (Baz) Landry, M.B., died in 2006, before Janice's first book was published. She now dedicates much of her energy to honouring Baz's work and memory, by supporting our country's first responders, emergency personnel, members of the military, and their loved ones — through her writing and speaking engagements.

That passion has led to her receiving a 2017 national Media Award for her efforts. Janice is also honoured to have won the prestigious 2018 Canadian Resiliency Award for her book, The Legacy Letters. *Please visit: janicelandry.ca.*

LETTER TO CANADA

Lesley Choyce

DEAR CANADA,
First off, let me thank you for taking me in. In 1978, I was a restless and rebellious young man living in New Jersey looking for some other place in the world where I could feel more at home. I'd spent time in Nova Scotia already and it seemed like a haven from much of what I thought was wrong with the world: crime, corruption, consumerism, pollution, blind patriotism, and paranoia.

And it was just that. And to some degree still is. But I was an idealist then and today I am more of a realist. We've been infected here over the years by those things on my list. But we haven't been overrun by them. So, we'll need to be vigilant.

In order to live in Nova Scotia, I had discovered in the mid-1970s, I had to become an immigrant to Canada. Canadian immigration turned me down for two years running and I couldn't figure out why Canada didn't want me. I was young, educated, fairly bright (in a goofy head-in-the-clouds sort of way), ambitious, and healthy. In fact, it looked fairly certain that Canada would never let me in. I simply wasn't wanted.

The explanation was that I would be taking a job away from a Canadian. The rule at the time was this: I had to be able to prove that I had a job skill that no other Canadian possessed. At the time, I had schooled myself in low-tech "alternative" energy: passive solar, wind, biomass, and such. I even had a job offer from a small Nova Scotian firm.

Nope. Canada is not for you, the form letter said.

But I was persistent and eventually was granted an interview at the consulate in Manhattan — it was in the Exxon Building if I remember correctly. I even got a haircut and borrowed some shineable shoes for the event. I was trying that hard.

The consulate official who interviewed me kept asking me why a young, educated, fairly bright, ambitious, and healthy young man would want to move to Nova Scotia, for god sakes. It seemed he viewed the province as a backwater, lacklustre place but admitted he'd never been there. I gave him my reasons and he still shook his head. But, as he stared at my rather thick file of documents and letters that had been building up for two years, he finally just threw up his hands, admitted he still didn't get it and signed the paper, saying I would be allowed to move to Canada. (He still thought I should reconsider the Nova Scotia part.)

And that was it. I was in. I became a landed immigrant and a few years later took a test to see if I was worthy of citizenship. One of the questions asked was this: "What level of government collects the garbage?" I nailed the quiz and found myself swearing allegiance to the queen. Really? Canada has a queen? What the heck.

And it all worked out rather nicely.

Like so many other immigrants I had this wonderfully positive view towards the country and the people. I still have it today.

So thank you, Canada. You reluctantly took me in, allowed me to write books and travel the country, gave me a teaching job, provided a damn fine place to raise kids. (You mean the country pays you to have children? Well, yeah, sort of. Holy Mackerel!) You did that and more for me. Thank you, Canada.

Okay, I'm gushing. It's not exactly what I meant to say.

For the record, Canada, let me say the whole Canada 150 thing seems a bit, um, artificial. There's evidence that early peoples were living in Debert, for example, well over ten thousand years ago. Let's start planning for Nova Scotia's eleven-thousandth birthday now, maybe. That would be a blast. And I am well aware that many other Indigenous Peoples across this vast land can trace their ancestors even further back. In April of this year, for example, archaeologists on Triquet Island in BC found artifacts from a village that was 14,000 years old.

Just a few years before 1867, most Nova Scotians, including Joe Howe, were opposed to confederation but through some fancy political finagling on the part of Charlie Tupper the province was signed up anyway. And that's probably been a good move, which prevented this fair province from being absorbed by the Americans and turning it into something, well, much more American.

But today there is still a lot to celebrate. The whole 150 thing may be a bit of a gimmick, I admit. I'd rather not fight it, however, but find other more significant ways to give the true ancestors of this land the respect they deserve.

In 1995, Cynthia Good, editor at Penguin Books, asked me to contribute to a book she was putting together called *If You Love This Country* along with other contributors such as Joe Clark, Peter C. Newman, Stompin' Tom Connors and Roberta Bondar. Around that time there was a good chance that Quebec was going to leave Canada and this book was a kind of communal plea to Quebecers to stay with us, please.

I wrote about my recent author tour of the lower North Shore of Quebec from Sept Isle to Blanc Sablon. Early on, I discovered that the farther away I travelled from the urban core of Canada (Toronto, Ottawa, etc.), the more Canadian everything felt. That was especially true of Harrington Harbour, Aylmer Sound and Tete-a'la Baleine. But it was in a motel room in Blanc Sablon, just shy of the Labrador border, where my Quebecois host sneaked into my room at night while I was sleeping and positioned a stuffed seven-foot black bear in an attack posture.

When I awoke in the morning, there was the threatening bear seemingly ready to pounce. It was a joke, of course, and a good one. And everyone at the motel who knew about the prank were hoping I (a "southerner") would wake up with an ear-piercing scream and scared out of my pyjamas. But, for some reason, I didn't. In the end, however, I felt rather privileged that someone was willing to go to so much unique trouble to provide me with a truly Canadian experience.

Both then and now, I must say, I like Quebecers and most everything about *la belle province* and sure don't want them to leave the party — which is you, Canada.

Pierre Trudeau was prime minister when I moved to Canada in 1978. Justin Trudeau is prime minister today as I write this. That year, Justin was just seven years old. Donald Trump is now president of the country where I was born. Donald Trump was a young lad of 32 hard at work amassing his fortune as I was moving north to get out of the rat race. The world moves forward in strange and mysterious ways.

Today, I continue to reflect on a young man's decision to go north when many of his peers back in 1978 were going south — because it was warmer — or staying put in New York — because that was where the money was, or going west to California — because that was where the action was.

I reckon I went north to Nova Scotia, Canada, because that was where the money wasn't and because that was where the so-called action wasn't as well. And hey, I was young and tough, and so what if it was a little colder in the winter? Once I planted my flag in Canada, I knew this was where I was meant to be.

I like the benign patriotism we have. I like the kindness currently shown to refugees — even though the immigration process had roughed me up a little. I like the adventures and misadventures that Canada has provided for me, the experiences that have help shape who I am.

To that end, a list. I know I am a Canadian because:
1. I have gone hiking and found myself hopelessly lost in a Northwest Territories wilderness with a veritable tornado of black flies descending on me from above;
2. No one showed up to my poetry reading in Lloydminster, Saskatchewan because Professional Outlaw Wrestling was in town that night;

3. I have surfed in Nova Scotia in January until the salt water froze on my forehead and my jaw muscles were so frozen I couldn't speak;
4. School kids on Vancouver Island dared me to kiss a 25-centimetre long banana slug on the forest floor near Tofino and I did;
5. During a February blizzard, I walked down a rural country road with my kids tied to a rope so they wouldn't blow away;
6. School kids across all Newfoundland addressed me as "sir" — except for the one feisty lad who preferred to address me as "Shaggy;"
7. I've raced the tides of Fundy across a muddy sea floor with water lapping at my feet and shoes sucking red mud with every step;
8. I holed up alone in a motel room in Sudbury one dark stormy night, feeling like the loneliest person on the planet;
9. I watched a man in Happy Valley, Labrador try to bring on spring by using a lawnmower to break up the deep snow in his front yard in May;
10. I sat in the Saskatoon Bus Terminal at 8 a.m. on a Sunday morning watching old grizzled men eat toast and bacon while I wrote a poem;
11. I dutifully carried an umbrella over my head on a perfectly clear morning in Banff to bluff a posse of elk into thinking I was bigger than them; and
12. I once woke up near the shores of the Strait of Belle Isle with a bear in my bedroom.

So, on this, my 39th year in this northern land, I reflect on these and many more images of your multifaceted self, Canada.

And by the way, thanks for the memories. And have a good one, eh?

Sincerely,

Lesley Choyce
Lawrencetown Beach, Canada
July 1, 2017

Lesley Choyce is the author of more than 90 books of literary fiction, short stories, poetry, creative nonfiction, and young adult novels. He runs Pottersfield Press and has worked as editor with a wide range of Canadian authors. He has edited a number of literary anthologies and hosted several television shows over the years.

He has taught Creative Writing at Dalhousie and other universities for more than 30 years and has acted as mentor to many emerging writers during that time. He has won The Dartmouth Book Award, The Atlantic Poetry Prize, and The Ann Connor Brimer Award. He has also been shortlisted for the Stephen Leacock Medal, The White Pine Award, The Hackmatack Award,

The Canadian Science Fiction and Fantasy Award, and The Governor General's Award. He was a founding member of the 1990s Spoken Word rock band, The SurfPoets. He surfs year round in the North Atlantic.

His website is at lesleychoyce.com.

This item originally appeared in the Halifax Chronicle Herald.

A HOMECOMING

Ian Colford

"NO, POP. YOU DID THAT ONE."

He's reaching a finger toward the painting. My parental alarm bell goes off. I tense, almost yell at him to stop. But I choke it down, force myself into that state of false calm with which I'm becoming very familiar. It's his painting. He can touch it if he wants. I'm only glad there are no museums or art galleries on our itinerary today.

"Really?" he says. "I did?" Fingering the surface.

"Yeah. Look. See the name in the corner? That's you. William Clifford."

He leans over and squints, and I realize I don't know where his glasses are.

"You got your glasses around here somewhere, Pop?"

It's a small apartment: kitchenette, a tiny sitting room and an even smaller bedroom. I leave him in the front hall gawking at the painting and check the obvious places: bathroom counter, bedside table, dresser.

When I get back 15 seconds later empty handed he's saying, "I was really good, wasn't I?"

"You were, Pop. You were. Any idea where your glasses are?"

"When did I do this?"

"Um, I'm not sure. Twenty years ago, maybe?" The painting's been hanging in the same place for years. He walks by it every day.

"I should get my paints out again," he says, nodding, assessing. He strokes his chin and for a moment his eyes clear. He looks like his old self, the wise professor, the font of advice and reason. "I wonder why I stopped. All that stuff's probably still down in the basement."

"Pop, your glasses? Any idea —"

"Oh, don't worry about the glasses. Your mother will find them."

My mother died last week. A stroke. That's the reason I've come back from Toronto.

"Well, we should go, don't you think?" There's a small round stain on the front of his jacket. A wet spot, and it's wet because he's drooling. The last time I tried to wipe his mouth he almost punched me. I pull out a couple of tissues and push them into his hand. Automatically, without acknowledging what I've done, he bunches them into a wad and swipes his lips dry.

He opens the door and I'm about to follow him into the hall but pause in front of the painting. It's a typical Nova Scotia scene: a craggy coastal view with high white water crashing against grey rocks. The sky is a mass of brooding, angry cloud, charcoal black over a yellow haze. The horizon is fogbound, invisible. As the water foams and churns a few birds circle above, serenely unaffected. You can see the wind, if that's possible. When he did this he had just entered his knife-painting stage. He completed these paintings in no time, slathering on the paint in broad, heavy strokes, layering the colours thickly one on top of the other, giving his pictures density and heft, capturing the raw ferocity of nature, leaving the energy he put into it palpable on the canvas. My father was always emotionally reticent, thinking before speaking, editing himself constantly, and I remember being astounded the first time he showed this painting to us — me, Mom, and my sister Jackie. The passion it expressed was out of character. He seemed embarrassed by it, by the part of his private self it exposed. But it might be the best thing he ever did.

"Hold up, Pop."

He stops halfway down the hall and waits. It's a bland, narrow passageway, rank with food smells that linger in the closed space. Despite the best efforts of custodial staff, there are spill stains on the carpet and walls. On Saturday morning I can hear television voices blaring behind several apartment doors, but we don't meet any of the other residents. At the front desk the young woman on duty nods solemnly.

The Viceroy is an assisted-living facility. My parents moved in three years ago, before my father's dementia had begun to seriously manifest itself. Jackie and I had already talked with them about selling the house, but we'd done it gently, expressing no urgency, simply to plant the seed, strategizing the conversation beforehand to suggest that such a move was still a few years down the road. They were both closer to 80 than 70, not young by any means, but from our perspective neither of them seemed old. They went for walks every day. They both still drove and there had been no mishaps. But we'd noticed some physical decline and mental confusion, some difficulty keeping the house in order and the refrigerator free of expired condiments, mouldy cheese and the musky decay of neglected fruits and vegetables.

My mother had stumbled on the stairs and sprained her wrist. Still, no real cause for concern. But I was taking a teaching job in Toronto and moving my family there, and Jackie has three kids and a demanding career as a loans officer at Scotiabank. We couldn't necessarily be there for them at a moment's notice. The conversation seemed necessary, and we expected resistance. So we were surprised when they accepted our concerns as valid, and astonished when, a month later, they found a realtor (the son of a family friend) and had him list the property. I can still remember the first-time shock of seeing a For Sale sign on the front lawn of the house where I'd grown up and fighting back tears.

Later on the truth came out, after the house was sold and the move to the Viceroy complete. Over lunch — at the Athens on Quinpool Road; my father was sitting next to me — my mother confessed that Pop had been losing his grip for a while, but had become adept at covering his lapses, and that she had agreed to keep his condition secret for as long as possible. But the disease progressed more rapidly than expected, and after several heated discussions, she'd persuaded him that the stress and worry was too great and that assisted living was the only move that made sense. My father smiled and nodded over his spaghetti and meatballs. He didn't deny a thing. In our family, concealing weakness had always been a point of pride.

Now my mother was gone and it was clear that my father needed closer monitoring than staff at The Viceroy could provide.

It's one of those bright, clear, cool October days that Nova Scotia is famous for. On days like this you can see for miles. On days like this anything seems possible.

My assignment is simple: keep my dad occupied while Jackie oversees the move of his things into an "enhanced care" facility called Greystone Arms. In the past week, I've grown familiar and almost comfortable with concepts that at first seemed alien and repugnant. Assisted living is one thing. The Viceroy provides its residents with an independent residential space, but there's also a cafeteria and a communal social area. Staff intervention is minimal and my parents, while enjoying freedom of movement, remained responsible for keeping their apartment clean, for doing their laundry and taking care of their own shopping. There's an in-house doctor and nurse, but residents have the option of visiting their family physician if they so choose. The building is in the south end of downtown, minutes away on foot from two grocery stores, two shopping malls, a public garden, and countless other urban amenities. There are a dozen bus routes that go everywhere. I toured the place when they first moved in and remember thinking, *I could live here.*

Greystone Arms is a whole other deal. They don't use the term "nursing home" anymore, but that's what it is, and it's likely the last stop for my poor confused father. At Greystone he'll occupy a single room with a television and private bath. He'll sleep in a hospital-style bed. His diet will be regulated, his meds monitored, and his movements restricted to one floor of the building. He will engage in "activities" the like of which would probably drive a four-year-old insane with boredom, but since his short-term memory is pretty much gone, will seem fresh and new with each recurrence.

Luckily, he's exhibited none of the aggression common in dementia patients, so for now will have unfettered access to other residents and the common facilities on his floor, and supervised access to the park-like grounds surrounding the building. In fact, as the disease has progressed, he's grown increasingly trusting and docile, accepting everything that's being done on his behalf without comment. But the doctor has warned us that this can change in a heartbeat, and that staff are trained to watch for shifts in mood and personality that might signal the acceleration of the downward spiral.

He gets in the rental car and doesn't ask where we're going. I swing down to Water Street and head toward the Macdonald Bridge.

It seemed inevitable that today's excursion would take us along the North Shore, in the direction of villages like Porters Lake, Gaetz Brook and Petpeswick. My father's family lived in those parts for generations — probably still live there, though we long ago lost contact with any relatives who might remain in those communities. A hundred years ago Pop's dad was a fisherman and subsistence farmer, among other things. In those days it was foolish to pretend that you could survive on the income from a single activity. You did whatever you had to in order to put food on the table. So my grandfather also hunted, worked as a carpenter, a logger, miner, well-digger, and occasional rum-runner, and did anything else that needed doing in a remote rural community populated by similarly multi-talented and resourceful men and women who were raising families and getting by on whatever they could pull out of the ground and the sea.

My memories of the old house where Pop grew up are vague, but it was solidly constructed by local craftsmen from local materials and provided the Clifford family with shelter from the cold for 80 years or more. We visited a few times when Jackie and I were very young. By that time, Granddad was dead and Pop had rented the place out to a family with several youngsters close to Jackie and me in age. I can't remember any of their names. The father kept pigs and fancied himself a butcher, but I think mostly he was a drunk. My last memory of the Clifford homestead is of a vacant, dusty, derelict property bearing the full weight of nearly a century of summers and winters, awaiting demolition to make way for a highway off-ramp.

Pop perks up after we pass through Dartmouth along route 107 and leave the city in the rear view.

There are a few wispy clouds hovering above us now. The four-lane highway rolls along without dramatic curves or inclines, placidly following the contours of the land. We climb modest hills and descend steeply into valleys, then ascend once again. We're too far from the coast to catch any more than the occasional glimpse of water, so there's not much to see except trees, but the autumn colours are ablaze and provide a stunning and welcome distraction. I notice that Pop now has his glasses on. I can only imagine that he pulled them out of his pocket at some point when I wasn't paying attention.

He's watching the scenery closely. The autumn foliage was always one of his favourite subjects. He must have produced hundreds of autumn scenes, brilliant with flaming reds, incandescent yellows, and luminous oranges. I remember reading the labels on his tubes of paints, marvelling at names that evoked exotic sun-drenched places and strange compounds: Burnt Umber, Burnt Sienna, Vermilion, Cadmium Yellow, Phthalo Blue, Titanium White.

"I know this place," he says.

The exit sign coming up on the right says Lake Echo.

"I thought you might," I say.

He turns to me then and asks, "Are we going home?"

I smile. "If you like."

He was always sensitive to the visual elements of his environment, to colour especially, and at odd moments — in the middle of a conversation about something else altogether — would comment on the angle of sunlight or point out how shadow gave depth to the scene in front of him. Years before retiring, he started carrying a camera with him, recording vistas that he would paint repeatedly for a decade or more. I don't know where his mind is now but he seems okay with what's happening. I had debated the wisdom of taking him somewhere familiar. If memories started crowding in on him, tumbling over one another, he could become agitated. Medications have blunted his emotions, but it seems unfair to keep short-changing him in this regard. In whatever time he has left, he should be allowed to feel something.

We drive for another 20 minutes or so before reaching the junction where the 107 highway ends and you have to turn either left or right on the old two-lane Route 7. This is where my own memories begin, but nothing looks like I remember it. The picture in my mind is of a sparsely populated settlement, mostly trees with houses and cottages dotting the landscape. But what I'm seeing is row after row of conjoined townhouses, a strip mall with a mini-mart and dry-cleaner, gas stations, a school, a playground behind a chain-link fence — all carved into what used to be untouched woodland. Other roads, also lined with houses, link into the main road on both sides and snake off into the distance. It's become a community of commuters. Pop doesn't seem bothered by the encroachment of urban development upon the rural domain of his ancestors, but I find it oddly troubling, though I realize I should have seen it coming. Not everyone who works in the city can afford to live in the city. In Toronto people travel for hours to and from their jobs. The city spreads its tentacles for miles in every direction. No surprise that here in Nova Scotia, Halifax and Dartmouth are doing the same.

Pop's tapping his fingers on the armrest, humming tunelessly, nothing that I can make sense of. Now that we're here I had thought he'd have more to say.

"Recognize anything?"

He shakes his head.

"Nothing?"

"I wonder where all the animals have gone," he says.

"Huh?" I don't know what he means. Maybe he's tired.

"Hey Pop, have you had enough sight-seeing? Do you want to head back?"

"Stop here!" He's shouting. "Stop, damn it!" Shifting around in the seat as we shoot past a gas-station-strip-mall combo.

"Okay, okay!"

The sign above the store entrance reads *Kwik Way* in prominent red letters against a yellow background. It doesn't look like much, but we're past it in an instant so I can't see what it is that's caught his eye.

He's upset, twisting himself in the seat, trying to look back the way we came and groaning from the effort. Along this stretch, houses and other structures line both sides of the highway. I pull into a church parking lot, swing the car around and back out on to the road.

"You okay, Pop?"

He doesn't answer, but when the *Kwik Way* comes into view he says, "Stop here."

I pull past the Petro Can and into the lot in front of the convenience store, and only then do I see what probably caught his attention. Attached to the *Kwik Way* — actually, part of the same structure — is another establishment featuring a single glass door and a display window about four feet square. Behind the window sits an unlikely, seemingly random and somewhat pathetic array of items: a glass jar filled with marbles, a collection of five green glass buoys still in their netting, a small wooden crate with several rusty tools and yellowed rolled-up papers sticking out of it, a small child's rocking horse.

Everything looks dusty and sun-bleached. Then I see the hand-carved wooden sign tacked to the shingles above the door with the word "Mullins" inscribed in black paint in a careless script, an afterthought it seems. But it comes back to me and I realize that I've been here before, many years ago, when Jackie and I were children and Mullins General Store was the only game in town, the place everyone went to stock up on whatever they needed: food, hardware, farm implements, cigarettes. If you wanted a fishing rod and bait, Mullins was the place to go. Antiques? Curtains? Furniture, new and used? Mullins had it all.

I can remember standing in front of the store on the wooden steps — there was a sheltered porch too, with a rocking chair and next to it an old barrel that was used as a table — sucking on one of those striped rock-candy sticks: the taste of it comes back to me, a cloying, overly sweet essence of citrus and berry. I remember the sensation of the candy in my mouth, crunching down on it and savouring the syrupy but immensely satisfying flavour burst that resulted, with its undercurrent of tartness.

Pop's pushing on the car door. I release the lock and he's out before I can switch off the engine.

"Hey, hold up a minute."

His other health problems have not seriously affected his mobility, which is a plus. But because he has a habit of wandering, he has to be watched at all times.

I hurry out of the car and get to the door to Mullins just ahead of him. A bell tinkles when I pull it open.

There's a step-up, but he manages this and, once inside, roughly shakes my hand off of his elbow as he lumbers forward, down a narrow aisle lined with tables crowded with items for sale and bins and boxes of various shapes and sizes. Bull in a china shop, like always.

"Careful, Pop." But he ignores me.

The arrangement is haphazard and any number of obstacles could trip him up. I almost go after him, but he stops and picks up what looks like an old oil lamp, puts that down and lifts the teacup that sits next to it.

Every kind of imaginable thing seems to be on display: lamps, clocks, all kinds of furniture for every room in the house, tools, mirrors, toys, paintings. There's a 1960s-style television, the top of the wooden case marked with overlapping moisture rings from numerous wet glasses. There's a guitar with no strings. There's one of those ancient wringer washers, the tub dented, the white paint pocked and rust-spattered. There's an old stereo console, the all-in-one style with the turntable, radio, and speakers built-in and storage for about a hundred LPs. There's a curio cabinet, every shelf crammed with cheap-looking knick-knacks and figurines.

I drift down the aisle opposite my father — whose attention is drawn to almost every object before his eyes — and try not to seem like I'm watching him. No sooner is he fascinated by one thing than he's dropped it and moved on to the next, exchanging a battered potato masher for a round brown-glass ashtray, and that for a small pillow embroidered on one side with a scene of a house and pine tree layered in snow and a poem or slogan on the other. He seems okay so I give myself a momentary reprieve and glance around. Overhead, two rows of fluorescent lights spray their stark white light over four long rows of creaky display tables crammed with items. Larger objects and furniture are backed against the wall or pushed into corners. We're the only customers in the store. The checkout counter is behind us, at the front, to the left of the door where we entered, staffed by a bored-looking girl with her nose buried in a book.

The linoleum floor is crumbling in places but it seems clean. Nothing smells bad exactly — no hint of rot or decay — but there is a pervasive mustiness that makes me think of old houses, closed windows, ancient dust, and trapped air.

Pop's moved on down the aisle. I back off to give him some space and take out my phone. I dial Jackie.

"Hey."

"How's it going?"

"Pretty much done," she says, and sighs. "There wasn't much to move. Most of it we threw away. It's sad, you know, doing this. Sadder even than when they moved out of the house. I'm trying not to think about how sad it is."

"I know. I'm sorry."

"Where are you?"

"Somewhere near Musquodoboit Harbour. He wanted to come into this antique shop."

"Well, watch out he doesn't buy more junk he won't have space for."

And with that I'm reminded of all the times Pop returned home from one of his buying expeditions — or, less often, an auction — rapturously displaying a trunk filled with treasures. Or crap, depending on your perspective.

We hang up. Pop and I can head back anytime. His new place will be ready when we get there.

He's still distracted by the variety and sheer number of objects, picking up and putting down. I watch for a minute and then head to the front of the store. The girl doesn't look up from her book, though I sense her posture stiffen as I approach. The book, I see now, is a school textbook. No one else has entered the store. I'm beginning to suspect that Mullins being empty of customers on a Saturday morning in October is not unusual.

"Good morning," she says, meets my gaze and smiles. She has the clear skin and straight teeth of someone with no bad habits. Blue eyes. Her glossy brown hair is braided down her back. She could be anywhere from 16 to 25. "Find anything you like?"

"I'm done, thanks. But if you don't mind," I say, jerking my head, "I'll wait here until he's had a look around. Shouldn't be too long."

I see her gaze shift to the back of the store, to the white-haired man fumbling with one object after another. Her brow wrinkles briefly.

"If he breaks anything I'll pay for it."

She smiles, still looking his way. "No worries."

"What are you studying?"

She hesitates — surprised perhaps at my interest — then lifts the book so I can read the cover: *Electrical Engineering for Non-Electrical Engineers*.

"Whoa!"

"Not what you expected?"

I shake my head, shrug. "Sorry. Just way beyond me. Science was never my thing."

She lowers the open book to the counter and rests her elbows on it. "You're a teacher?"

"Why do you say that?"

She shrugs. Her gaze drifts to the space beyond my shoulder where there are sounds of scuffling and some muttering. Something goes clunk. I resist the urge to turn.

"You're right. I teach history at University of Toronto."

She nods.

"In town to visit my dad."

She doesn't comment. Though she's still smiling, I sense her interest fade. I look down at my feet and the next minute or so passes awkwardly in silence.

Then Pop is standing behind me, right up against me in fact, almost breathing down my neck.

"Is Grant around?" he says, barking out the question.

"Sorry?"

"Pop, don't …"

"Grant Mullins. He owns the store."

"Not for a while …"

"Well, if you see him, tell him Bill Clifford came by asking."

She looks to me, baffled.

"My dad grew up around here," I tell her, raising my voice a bit so he won't interrupt. "Used to come in all the time when it was a general store."

"Thank you," he says, his tone icy with sarcasm. He's staring at me. I'm concerned for a moment that he might not know who I am.

"Sorry, Pop."

"We'll take these," he says, plunking his selections on the counter none too carefully: two framed paintings, one about a foot and a half square, the other a bit bigger.

Now he's patting his pockets, flustered. "Damn it. Where's my wallet?"

I touch his arm. "Don't worry, Pop. My treat." I stare him down. A second later I watch the belligerence melt away. This is replaced momentarily by confusion before a sort of cautious understanding takes over. He knows his wallet is in his pants pocket. It contains everything anyone would need to identify him, but only a small amount of cash and no credit or debit cards. "Remember?"

"Oh," he says. His shoulders slump as he calms. "Right. I forgot. Sorry."

All smiles, playing my role flawlessly, I pay for the paintings while he stands back, silent now. The girl rings them up with detached efficiency. Both paintings are crudely executed: oil or acrylic on board, framed in stock wooden frames. The smaller of the two depicts a harbour scene, with lobster traps piled on a wooden pier and in the background a few boats floating in the water, but there's no skill in the colour mix and the perspective is off. The other shows a white bungalow nestled amidst a bower of leafy green trees, smoke spiralling from the chimney, picket fence, car in the driveway, sun in the sky, cartoon family standing out front, hands linked in a chain. It's done in a naïve style that's closer to folk art than realism, but lacks the charm of the first and has none of the precision of the latter. I don't know why he wants them. His critiques of work he regarded as substandard, which these are, were always pitiless. But at this point, I'm not questioning anything.

"Thanks."

She follows us outside and watches as I steer Pop into the car and put the paintings in the trunk. She's thin and appears childish in an oversize blue shirt, jeans and brown lace-up work boots.

As I'm getting into the car she says, "He took me a bit by surprise."

"I'm sorry about that. He can be … abrupt."

"No. It's just that Grant Mullins was my grandfather." She brushes a stray hair away from her face. "I never knew him. He died before I was born. Thirty years ago it must be. But this was his store. It's not anything like it was."

"Not like I remember it from when I was a kid," I say. "That's for sure."

"I'll tell my dad you were here. Bill Clifford was it?"

"And I'm Andrew. Thanks."

She smiles, lowers her eyes and turns away. I hear the tinkle of the bell as she returns inside.

We set out again. I drive farther along the meandering highway, but there's nothing of significance to see, and it isn't long before I notice Pop's head nodding. Soon, I hear him softly snoring. I had thought we'd stop somewhere for lunch, but the brush with his past has left him exhausted.

I'm looking for a place to turn around when I spot a sign that says West Petpeswick Road. I take the turn and after a few moments follow a left turn down Clamshell Road. I'm desperate, I realize, for a glimpse of water. Clamshell Road skirts the head of Petpeswick Inlet. I haven't given these places a single thought for years, but I don't even have to strain my memory for it all to come back. Where the trees thin and road begins to bend: this is where the water emerges into view. Pop sleeps on. There are houses along this stretch, but I pull off the road, get out of the car and wander down an empty driveway and across what is obviously someone's lawn.

The scene is unassuming: a small grey house on a flat patch of stony earth and sparse grass that slopes toward the shore, a rusty swing set, a picnic table, a few trees. But I didn't come here expecting anything spectacular. The water is flat and untroubled and provides a true reflection of the sky, which I notice has turned overcast. There's a winter chill in the air. I've missed this, the tranquility of empty time and space, of seconds ticking by unhurriedly with nothing to distinguish one from the next. The only sound: the lapping of water against stones. I'm looking at ocean water, but the inlet extends about three miles southeast from where I'm standing before widening at the mouth.

I miss this place more than I can say. My Toronto life is eventful, often frantic, and deeply satisfying. You can't escape the commotion. We drive north sometimes, into what my wife calls the outback, but there are always so many cars, so many people bringing the city, its anxieties and urgencies and endless demands with them. I do it myself. I've done it today, here, right this minute. I feel the tug. I'm where I want to be, but everything I left behind has followed me to this patch of ground on the head of Petpeswick Inlet. I can't disconnect. I'm not sure if I want to.

I get in the car, swing it around. We head back to the city. Pop has settled into a twitchy slumber. In 45 minutes, I'm pulling into the sprawling lot of Greystone Arms.

The transition goes more smoothly than I'd hoped. I'm fully cognizant of the subterfuge we've employed today and expect some pushback, but Pop accepts his new circumstances with a kind of steely resignation and without much curiosity. His room is simple and private and beige, with a chest of drawers, a sliding-door closet, comfy recliner, flat-screen television. The crashing waves painting is prominent on the wall next to the only window, which offers a view of a carefully manicured garden, leaf-strewn today. Standing in the doorway of his new residence, stooped and looking somehow reduced, he acknowledges the ascetic prospect before him with a quick nod. Jackie takes his arm and leads him down the hallway to the dining room and common room for movies, reading, and games. My stomach feels hollowed out by the forced lilt in her voice, the false brightness and phoney cheer.

Then I remember the two new paintings, still in the trunk of the car.

I dawdle in the parking lot, take out my phone in order to look busy and struggle with the guilt and second-guessing I thought I was prepared for. I try to convince myself that it's not so bad. The place is clean and modern and the people friendly and competent. He'll get great care and all the support he needs. But the truth is that it's depressing. No one would want to stay here if they had a choice.

When I return, the crashing waves painting is on the floor, propped against the wall. Pop is leaning back in his recliner. Jackie stands over him, her thin lips pressed together. There's a nurse hovering in the background, pretending to fiddle with something beside the bed.

"Andrew!" he says. "I told Jackie where we went today. Good, you brought them."

He pulls himself out of the recliner, surprisingly nimble. Jackie stretches her arms toward him, but he's on his feet, grabbing the paintings out of my hands.

"You don't see it, I can tell," he says, lecturing, holding them up. "But the seed is there. If you study the colours and the way the scenes are constructed. Someone gave it a lot of thought. It's fair to say the execution is lacking, but there's more than that to a good painting. We can still enjoy it."

He bustles over to the wall, sets the family painting on the floor next to the crashing waves and starts fumbling with the empty hook, trying to hang the harbour scene. But the nurse is at his side. Somehow, with her air of professional equanimity and easy smile, she seems to move quickly without seeming hurried or even particularly concerned.

"I'll do that, Mr. Clifford," she says. "You stand back and see if you like it."

Pop doesn't argue. He lets her take the painting and comes over to stand between Jackie and me.

"I like it," he says, giving an emphatic nod.

He returns to his recliner. Jackie and I have agreed to the recommendation of staff that we leave and give him a chance to settle into his new environment free of distractions. We'll return for a brief visit this evening.

"One of you take that other one," he says.

"What, Pop?"

He's pointing at the crashing waves.

"I'm sick of it," he says, an edge to his voice suddenly. "Take it, one of you."

In a minute, he's dozing. We leave. I've got the crashing waves under my arm.

We've made it this far. It seems a miracle. Certainly, it's been a whirlwind. A week ago we buried our mother. Now our father is in a nursing home. People have told us we were lucky to get a spot so fast. If that's so, why don't I feel lucky?

Jackie gets into her car. I get into my rental. We don't say goodbye. My wife Sandra took the kids back to Toronto after the funeral and to save money, I moved out of the Weston and into in the spare room in Jackie's house, where I've been sleeping on a fold-out bed. Tonight's discussions will be real and probably difficult. There are countless questions to consider. I wonder, should I stay for another week? Before deciding I'll talk to Sandra, and to my department chair, Christine Paulson. If I stay, I'll check back into the Weston. I've imposed on Jackie and her family long enough. Both of us have to return to our lives. Somehow, we have to put the stamp of normality on all of this, build the new reality into our routines.

The crashing waves are next to me in the passenger's seat. Pop didn't like to keep his own paintings around. If he couldn't sell it, he'd give it away. It was vanity, he said, to have your own work hanging on your walls. But Mom wanted the crashing waves, so he conceded that one for her sake. Jackie and I each own a few of his paintings — some are good, others not so much — and if Jackie wants this one, of course I'll let her keep it. But maybe I can persuade her that it's a piece of Nova Scotia that I have to take with me, a piece of Pop that my children need to see every day, that I need to see. A reminder of place and home.

I'll bring it up tonight, see what she says.

Ian Colford lives in Halifax. His stories, reviews, and commentary have appeared in Canadian literary publications from coast to coast and in journals published online. From 1995 to 1998 he was editor of the literary journal Pottersfield Portfolio. He has served on the Steering Committee of One Book Nova Scotia and the board of directors of the Writers' Federation of Nova Scotia, and and was for several years recording secretary for the Atlantic Book Awards Society. He has completed residencies at the Hawthornden Castle International Retreat for Writers and Yaddo, an artists' colony in Saratoga Springs, New York.

Evidence, a collection of short fiction, was published in 2008 by Porcupine's Quill, and won the Margaret and John Savage First Book Award; Evidence was also shortlisted for the Danuta Gleed Literary Award, the Thomas Head Raddall Atlantic Fiction Prize, and the ReLit Award. A novel, The Crimes of Hector Tomás, was published in 2012 by Freehand Books and won Trade Book of the Year at the 2013 Alberta Book Awards. Perfect World, a novella, was published by Freehand in 2016 and shortlisted in the book design category at the 2017 Alberta Book Publishing Awards.

THE COME-FROM-AWAY SPEAKS ABOUT FAMILY LIFE

Phil Milner

IT IS A LITTLE AFTER 10 p.m. on December 21, the longest night of the year. It is also the night a St. Francis Xavier University professor's Christmas marks are due.

I drop my marks into the Nicholson Hall lockbox — long official typed sheets of paper in this pre-digital era — and hurry home.

My wife has been packing, cooking, and arranging all day. I place our suitcases and gifts on the roof rack, put the tarp over them, and bungee everything down.

I fold the backseat down, cover the hatchback floor with a foam pad, then blankets and pillows. The kids pile in and find their place on the nest that covers the backseat. They wear their pajamas and warm socks. They are excited, but will be asleep before Truro. With luck, we'll cross the border at Calais, and reach Bangor, Maine, before they wake up.

We've done this before. The plan is to keep driving, to eat in the car, to stop only for gasoline and pee breaks. The hope is to make the 2,500-kilometer trip in 30 hours.

If we don't have to stop, if nothing goes wrong with the car, if snow doesn't force us to spend a night in a Buffalo or Cleveland motel, we'll be home in 30 hours with money to spend.

It begins to snow shortly after we pass Moncton. I make the left onto Road 1 South near Sussex, and negotiate the two-lane highway toward St. Stephen and Calais.

Shortly after first light we pass a cut-your-own-Christmas-tree lot. "Comme ci, comme saw," the billboard proclaims. An only-in-Canada moment. We read the sign and laugh, happy to be in on a Canadian joke.

We cross the border at St. Stephen, buy a tank of cheap American gasoline. The land of the free and the home of the brave. Home again. We take the twisted Airline Highway to Bangor, and continue south on the Interstate. South of Boston we make an enormous right turn onto Interstate Highway 90. It takes us across Massachusetts, New York, part of Pennsylvania, Ohio and into Indiana.

The states have different names, but from the Interstate they are all — except for Ohio and Indiana — cornfields, rocks, small mountains, odorous refineries, and the backs of shopping malls. In Ohio the landscape flattens, more farms, the 16-acre squares of corn and wheat and soy beans I grew up with.

I am the all-night driver. I drink from my coffee thermos, sing along with the radio, slap my face when I hear the rumble strip, and think about our family in Indiana.

My wife sleeps beside me for now; the three kids sprawl in the hatchback. I feel strong and competent. I am, in the 1975 language the Canadian government spoke then, the "head of household."

When I veer onto the rumble strip a second time, I pull onto the breakdown lane, stop, and nudge my wife. We open our doors, walk around the car, and change seats. The snow has stopped.

She drives. I fall into a jumpy sleep, full of dreams.

Twenty-eight hours after we started, we arrive at my mother-in-law's house on Walnut Street, in Plymouth, Indiana. How sweet to again be in a place we know.

We know the flat geography of Indiana farm country, and we know the rules, and we know the people there. This is where we grew up.

These are the people who know what we are, and they trust us. As our short time in Nova Scotia has taught us, we don't have that acceptance in Nova Scotia.

Though it is after 3 a.m., my mother-in-law's Christmas tree glows behind the picture window with silver and green and red light. The porchlight is on.

The tree has bubble lights, silver bulbs, foil icicles, half a hundred ornaments, and an angel on top. I cannot see it from the car, but I know my mother-in-law's living room. To the left of the tree, on a card table covered with a white blanket, there is a nativity scene.

The stable has wise men on camels approaching from the west. There are cows, oxen, sheep, a stable with a manger. Mary and Joseph wait beside the empty cradle for the birth of the Jesus.

Our kids rush in, hug their grandmother, and pick up the plastic animals from the nativity scene on the card table, set it carefully back. We all go into the kitchen and eat sandwiches and sweet things.

This place, in Plymouth, Indiana, is the place where life works the way we all remember it working. This is where we love, and are loved. Home. The word says everything.

I went to Antigonish for a pay cheque. St. Francis Xavier wanted me because I was nominally Catholic (1975 might have been the last year that being Catholic mattered), possessed papers that certified me as an expert in literature and language, and, because I had a grad school buddy who taught at St. FX and made the case to the English Department that I knew American literature, and would become, in time, a great teacher and scholar.

Seven months after we moved to Antigonish, my wife's sister died of cancer. She left a husband and five young children behind. My wife hurried home without me for a short week. She did what she could. It wasn't enough, but she had three kids in Antigonish here who needed her more.

Fourteen months later, my only brother, Dick, disappeared in the mountains of Colorado in July. We drove home, the five us, "straight-through" again, to do what we could.

Shortly after crossing the Indiana-Ohio border that late-summer night, the radio announced that a mountain climber had been found dead in Colorado, name withheld until kin were notified.

We began a phase of our life where we were 2,500 kilometers away from people who needed us. We were not much help, and they had nobody else. Our arrivals in Indiana were occasions of joy for our Indiana kin and for us. Our departures back to Antigonish left them devastated.

What were we doing up there in Nova Scotia, where, face it, we didn't know anyone very well?

I had a good job. People there were nice. That's why we were there.

In Antigonish 20 to 100 students would drift into my lecture room. I would tell them about 19th-Century American literature. They would drift back out after 50 minutes, usually giving me friendly nods. They would come to my office when they had problems with their understanding of American lit, or couldn't figure out what, exactly, I was demanding of them. I would address their intellectual problems, and they would leave.

"Ivory Tower" is the cliché for where professors reside. The term is accurate. I spent my days on the fourth floor of Nicholson Tower, as students called it.

Our life consisted of my professing English and American literature, my wife's leadership in child-raising, her part-time job at the local newspaper, and round after round of university dinner parties. We were new fish in the bowl. We were in demand — the new American professor.

In my second year, a Canadian poet from Cornerbrook visited Antigonish to read his poems. I had the happy task of taking him to the Lobster Treat for dinner on the university's dime, then introducing him.

"I could take you to Cornerbrook," the Canadian poet bragged, "and we could walk down the streets, and I could tell you what they're eating for supper in every one of those houses."

He felt that this kind of knowledge about his hometown was a key to his poetry-writing.

I hadn't thought about it, but in Plymouth, Indiana, I knew pretty much what people ate for supper. I stay overnight with my friends sometimes. I had a series of paper routes where I entered homes every Saturday morning and collected money. I went to my classmates' houses after school from the time I was six years old until I left town for good at age 18. Mom brought home stories from the courthouse, where she was a court reporter. Dad knew all the fishermen, hunters, and purchasers of paint and appliances in Marshall County from his sports and hardware store clerking, and I'd go with him to people's houses.

In Antigonish, I knew what the professors were eating at dinner parties. They were eating superior meals of a quality beyond the dreams of most Antigonish or Plymouth citizens. Otherwise, I didn't much know what Antigonishers ate.

We joined the dinner-party circuit with trepidation. Tenure and promotion seemed to be linked to serving up good food and providing a venue for sparkling conversation.

We ate the first lobster of our lives at a dinner party. Other nights we were served crème brûlée, chilled soups, lobster bisque, and Jamaican fish soup at others.

When it was our turn to host a dinner party, my wife dropped her life for three days in order to prepare a spotless house (no small feat with our ancient rental) and cook the meal. After our guests left, it took two hours to restore order and wash the dishes.

Never had I been more quickly welcomed into a new environment than we were accepted into the tiny world of St. Francis Xavier University faculty — intellectual discussions, dinner parties, "research" that connected with nothing the town or professors in other departments cared anything about.

If anti-Americanism existed in Nova Scotia, I encountered it exactly once. That was during my first year in Antigonish. To give my wife some peace, I loaded the three kids into the car and we carried garbage bags and broken grad school furniture to the dump. We threw it into a deep slit the bulldozer had dug.

Our work done, I sprung the kids to breakfast at Gentleman Jim's. I wore my old army field jacket. It was the coat I'd been wearing without drama for dirty jobs ever since my discharge from the army seven years earlier.

The patch on the left shoulder said, "US Army of Japan." Above the patch was a small icon of Mount Fuji. There were two Spec5 patches with stripes beneath them to indicate my army rank. "MILNER" was stenciled in black capital letters above a pocket.

That coat might have been the toughest, most durable, and best designed piece of clothing I ever owned. I'd earned it. I cleaned garbage cans, marched all night, and did pushups for punishment in that coat.

When I got to grad school, I resented the callow Notre Dame undergraduates who wore army surplus field jackets as fashion statements. They had no right to wear it. I'd earned it. There was honour in that jacket, if not in the Vietnam War that caused me to own it.

We sat at a table. The man at the next table began talking to the waitress in a voice that was louder than necessary. He didn't seem to notice us.

"You know, these Americans come up here and take the good jobs," he explained to the waitress. "Vietnam veterans, too." This, and much more. We ate quickly. I drove home, mildly shaken.

I haven't worn that field jacket off my property since. Happily, I have not heard an anti-American sentiment aimed at me or my family since.

Our Hawthorne Street neighbours — a Sears washer repairman, a mechanic at Keltic Ford, and a clerk at Central Supplies — invited us into their kitchens. They took our kids places, fed our cat, did our babysitting, told us where to go for repairs, and performed every kindness that could be performed for a family they didn't know from Adam.

They didn't even know they were being nice. They were doing what people in Antigonish do for neighbours. Theirs were among the few non-professor's houses that we were free to walk into, sit at the kitchen table, and talk.

My wife was a "faculty wife," a term that was loaded with meaning in 1975. The professors — apart from a few nuns, the Phys-Ed Department, the Nursing Department, and one noble history professor — were male. Wives raised kids and supervised a complicated social life, and joined together to spring the university to a Christmas Party, some open bars, and a lobster feed in the spring.

Our non-professing neighbours and quasi-friends all had complicated networks of sisters, cousins and in-laws in Antigonish, with uncles and aunts and brothers in Ottawa and Alberta. Relatives living away seemed to show up in Antigonish every time the wind changed. Our neighbours disappeared into these extended families on the weekends. It looked wonderful and impossible to our nuclear family of five.

We would go to the beach and look for starfish. We'd drive out to Barney's River for maple syrup, see a movie in New Glasgow or at the Capitol Theatre in Antigonish. We'd picnic on Eigg Mountain, find a lobster festival, a blueberry festival, a university play, or similar touristy entertainments.

"When we meet someone new, the first thing you should do is figure out how you are related to each other," our neighbour told us.

Everyone seemed related to everyone else except us.

But time passes, and without realizing it, we'd been nudging our way into the community from the day we arrived ... "Me 'n' the wife" have been here more than 40 years.

Besides, through a daughter's marriage, we are technically kin to a cross-section of Antigonishers. Right here in Antigonish, we have become "second-cousins by marriage once removed" to lots of people ourselves.

And when the other two come home, their buddies come to our house and assemble at our table as though it were 1985 all over again. We are not connected to these people by blood, but we feel toward them (and flatter ourselves that they feel toward us) like aunts and uncles in their lives.

Over the past 40 years, we coached them on kids' softball and basketball teams, took them canoeing on the West River, assisted with scouts and girl guides, scrutineered elections for our political party (not simple when you come to town knowing about only Republicans and Democrats), and both my wife and I, as teachers, had a lot of our kids' friends pass through our classrooms.

The *Antigonish Casket*, after 35years of turning down everything I offered them, invited me to write a column. True, it is a shadow of its former Scottish Catholic self but with the Bishop of Antigonish no longer publisher, there was at last room for a cafeteria Catholic with roots in another country.

Antigonish is where we belong. It would be sappy and incorrect to push this observation too far, but our experience here counts.

We are still Americans and have the papers to prove it. We are also Canadians and have papers that prove that too. As I write, three generations of us are walking around Antigonish. Happily, none of us are in the ground yet.

Only two adults in Antigonish (my former graduate school buddy and his wife), and not a person in the rest of Canada knew us before we moved here.

Our kids found their places immediately. Meals at friends, sleepovers, cub scouts, girl guides, Grade Three romances, pictures in the paper for every minor accomplishment, sport teams, playing at the rocks in the Brierly Brook, and more.

My wife, Marilyn, got a job teaching Grade Five at MacPherson Elementary. My mother-in-law moved to Antigonish from Indiana. We bought a house on the other side of the Trans-Canada highway one kilometre from the Trans-Canada highway stop light.

We paid off loans, replaced our beaters. We bought new washers and new mattresses whenever we needed them.

Our kids graduated from schools, and left town — one daughter moved to a waitressing job in Vancouver, then to Korea with her Antigonish County boyfriend where they taught English. Her sister moved to Indiana and then Boston and a career in business. Our son moved to the Yukon.

One day our daughter and her husband — after teaching for two years in Korea, then using my daughter's dual citizenship to land teaching jobs in New Hampshire — returned to Antigonish. They brought with them three kids between the ages of eight years and one year.

They'd given up good jobs, and came home with nothing but hope and a theory of where they wanted to live. They came back because Antigonish could give them the very thing Antigonish couldn't give Marilyn and me when we came here. They came back for friends, support, community, and the mores and norms they grew up with. They came back because this was the place everyone knew them, and people loved them. Mostly, they came back for the MacIntoshes and the Milners.

They lived with us for a while, found teaching jobs, bought the house we'd raised our kids in. All at once, everyone's lives were different.

We all at once were again watching kids, attending elementary school concerts and sports games, babysitting, getting help on the wood pile, and more. They came back for roots, family, memories, and a thousand ties of love. We got some of these things, too.

My mother died in Indiana. A year before my father died — I'd been making whirlwind trips back to Indiana for several years — I flew home for what felt like the last time.

Mom and Dad were keepers. Their basement contained every radio, television set, iron, mixer, and toaster they ever owned.

I carried most of it to the dump. I took their ancient sagging furniture to Goodwill. Goodwill wanted only the crutches, special chairs, bathing equipment, and walkers. I received a tax receipt for a charitable donation. It turned out to be worthless in Canada.

I held a yard sale — took in $200 and gave away what nobody would pay for.

I spent a long day sorting through picture albums. I thought of taking all the albums back to Nova Scotia, but who would look at them except my wife and me? I ended up throwing most of them away. My father had lovingly saved every letter I wrote him for 40 years. I pitched them, too.

My brother had been a local sports hero, and Mom had gathered his PHS honour jackets, medals, pins, and clippings, into a single box.

I took the box to my brother's best friends' office. Dick and Rick had played football and basketball games together for nine years, and stayed in touch afterwards. Rick wasn't in. I told his secretary who I was, that I wanted Rick to have his sports mementos. So much for my kid brother's life.

My half-sister, who lived in Arizona, came to town for a long day. We opened my parents' safe-deposit box, sold the home they'd lived in for half a lifetime for peanuts. My half-sister's husband was a hunter, like my dad. She took Dad's gun collection, minus his finest rifle, which Dad wanted me to have.

"Promise me you won't sell it," he said when he gave it to me. That hurt.

Dad's gun collection turned out to be the most valuable thing my parents owned except for the house.

She insisted I take my parents' car. I loaded it with picture albums, some knickknacks I thought my adult kids might want, and the deer rifle (a beautiful thirty-ought-six). I put it in my basement when I got home. It hasn't moved since.

I made the long twenty-five hundred kilometre drive home in Dad's Dynasty for perhaps the last time.

My wife and I had always had two homes — Antigonish and Plymouth. Now we had one.

The two contradictory sayings about home ran through my head several times on the long solitary drive home.

"If we don't belong in Antigonish, we don't belong anywhere."

"You need three generations of your family in the ground in Antigonish before you can claim to be an Antigonisher."

On a warm day in May, six months ago as I write, my son-in-law did me a solid I'd never have guessed he'd do.

He came home and asked me to go to lunch with him. I was baffled. He and I spend a lot of time together. We both love sheds, the outdoors, and the West River. We both feel drinking beer is most fun and instructive if the other is involved. Our front doors are 100 meters apart. Our wives criticize us both for thinking that Church Street Extension on the far side of the Trans-Canada Highway tunnel is the world.

We'd never gone out to eat together without our wives before. Something was up.

"I'll drive you," my daughter said.

I climbed into the back seat of their Toyota. Billy sat in front, a 12-pack of Keiths in a plastic cooler on his lap. My daughter drove us to a newish house in the new Bantry Lane addition to the town.

A dozen men were standing in the garage. Most were wearing kilts. It was the day of the Keltic Classic Golf Tournament. You couldn't have the radio on or read a paper in Antigonish without knowing that, but I don't golf.

They welcomed us. Most were much younger than me. Lots of school teachers who worked with my daughter and son-in-law, some businessmen who hovered in the background while I patronized their stores, friends of my kids, a farmer I knew of, other faces that offered friendly half-nods when I made eye-contact at Pipers Pub, but, whom, unless I was with my son-in-law, I wouldn't think of joining.

The guest-of-honour was a former hockey coach for the Antigonish Bulldogs. He won hockey championships, was famous for not tolerating mistakes by his players. "Legendary" would be the word.

Though I was pretty sure that, if the coach saw me at all around town, it was as just another effete come-from-away professor, he gave me an almost affectionate smile of recognition.

I gloated for a moment. Here I was — my son-in-law's father-in-law and not a professor — almost a guest-of-honour at this gathering of real Antigonishers.

During lunch, the coach told a series of funny hockey stories — flying sticks, bullying refs, smashes into the boards, weird strategies that backfired on the Bulldogs, legendary crazies who pulled crazy stunts, broken-down buses.

I wish I knew hockey well enough to re-tell one here, and get it right.

Then the younger generation swapped stories. These guys built forts in the woods together, dated each other's sisters, swam and fished the river behind the hatchery in summer and skated there in winter. They played hockey together for the same teams, and made the same road trips. They remembered the same teachers, priests, and coaches. Between themselves, they seemed to know where every person of their generation was now. They mostly went to St. FX together, and a few of them sat in the very back of the room in my English 100s.

Most wore kilts today because they were going to go and golf together.

I basked in the company and the venue. Here, at last, I remember thinking, on the deck in party mode with real Antigonishers and real Nova Scotians. They are tied together with a thousand bonds of family, sport, neighbourliness, and blood.

The depth of their knowledge of each other and the town, the dense unstated experience they share, the deep affection and understanding they feel. ... These are lovely things.

"Locals," the faculty word for those born here. In Plymouth, I went all the way back with everyone. I opted for adventure, novelty, the next hill, the hope for more and different somewhere else.

My daughter and son-in-law go all the way back with the people they know. Like her brother, who couldn't wait to leave town and head west, she knows where the apple tree with apples that ripen in August is (actually, they cut it down when they put the new highway through), and where you can still find blackberries.

You have one home, one family, and one place you fully belong. Leave that place, and life will never be as clear again. You'll see a world that is different from what your neighbours see. This is my home, too. I see things in a different way than the natives. Alienation will do that to you, but (am I flattering myself?), alienation contains a wisdom and perspective of its own.

Often, you don't know what is obvious to your neighbours. If all you know is Antigonish, you don't know that.

I've not lived my life with as much wisdom as I wish I had. I'd do lots of things differently if I could. I miss my Indiana kin more than I thought I would. I'm grateful for the places Marilyn and I have lived — Indiana, Tennessee, Japan, and Notre Dame.

We thank our Smiling Providence that brought our family to Antigonish and Canada to live our days the way we have been privileged to live them.

Phil Milner was born in Plymouth, Indiana. He graduated from Vanderbilt University, and was drafted into the American Army a year-and-a-half later. The army sent him to Tokyo instead of Vietnam. He got a Ph. D. from the University of Notre Dam, and came to Antigonish, Nova Scotia to teach American literature. The books he claims are The Yankee Professor's Guide to Life in Nova Scotia *and* The Antigonish Book of Days. *He married his high school sweetheart, Marilyn, when both were too young. Their grown children Ellen, Bethany, and Paul live in Antigonish, Boston, and Jackson Hole, respectively. He is an enthusiastic, if not particularly competent, biker and beekeeper. He tells Canadians who think he is an American that he has lived in Canada longer than they have.*

SAVING HOME

Janet Barkhouse

I.

I was born in fairyland,
The Valley, in the spring,
When all along her winding roads
The trees were blossoming.*

WE'D MOVED AGAIN, THIS TIME to Montréal. We were all homesick.

Mummy hung up the phone. Her face was pink, and her eyes looked shiny. "Daddy's got two weeks' holiday. One whole week in Nova Scotia."

For my mother, home was Kinsman's Corners in The Valley. For my father, it was Bridgewater on the LaHave, "The most beautiful river in the world." For my brother, it was Berwick. For me, it was Harbourville, over the North Mountain from Berwick. Home was Nova Scotia.

My father was a banker, and, in the early 1940s, bank employees were poor. He'd had to ask the bank for permission to marry my mother because, according to his contract, he didn't earn enough to support a family. The bank raised his salary to a thousand dollars a year, and as a result my brother and I were born. Twelve years later in Montréal, on the day of the phone call, my father was earning just enough to get a loan for a used Chevy.

That summer in 1955 we drove for three days over winding, bumpy roads, tenting at night, eating egg salad sandwiches or wieners and beans heated on a Coleman camper stove. At least that's how I remember it. And I remember my father coming to the Tantramar Marshes and inhaling deeply with delicious appreciation.

My Nova Scotia Home · 203

"Ahhhh. We're home!" Although I didn't much like the rotten salt-marsh smell, I thought it wasn't any worse than the air in the car, filled with fumes from my father's MacDonald's cigarettes and our egg and bean exhalations.

II.

I dream Harbourville's weir,

look down from a crossbar near the tops of those peeled trees, poles tall as schooner masts braced to withstand Fundy tides. Green jade water, blue salt sky.

I don't think it would be possible to overstate the depth of love I felt for Harbourville as a child. Coming up the North Mountain by way of its thrillingly steep ox-bow bend, kneeling to look out the back window at the gloriously green valley below, then leaping up and hanging over the front bench seat, straining to see the Bay of Fundy so I could be the first to chant, "I see the water! I see the water!" — all that was just forerunner to the actual magic of being there.

Barefoot, without grownups, my cousins and I ran down the cliff road to the beach. There we lit driftwood bonfires and steamed periwinkles in rusty tin cans, a most useful part of beach litter then. We hunted for amethyst, geodes, rocks with perfect circles on the top (they were good luck), rocks with a "sandwich" filling (more good luck). My mother was wont to say, "This is some of the oldest exposed rock in the world," which I didn't entirely credit until I saw a display in the Royal Ontario Museum in Toronto with rock specimens sitting on black velvet under glass, labelled with strange geological names, many listed as being from "Harbourville, Kings County, Nova Scotia."

There was a weir, a constant source of fascination. Its owners were hard-working farmers who every spring built a tidal weir at Harbourville. Twice every 26 hours all summer they drove from their farm on the Rooshie Road to empty the weir of the many different fish it trapped. I might be sent down by my mother or grandmother with 50 cents or a dollar to buy enough mackerel or flounder or salmon for supper, but mostly I climbed high up the weir to point out salmon, as the men waded after them with their nets.

According to my mother, Fundy's tides were "the highest in the world." During spring tides, when the ocean seemed to retreat almost to the middle of the Bay, we wandered out to exposed mud flats to poke about in tidal pools. There were sea slugs, brilliantly pink or turquoise or polka-dotted or speckled or striped or iridescent; tiny crabs and shrimp; sea worms leaving delicate trails in the mud; whelks and periwinkles snailing about; barnacles opening their sunroofs and sticking out their grasping fingers: all seeking food, as we humans did at the weir.

III.

"I must go down to the Valley to see what is going on with the Red Coats. Be careful, Grandmother, and do not let anyone into the wigwam."

The Grandmother promised, and Little Marten armed himself with his bow and arrows. The bow was so tiny that the string was made of a single hair, and the arrows were fashioned from the smallest twigs of an ash. But Glooscap had made the bow and arrows, and so you may be sure that they were much more powerful than they appeared.**

Along with her geological knowledge, my mother was a wonderful storyteller. Her Bay of Fundy was rich with history and legend. We heard how Champlain sailed up the Bay and, seeing fool's gold sparkling in the cliff directly across from our cliff, named it *Cape d'Or* and reported back to his King that the land was rich beyond imagining. *Isle Haute* was named by Champlain, too, but earlier still it had been a giant moose swimming away from the great "Micmac demigod," Glooscap, who had lived in a wigwam on Cape Blomidon, but had had to leave home because the White Man had come and desecrated his holy places and destroyed his hunting grounds. He would need food for his journey. He shot at the moose, but in his distress, shot wide. He was so furious he turned the moose to rock.

How I identified with Glooscap's outrage. To have home taken away! Of course he would be fiercely angry. That same distress was responsible for other land formations, too. As Glooscap broke camp, he threw out his cooking pot — there it still was, perfectly round Pot Island. He took a great club and smashed his beaver dam — and there at the farthest end of the Bay was Cape Split, its sharp broken peaks visible on a clear day. My mother wrote stories of Little Marten, a Mi'kmaw elf of sorts, a shape-changer, who lived with Grandmother in a secret home under Glooscap's wigwam pole, and who got up to all sorts of mischief.

Today I understand that these stories were appropriated. They were not our stories, but they made us aware of the ancient nature of the land, its delight and wonder. My mother's version of the story included the belief that Glooscap would return when there was peace in the world, and people stopped destroying the Earth — and that dream has stayed with me throughout my life.

IV.

All those strawberries my brother picked, 5¢ a quart,
when he was 10, flats and flats, eight quarts to each, while I
swung from a long hemp rope into the swimming hole
nearby, bubbles soaring up and up, my fingers
wrinkled white—his stained red from picking clean.

If the land came first in my early sense of home, family was the next anchor for a child who moved every two or three years, perforce leaving old friends behind. My mother had four siblings, three still in The Valley, each with a daughter my age. Every summer, there they were, the same dear cousins, ready for shared adventures. Sometimes I played or slept over at one of their homes in The Valley, where we might pick strawberries, theoretically for money — a nickel a quart — for an uncle who owned a farm, but more for the deliciousness of eating them ripe and hot under the July sun. When berry picking palled, there was a brook at the farm with a pool big enough for kids to swim in.

My mother loved her parents, her siblings, and all her siblings' children, with unwavering devotion. "Family" was sacrosanct, to be supported through whatever difficulty it found itself facing. (My father adored his family, too, and often went to see them without us in tow, because one week's holiday was proof positive that time shrivels in proportion to how much it is craved.) There was plenty of dysfunction to go around in our family, but we didn't let it change how we felt about each other. "We don't love people because they're perfect," my mother would pronounce.

My mother's siblings obviously felt the same way, and passed the paradigm on to their children. Recently, my middle-aged daughters and I organized a "cousins" picnic on the beach at Harbourville, where we are now part owners of a family cottage. By "organized," I mean we put the word out to say we would be on the beach with a fire going at 3 on a Saturday afternoon. Despite being rained out and having to reschedule at the last minute, 37 of us gathered the next day — three generations of cousins.

Like many families today, we are spread across the Earth, but we visit enthusiastically when we can. One of my granddaughters, who lives in Toronto, texts all year with one of her third cousins, who lives in Berwick. What could these children possibly have in common, living miles away from each other, physically and culturally? They are family. They are *at home* with each other, despite being together only briefly each summer, just as I was with my cousins, 60-plus years ago, and am still today.

V.

You're crazy, you tell yourself,
to have this pervasive sense of knowing, of naming,
of rolling the small round "my" over your tongue like a warm marble.

Given my passionate childhood love for Harbourville, perhaps it seems odd that I didn't settle there. When I was making a typical mid-life change — in my case, divorcing both my husband and my theatre career, and moving to Nova Scotia from Toronto to "live off the land" and write — my brother was living in Lunenburg. He had moved "back home" to Nova Scotia as soon as he could, in his early 20s, to get an education degree, and teach. He went where work was, of course, but it's interesting to me that ultimately that was on the South Shore, where our father was born. My brother and his wife praised the school system here, so it seemed sensible to me as a mother of young children to offer them a solid education, at least, while I was ripping up their city roots and planting them in the country.

Living off the land proved way too tough for a city-bred actor, so I went back to school for an education degree, and got a job at the school where my brother taught. When my mother in her old age moved to Bridgewater to be near us, there we all were, living or working beside the same "most beautiful river" my father so loved. My father died young, at 53, so there was nothing to pull us there except coincidence — and, perhaps, my brother's and my genes.

I wonder. Is "home" part of our human inheritance? Geneticists think we may pass deep learning on to our offspring. It seems to be so for migrating animals. Certainly Atlantic salmon know the exact river where they were spawned. My oldest daughter's fascination with genealogy led me to have my genetic heritage analyzed recently, and I discovered that a fifth of my ancestors were Irish. When I visited Ireland years ago, I had a vivid sense of belonging that seemed to come out of the very soil I was standing on. So compelling was the feeling that I wondered aloud if Nova Scotia had once been connected to Ireland when Pangaea formed the world's land mass. It hadn't, so I shrugged off my strange feeling as an anomaly.

If home is encoded in our genes, what does that mean for those of us forced to find new homes? What of the millions of people living in refugee camps? In October 2017, Statistics Canada reported that 22 percent of Canadians are recent immigrants. We are experimenting in Canada with a system of government that (in theory, anyway) welcomes newcomers, honours their language and culture, supports them until they find themselves putting roots into new soil. I know how imperfect the experiment is. I know as well that here in Nova Scotia we are welcoming immigrants to live on the unceded territory of the Mi'kmaq, the land my ancestors appropriated, forcing Glooscap out.

We have a long way to go.

And, according to more than fifteen thousand scientists in 184 countries, we don't have much time for the journey. In November 2017, they issued a "warning to humanity," that our greed and sense of entitlement are pushing us ever closer to mass extinction.

VII.

I know, at least in part, the grief of having to move away from home. But I also know that notions of home don't have to be exclusive. Before it was taken from them, *home* for the early Mi'kmaq was all of Nova Scotia, parts of New Brunswick, Quebec, PEI. My own childhood love of Harbourville expanded to include the South Shore of Nova Scotia, and I still remember feeling the pull of home in Ireland. My pioneer ancestors exchanged their European and

American homes for places in Nova Scotia. So I know that we *can* move, put our roots in new soil, adapt, and thrive.

But ultimately, the only reason we have other places to settle is because the Earth sustains us.

My mother often quoted Sir Walter Scott's "Breathes there the man, with soul so dead / Who never to himself hath said, / This is my own, my native land!" It's long past time to let that kind of nationalism go. Like the intertidal creatures at low tide on the Bay of Fundy mud flats, the berry pickers in the Valley, the fishermen at the weir, we are all seeking nourishment. That weir no longer exists, not viable because of overfishing. The Earth can withstand only so much exploitation.

If we can embrace our human counterparts as family, despite cultural and geographical differences, and share Earth's bounty, wisely, we all stand a better chance of survival. We are none of us perfect, but "we don't love people because they're perfect." Where there is generosity and openness, there is hope. What hope is there for our human family otherwise?

> *And it's going to get worse, a lot worse, because thunder*
>
> *is drumming the storm closer. Surely there's something intelligent*
> *you could be doing instead of blundering deeper into the mess*
> *you've put yourself in, so smug, so sure. You're windfall,*
> *leafmold, not even a speck on a satellite map. This*
>
> *is when it hits you hard in the belly, when you sag*
> *to the mossy forest floor, beg God to see.*

ACKNOWLEDGEMENTS:
* Excerpt from Joyce Barkhouse's "Annapolis Valley" published in *Whispers of Mermaids and Wonderful Things: Children's Poetry and Verse from Atlantic Canada*, ed. Sheree Fitch and Anne Hunt. Halifax: Nimbus, 2017.
** Excerpt from Joyce Barkhouse's "Little Marten," unpublished children's story, 1955.
All other poetry fragments by Janet Barkhouse, some from poems published by *The Dalhousie Review* and *Galleon*, and in her debut book of poems, *Salt Fires* (Pottersfield Press, 2018).

> *By the time you're in your 70s, a "bio" can be a bit of a farrago. In my 20s, I married and had two children, got a Master's degree in English, acted in theatres across Canada. In my 30s, I divorced, remarried, moved to rural Nova Scotia to farm, worked at a fruit stand and a library, got an Education degree. In my 40s and 50s, I taught high school English and directed students in musicals and plays. In my 60s, I retired, promptly fell*

in love with writing poems, helped start a list of Sable Island's fungi, wrote and published poems, children's books, short stories. In my 70s, I'm still writing and publishing, engaging in the Writers In The Schools *program my mother, Joyce Barkhouse, CM, ONS, helped start when she was in her 60s, still living in the home my partner and I found in 1981.*

What a lucky, astonished and humbly grateful human I am, to have been born when and where I was, with ancestors who thought women mattered enough to educate, then listen to what they had to say.

PLACE IN EIGHT ACTS

Alice Burdick

ACT ONE

IT BEGAN WITH A TRAVELOGUE — to the South Shore, to the Valley, to the Eastern Shore, with great music, open windows, salt wind in hair, lobster butter on fingers, the warm feeling of welcome. An impression of no fences, rolling hills, sparse population, small roads, artists getting by on little, but a sense of expanded time and room for roaming, physically and mentally.

It was the best I'd felt for a long time. My boyfriend of five years had died two years before, and five years before that, my mother. My life in Toronto was full of reminders of love and loss, and the physical markers of these memories, internal memorial plaques, street by street.

ACT TWO

Back in the big city of my upbringing and ongoing life, on the way to work, a garbage bag that somehow made me think: bomb. A brilliant blue sky. Minutes later, through the various codes into the workplace of many currencies, a strange quiet in the office and on the streets outside.

The towers of 9/11 hit and falling. I walked home, under the dome of the glorious blue sky, a dreamlike, eerie quiet, through streets of tall buildings and dense housing, and thought about what is worth living for and what is worth dying for. The answer: poetry — my first perfect-bound collection to come out the next spring: worth living for, worth a continually changing life.

Worth living for: an expanded life, a chance taken, a move away from the familiar. A job in currency exchange not worth possible death due to affiliation.

ACT THREE

A quick trip to Halifax, a blustery rainy autumn, to look for a place to live. Within four or five days, I'd found a flat near to all four of the friends who made Halifax a friend-formed home. The landlords kept a collection of cuckoo clocks and pianos upstairs.

On January 1, 2002, my brother drove me and my old cat Ed (who had been a mouser at a cheese store where I worked in Kensington Market — Cheese Magic) all the way to Halifax, from Toronto. I settled into a new existence in the new old city. I walked around the city repeatedly, from the North End to Point Pleasant Park especially, to get a feel for the place, and enjoyed the adjustment.

I'd saved money from my job, and had a small inheritance from my Grandfather Clifton Paisley, that allowed me a few weeks of writing, reading, editing, and adjusting before looking for a part-time job.

ACT FOUR

The only way I really start to know a place is to walk around it, repeat routes and try new directions to various places. I had heard nothing about the Halifax Explosion from my history classes in school, but here in the North End especially there was much to learn from. I walked to Fort Needham and saw the memorial bells there; saw the Hydrostone with its impressive stone buildings, remarkable as they stood out from the predominantly shingled and clapboard covered houses of the region.

I'd heard about Africville when I lived in Toronto, not in school, but from activists — there were lots of African-Canadian people who'd moved from Nova Scotia to Toronto at various times. The history of the Mi'kmaq was also not taught in Ontario — except in the typical way of implied extinction (in line with how the histories of all Indigenous Peoples were taught, at least in the 1980s).

It was a winter when I walked and felt the swerve and curve of the hills, forced up and down, sliding on ice, pushed by a fierce wind with the ocean in its blow. One night, that massive wind felled a huge tree the full length of the backyard of my apartment — its crown just cleared my back door. The raw winter opened into spring, an easing of the wind, a raising of the face as the wind's whip withdrew.

ACT FIVE

After returning from my trip to Ontario to launch my first collection of poems, I enjoyed my first full spring and summer in Nova Scotia. I'd been able to get away without a driver's license up till then, but it was a big deal, living in Halifax — the closeness of the beaches, inaccessible without any transportation system that regularly travelled outside the city.

I took a course at Young Drivers of Canada — the oldest person in the class, at 31 years old — and got my learner's permit. Still couldn't drive — no car — but friends let me use their vehicles on occasion. It was a summer of writing, music, walking, friends, silence, and parties, and I met the man who would eventually become my husband.

I started travelling out to First Peninsula when I could, to visit him, and I realized that my life was very portable at this time. My writing could happen anywhere, and it didn't need to be in Halifax. By the following spring, I moved out to live with him, in First South, just outside of Lunenburg.

ACT SIX

The move from Fuller Terrace to Grimm Road was bigger than I anticipated. I had lived in small places before — a small town called Espanola in Ontario, and an off-grid cabin near Robert's Creek in BC — but I was born and raised in Toronto. A dense urban landscape, full of people, noise, and movement, this was my hometown and comfort zone. I also always had long-established friends and family there. Halifax had some great old friends, and I met new folks there too, through those old friends, and through poetry.

Grimm Road was hard. My first job out here was at the LaHave Bakery branch in Mahone Bay — the graveyard shift, which I worked alone, making bread from the wee hours into daylight. It was nice — I met people who came in to buy the bread — but no friendships took hold there. I was the solitary sleepy seller of hand-hewn loaves.

I got other work after this, and there I met a friend or two, but also for the first time the friends I was making were new parents, had their own busy lives, and so just meeting up on the fly didn't happen. I found a reticence in people here. As always, I walked to learn a place, to feel it and see what made itself available to my eyes. There were actually curtains drawn, eyes peeking out, a suspicion that emanated from these things. Very few people were friendly, even to my straightforward "Hi" — they didn't know who I was, what my context was, how long I was going to be around.

As the seasons turned, they must have figured out that I was sticking around through the dire months, but a woman walking alone? Maybe I just seemed essentially "wrong" — and as a poet this is my default feeling, which is not necessarily a negative — but it can distance.

The first few years in the area — let's say the first four years — were difficult. They got easier as I gradually met people, and had some good friends, but I had never felt so acutely weird and isolated as I did in those years. There were encounters with people who frowned at me, gave me the proverbial side-eye, actively ignored my smiles and greetings — specifically on the streets of Lunenburg. It was disorienting, and actually funny in a way, especially when there is still so much talk of Toronto being a cold place.

But what I realized over time is that this experience I had — of being the so-called "come from away" (which I honestly didn't hear to my face more than maybe once or twice) — is something a person could experience in almost any new place. I had to open myself up, be patient, play the long game — and also simply realize that whether in a big place or in a small place, there are people you might not want to be friends with, or people who will not want to be friends with you — it's all just so much more apparent in such a small population!

ACT SEVEN

I finally started to meet a wider group of people when I had my first child — suddenly a community of mothers and parents made itself visible and available — and it was my good fortune to meet a wonderful bunch of people, most of whom are great friends still. I do suspect that being known within a small community as a poet or an artist automatically makes a person, especially a woman, uniquely suspect.

My new identity as a mother allowed others to feel comfortable with me — to "understand" me — because I was fulfilling a role that is more universally understood. It's both a valuable, humbling experience, and a frustrating one — a good ol' dichotomy. I value the friendships of folks I've met here — and I'm happy to say that many of them are born-and-bred Nova Scotian, not just other newcomers like me.

I think it's key that folks not hunker down in their own comfortable class/place/hipness zones, and not assume the worst of others according to differences. The breakdowns in communication that I've seen in local politics, for example, often reflect an entrenchment of identities that come from feeling hurt and misunderstood — one side by the other, both and all defensive. It would be so great if we all could have the basic understanding that this place, the South Shore, is a place where many different people with a variety of incomes, backgrounds, beliefs, and aspirations, live together in imperfect harmony. It's perfectly normal for people to have a hard time understanding each other, but it's a good idea to try.

ACT EIGHT

I have now been in Nova Scotia for 16 years, and in that time I have gotten married, have had two children, separated from my husband, lost my old cat, gained two new cats, moved five times, and have had multiple jobs: in cafes and restaurants; managed an art gallery; designed; edited; acted as a simulated patient; have written in all forms, and have had five books, including a volume of selected works, published; served on various writing-related juries; and of course opened Lexicon Books in Lunenburg with a couple of friends, and this job itself is composed of around 10 other jobs!

Being a poet and used to a marginal income, I am probably an ideal candidate for life on the South Shore. I've always been used to working multiple jobs, and this is the land of multiple jobs, and seasonal employment. My business, although successful (it has to be a working business, not just an aspiration — I have lots of aspirations that pay me nothing) is marginal — we know that a bookstore isn't going to have us sleeping on beds of solid gold. But it is satisfying, and overall that's the feeling I have about life here.

It is a beautiful place to live — and that simple fact is a balm. This beauty — the oceanside, the pace of life, the love people share for the place, the big sky — lives here, alongside more complicated realities, because we're part of the world and its complications. It would be a massive delusion to ignore the complications that exist here in order to present a pseudo-utopia. It is not kind to ourselves as residents, or to those who fall in love with this place and want to move here, to ignore the big issues of employment, income, availability of childcare, healthcare, transportation, food security, schools, arts funding, etc.

Let's say there's a beauty in facing the hard stuff. I'm happy to face the hard stuff without also overstating it — we are lucky in many ways here. I love it here and want to stay. My eyes are open. My brain is working. My feet walk on, on trails and streets. My heart is open to this beautiful, complicated place.

Alice Burdick is the author of four poetry collections, including Book of Short Sentences, *published in 2016. A collection of selected works,* Deportment, *which came out in 2018 from Wilfrid Laurier University Press. Her work has appeared in many anthologies and magazines and was shortlisted for the Lemonhound Poetry Prize in 2014. She lives in Lunenburg and is a co-owner of Lexicon Books.*

MY HOME IN NOVA SCOTIA

Monica Graham

BLINDFOLD ME, TURN ME AROUND three times in my backyard, and tell me to point to the North Star.

I can do it.

My home in Nova Scotia is my compass, my centre of gravity, my nest, my hidey-hole. Despite that strong sense of being rooted here, I am not from here.

I was born in Newfoundland, a solid-enough rock from which my parents' itchy feet took our family to villages across Canada and back. I lived in quite a few places before I finished high school in a Cape Breton coal town.

I could have gone anywhere after that, but I stayed in Nova Scotia. I was done with packing up, saying goodbye and moving every few years.

Although the man I married had a job here that was too good to just give up and leave, he can't be blamed for digging me firmly into the Nova Scotia mud. In truth, he would have been happy to roam the globe.

No, it was my wish to park us in a Pictou County meadow, surrounded by forest and streams. Forty-plus years, three children, four grandchildren, and eight or ten dogs and cats later, I have no regrets.

And what is Nova Scotia, after all? Nothing but a name, a label on a hunk of land — a Latin name, not even English or Gaelic or French or Mi'kmaq or of any other tongue spoken by our ancestors. A name that recalls the heritage of a certain percentage of the province's inhabitants. It's odd that it gets translated into French when Ontario and Manitoba are not but, just chalk it up as one more idiosyncrasy.

My relationship is not with the name, but with this place.

This is home.

I know every inch of the land where I live.

That tree. This dip in the path. The shadows at breakfast time and the light slanting through the hardwoods at supper. Where the sun rises and sets in every season. Where the water sits when it rains hard, and where the snow piles itself against the fence. The night noises, and the schedules for the school bus, the snowplough and Canada Post.

I know who walks or cycles "My Road" for their health, and who does it because they don't drive. I know which dogs may bite, and which ones — mostly — only bark. I know where the deer cross, and where the coyotes chase them across. I can name the trees, flowers, birds, and rocks in all their seasons.

Ask me for directions to sandy beaches, photo-worthy views, productive fishing holes, rugged hikes and easy ski trails.

I have to qualify that boast — ask me about places close to home. Farther afield, my knowledge gets a bit hazy.

Still, there are few places in Nova Scotia that I haven't been, even if I've forgotten some details. Like Londonderry. I've been there to visit relatives. But all I remember is seeing a dilapidated building beside the railway, blueberry fields, and vague directions through the backwoods to get home. It being deep winter, we followed the highway.

I've been to Mary Ann Falls at least three times, and I have the photos somewhere to prove it, but I'd need a map to find it again. The same goes for the swimming hole somewhere near Yankee Line, and a series of small, shallow lakes on South Mountain. There is a beach somewhere near Darling Lake, a really good dirt road on Mount Thom that seems to have disappeared, and a band of shiny quartz streaking through an outcrop of grey rock just above high tide somewhere near Wine Harbour.

I promised myself I would return — if I can find them. They've receded into the tapestry of Nova Scotia, a tapestry that is as repetitive and as colourful as tartan.

Driving through Malagash, for about three kilometres it's easy to believe I am approaching Port Hood. Downtown Westville looks a lot like downtown New Waterford. Parts of Amherst could be picked up and plopped down in Antigonish or Kentville and few would notice. A mere glance at Clarks' Harbour might persuade me I was in Caribou or Canso.

I have a map of Nova Scotia, produced by the provincial government in about 1972 when I was a relative newcomer. For four or five years, I traced with black marker every road I took around the province.

Later, when I began skiing, snowshoeing, and kayaking around the province, the map was of little use for explorations off the beaten path to places like Cape Smokey, Fitzpatrick Mountain, Wentworth Valley, the islands around Tangier, the Mira River, the Fundy tides. An emerging interest in history took me to museums, from well-known national piles like Fortress Louisbourg to small community collections like the Stewiacke Valley Museum.

It's corny, but true: there really is a lot to 'sea' in Nova Scotia. So much is packed into this small province — where the benefit of being small is that it's all within reach of a day's drive.

But my life in Nova Scotia is about more than natural beauty, tourist attractions, sports, and homage to the past.

It's the people.

They are friendly to the point of occasional — but not quite — nosiness. They are helpful to the point of almost — but not quite — interference. They can relax, but not nearly to the point of laziness, and they can be intense, but nowhere near obsessive.

People in Nova Scotia are almost ordinary, except they are not. I know them. I know how extremely interesting they are. Each one is a living, breathing gold mine of fascinating experience, wisdom, humour, and stories. ... Oh, the stories!

Listening to people over the years has developed in my head a multi-dimensional and ever-shifting map. It tells me who lives where, where they work, where they take vacations, and which political signs they will put on their lawns come election time. I've learned to recognize accents from communities separated by just a few kilometres, by a hill, or by a cove. I know which families come from which parts of the province, and I can expect they know how they ended up in another part. I know that it's possible to meet people from here almost anywhere in the world and, by the same token, to walk down a street in, say, New Minas, and meet distant family or long-ago friends from another place.

Small world, we say.

Nova Scotia is the epitome of the term.

The connections of family and friendship are so entwined in the map of Nova Scotia that drawing lines among them would create a disorganized and convoluted web, as if woven by a spider on crack.

When disagreements of one kind or another disrupt the strands of those webs, the whole community has a ringside seat to a drama that may take years — even centuries — to unfold. Will a wronged spouse hold a grudge? Will the cheater look anyone in the eye, ever again? Will a robbery victim cross the street rather than meet the perpetrator's family on the sidewalk? Will anyone speak to the criminal after he or she has done his or her time? Can a mistake, misstep or crime ruin a person's reputation forever, and become a family burden for generations?

The answer to all those questions is yes, of course. The world was ever thus, and Nova Scotia history is certainly long enough to have accumulated its own excess baggage.

This is one of the earliest sites of European contact with Indigenous Peoples, yielding a legacy of broken promises and prejudicial policies. For about three hundred years, the province served as a proxy battleground for French, English, and Spanish empire-builders and their favoured fish merchants, mining magnates, lumber barons, fur companies, and religious organizations.

As a result, much of the natural wealth was carried off to Europe, and hard lines were deeply scored between the haves and the have-nots, the worthy and the worthless.

There is indignation among the wronged, allied with a sense that the world goes on and we must bury our hurt and go with it.

There is sympathy among the privileged, coupled with a feeling that past wrongs can never be properly righted, it's almost futile to try, so let's just move into the future with a vow never to repeat history.

Despite some nasty history — or maybe because of it — Nova Scotia has some notable achievements. Then a colony, it raised Joseph Howe, father of the earliest responsible government in what is now Canada, and also in what was then the British Empire.

As a result of abuse of miners and their families by coal companies and other industrialists, Nova Scotia developed labour laws well before some of our ten provinces ever joined Confederation.

Canada's first newspaper, and its first newspaper owned and operated by a person of African descent, were both published in Nova Scotia.

Canada's first airplane flight was in Nova Scotia.

The province has exported innumerable educators, scientists, lawyers, artists, business leaders, politicians, and clergy to the rest of Canada and internationally — while keeping enough for ourselves. Such dichotomy has the ability to energize, exasperate and inspire me all at the same time.

In my first years here, following any community tragedy or upheaval, I wondered if I could be normal (whatever that is) once the wonder of nine days had passed. Could the community that surrounded me be normal? Could we avoid condemning others? Could we avoid the censure of others? Could we just pick up our brokenness and keep going?

Ultimately, that answer, too, is yes.

I learned that being interested is not that same as taking sides. Caring is not the same as judging. Knowledge of another person's idiosyncrasies is not gossip. I discovered that interest, care and knowledge are community-building tools. Without their involvement, we are lonely, barren little islands.

Maybe it's like that everywhere, but not for me. I never lived long enough in any one place to watch how time, like water, can wear down the stoniest of hearts and the highest walls. Or how acceptance and tolerance can flow around a rock-obstinate point of view and carry on as usual, down the river of life.

That's what I see, here in Nova Scotia. I watched Nova Scotia for a long time to figure this out, and I may still be wrong. It wouldn't be the first time, and not likely the last.

My perception may be the result of more than 40 years' acquaintance with the province and its people. It could be my advancing age that I'm too tired to fight with it all, so let it be. It could be the way it is here in Nova Scotia.

Everyone matters — with exceptions. Everything is important, except for the things that aren't.

Maybe it's left up to each of us to determine our own priorities, and each of us lives with each other's choices. I don't really believe it, though. I believe tolerance is more natural to Nova Scotia than resignation.

A choice I have is to leave.

I think about it every now and again, adding up the pros and cons. I have family in the region, but I have family elsewhere as well. I have friends here, but they don't expect me to stay for them, any more than I expect them to stay for me. I have invested time and energy in making a home, making friends, putting down roots — but I know it's possible to start over, and it may even be an adventure.

My hobbies, activities and life's work can all be done wherever I am — but where would be better than here? While I'd like to see more of the world, I feel no need to go away and stay away.

The thing about going away is that wherever I may go, I bring my self with me.

I've travelled enough to know that every place has its display of light and shadow, its unexplainable contrasts between problems and benefits.

Once, visiting at a downtown Toronto apartment complex where the tenants outnumbered the population of a good-sized Nova Scotia town, I got acquainted with more people between the elevator and the parking garage than my hosts had met in two years' residency. Yet, that same standoffishness failed to distinguish among the various nationalities crammed into that building. To my surprise, when I came back to Nova Scotia I'd also developed colour-blindness. My eyes and ears slipped right over skin colour, garb and language, where, once, any unusual (to me) feature would have been intensely interesting, and I would have struggled to not stare.

As another example, Costa Rica has achieved fame for its positive environmental policies, but during a visit to that country I discovered raw sewage running down municipal ditches, and personal litter on the streets. The country is a medical tourism destination, yet public health officials here would be gob-smacked to see birds and lizards prowling restaurant floors for crumbs. There is no military, but the frequent highway tollbooths are armed to the gunwales.

Here, the land and sea and sky are heart-achingly bright and beautiful, yet Nova Scotia life is about the people who fill that landscape — people from every walk and situation of life.

The canvas we paint is a chiaroscuro of our characteristics: bright friendliness with dark borders of wariness, cheery welcome pocked with clouds of suspicion, energetic enthusiasm for new ideas tied to a crippling fear of change. There is a sense that in Nova Scotia we can do better, that we haven't yet arrived, that we must keep trying.

None of the facets are hypocritical or deceitful. The character of Nova Scotia is real, a natural outcome of who we once were, what we've become, and where we could possibly go. It's not more right than wrong, or more wrong than right. It just *IS*.

You notice I used the pronoun 'we.'

I belong here.

My hard-won ability to navigate Nova Scotia's cultural and emotional highways and byways gives me a sense of belonging and peace. It's a feeling of home.

It's a bit like snuggling into a favourite chair, shifting a hip in one direction to avoid a loose spring, an elbow in another direction miss the heavily-worn arm upholstery, and then tipping the chair back just-so-far — and no more. A book and a lamp, the television clicker and the phone, the mug and the plate, all within reach. Never perfect, but a fit.

Nova Scotia is where I fit, a comfortable place from which I can take on the world — on the days it's necessary to take on the world.

Other days, me and Nova Scotia, we just fit.

Monica Graham came to Nova Scotia in 1972 and has lived in the woods of Pictou County for most of the ensuing years. She is the author of nine non-fiction books including In the Spirit: Reflection on Everyday Grace, Fire Spook: The Mysterious Nova Scotia Haunting, Bluenose *and* The Historic Town of Pictou. *She has also written countless newspaper articles and several short stories, she is a former columnist at* The Chronicle Herald *and* Pictou Advocate *newspapers and is working on a first novel. Just for fun, she skis, paddles, gardens, hikes and sings.*